PESTS, DI

COMMON PROBLEMS

PESTS, DISEASES AND COMMON PROBLEMS

GEORGE CULPAN

HAMLYN

First published in 1995 by Hamlyn

An imprint of Reed Consumer Books Limited
Michelin House, 81 Fulham Road, London SW3 6RB
and Auckland, Melbourne, Singapore and Toronto
in conjunction with
Amateur Gardening, IPC Magazines Limited
Westover House, West Quay Road, Poole, Dorset BH15 1JG

Printed in Finland

ISBN 0 600 58427 5

A catalogue record for this book is available from the British Library

CONTENTS

INTRODUCTION

However well we grow our garden plants, it is extremely likely that sooner or later they will be subjected to attack by a pest, a disease or by some other ailment. If the plants are growing strongly they have a good chance, in most cases, of withstanding the attack, and there are measures that can be taken to prevent and to control most garden disorders.

As gardeners, it is up to us to decide how to manage pest and disease control. We can decide to ignore the caterpillars busily eating our cabbages, the black deposits growing on whitefly excretions all over our greenhouse tomatoes or the systematic defoliation of our roses by black spot, but most of us will choose instead to take some action. The aim of this book is to help the gardener to reduce the damage caused by pests and diseases by aiding identification of the various problems, providing guidance on preventing attacks, and also by giving advice on the various physical, biological and chemical measures that are available to control any attack that may occur.

The opening pages deal with general principles, including the various cultural practices that can be followed to reduce subsequent damage caused by pests, diseases and other problems, resistant varieties, biological control measures and pesticides. The remainder of the book deals with garden plants and the pests, diseases and other problems to which they are susceptible, along with detailed descriptions of those ailments and details of how to control them. The garden plants are divided into sections: ornamentals (including annuals and biennials, herbaceous perennials, bulbs and trees, shrubs and roses); lawns, indoors (including greenhouse and conservatory flowering plants and houseplants) and edible crops; vegetables (including vegetable seeds, brassicas, peas and beans, stem and leaf crops, onions, potatoes and other root crops and vegetable fruit); and fruit (including top fruit and soft fruit).

Each section has its own key to help with the identification of the particular problem being experienced. There is also an appendix listing a selection of commonly grown plants in alphabetical order, giving the pests and diseases to which they are prone.

Pesticides are referred to by their active ingredient name, and all the chemicals included have received full official UK approval for use as directed on the product label.

HOW TO USE
THIS BOOK

1. Your affected plant will belong to one of the following categories:
Flowers
Lawns
Indoors
Vegetables
Fruit

2. Within the general category, find the correct section from:
Flowers

- Annuals, biennials, bedding plants and other flowers grown from seed (see pages 22–33)
- Herbaceous perennials (see pages 33–44)
- Bulbs, corms, rhizomes and tubers (see pages 44–57)
- Trees and shrubs, including roses and conifers (see pages 57–81)

Lawns

(see pages 81–85)

Indoors:

- Greenhouse, conservatory flowering plants and houseplants (see pages 86–97)
- Edible crops grown under glass (tomato, pepper, aubergine, cucumber, melon, lettuce, climbing French bean, grape, peach) (see pages 97–107)

Vegetables:

- Seedlings and young plants (see pages 108–110)
- Brassicas (broccoli, calabrese, cabbage, cauliflower, Chinese leaves, kale, kohl rabi, sprout) (see pages 111–118)
- Peas and beans (runner, dwarf, broad bean) (see pages 119–124)
- Stem and leaf crops (asparagus, celery, celeriac, chicory, lettuce, lovage, mint, parsley, rhubarb, sea kale, spinach, spinach beat, Swiss chard) (see pages 125–129)
- Onions (bulb and spring); leek, shallot, garlic, chives (see pages 130–134)
- Potatoes (see pages 134–140)
- Other root crops (beetroot, carrot, Jerusalem artichoke, parsnip, radish, swede, turnip) (see pages 141–145)
- Vegetable fruit (courgette, gherkin, globe artichoke, marrow, melon, pumpkin, ridge cucumber, sweet corn, outdoor tomato) (see pages 146–150)

Fruit

- Top fruit (apple, almond, apricot, cherry, gage, hazelnut, fig, nectarine, peach, pear, plum, quince, walnut) (see pages 151–174)
- Soft fruit (blackberry, black, red and white currant, grape, gooseberry, raspberry, loganberry, strawberry) (see pages 175–190)

3. Examine your plant and compare its symptoms with those detailed in the key at the start of each section. Look at the roots, stems, leaves, flowers or fruit and vegetables and ask yourself such questions as:

- Roots: are they eaten, galled or rotting?
- Stems: are they wilting, carrying visible pests or fungal growths?
- Leaves: are they discoloured, holed or spotted?
- Flowers: are they distorted, discoloured or lacking?
- Fruits and vegetables: are they eaten, mined or spotted?

4. Having identified the cause, look it up in the alphabetical directory of pests, diseases and problems following each key. You will find details of the ailment and methods available to control and prevent attack.

METHODS OF PEST AND DISEASE CONTROL

Prevention of damage by pests, diseases and other disorders is best achieved by a combination of different measures, all of which are designed to produce healthy, well nourished plants. Then, even if there were to be an attack by pest or disease, the plants would be less likely to suffer severe damage.

Plants under stress from drought, poor soil conditions or lack of nutrients, on the other hand, are more likely to be severely damaged or even killed by such attacks. Good soil preparation is the first stage in control.

1. SOIL TREATMENTS

The incorporation of plenty of organic matter will help to open up heavy, clay soils and improve the water-holding capacity of light, sandy soils. This will encourage the development of a strong root system capable of supporting a strong plant. The organic matter could be compost made from selected garden and kitchen wastes or from straw, strawy animal manure or composted bark.

Manures, fertilizer and lime also have a part to play in the control of various problems. For example, club root disease that attacks members of the cabbage family (flowering types such as honesty and wallflowers as well as vegetable types including cabbages, sprouts and cauliflower) is most troublesome on wet, acid soils. Good digging to improve aeration, together with the use of lime to reduce acidity will also lessen the chance of a severe club root attack. Liming can be of benefit to cauliflowers for another reason, too. Under acid conditions the element molybdenum can become deficient and a lack of molybdenum results in a condition in cauliflower known as whiptail, in which the leaves are reduced to whip-like strips. On the other hand, potato scab disease prefers alkaline conditions, so the use of manure or compost and acid fertilizers would help to reduce damage from that source.

Slightly acid conditions are generally best for root crops as, with any excess of lime, the alkalinity tends to make boron unavailable. Lack of boron in root crops causes them to develop hollow or brown centres, a condition referred to as 'brown heart' or 'heart rot'. It is also found that carrots and other root crops tend to produce forked roots if grown on freshly-manured soil, so for a variety of reasons care is needed to relate the treatment of the soil to the plants that are to be grown. The easiest way to achieve this is to follow a set rotation of crops.

To check on whether the soil is alkaline, neutral or acid, soil testing kits are available, as are pH meters for really accurate readings.

2. CROP ROTATION

Particularly in the vegetable garden, but also to a lesser extent in the flower areas too, rotating the crop around in a set pattern will help to avoid build up of any crop-related trouble in a particular part of the garden, as well as giving the opportunity to provide ideal conditions for each different type of plant. In the flower garden, for example, try primulas, wallflowers and pansies for spring bedding in different years to reduce the risk of club root building up with regular annual plantings of wallflowers. With summer bedding, try not to grow asters every year to stop aster wilt becoming troublesome.

With vegetables, divide the crops into three main groups;

1. Onions, leeks, peas and beans, also lettuce, radish, spinach, celery, sweet corn and outdoor tomatoes.

These crops require the richest soil and the peas and beans put nitrogen back into the soil.

2. Root crops including carrots, parsnips, beetroot, plus potatoes if only a few are being grown.

These crops can be grown with just a light dressing of fertilizer, remembering that if fresh manure is added the roots tend to fork. Where several rows of potatoes are to be grown it is better to put them in their own plot which can then be manured before planting.

3. Brassicas including cabbage, sprout, calabrese, broccoli, cauliflower and Chinese leaves.

Brassicas, being mainly leafy crops, benefit from nitrogen and planting them to follow the peas and beans will enable them to use the nitrogen fixed by these crops. Where potatoes are to be grown on a larger scale, make their plot number four and add manure and/or compost before planting them.

For a three-year rotation, divide the vegetable area into three plots and treat them as follows:

THREE YEAR ROTATION
Year 1
Plot 1 Manure; grow onions, leeks, peas and beans
Plot 2 Fertilize; grow carrots and other root crops
Plot 3 Lime; grow cabbages and relatives

Year 2
Plot 1 Lime; grow cabbages and relatives
Plot 2 Manure; grow onions, leeks and peas and beans
Plot 3 Fertilize; grow carrots and other root crops

Year 3
Plot 1 Fertilize; grow onions, leeks, carrots and other root crops
Plot 2 Lime; grow cabbages and relatives
Plot 3 Manure; grow onions, leeks and peas and beans

The rotation of crops ensures that each area of the vegetable garden gets a regular supply of manure, lime and fertilizer, and also ensures that thorough soil cultivations are carried out at least every three years. This will also reduce the weed population, and as many pests and diseases of cultivated plants can live on weeds, there will be a two-fold benefit. If, for any reason, it is not possible to follow a precise rotation do try at least to alternate between 'above ground' crops and 'below ground' crops, and try never to grow a vegetable from one of the above three groups on the same site for two years running.

3 . WEED CONTROL AND HYGIENE

Good weed control and careful attention to garden hygiene both play a useful part in pest and disease control by removing alternative hosts and hiding places. Woodlice and snails abound under piles of old seed trays and pots under greenhouse staging, or among weeds at the bases of hedges or walls. Many pests and diseases of cultivated plants can live equally well on weeds and then spread from there to garden plants. In both the greenhouse and the outside garden it is a wise policy to have a really thorough clean up at least once a year. Most old plant residues can be composted quite safely, but where they are carrying diseases, or heavy populations of pests, they are best burned, or disposed of away from the garden.

4. RESISTANT VARIETIES

A further factor that can be used to reduce crop losses from pests, diseases and other disorders is the choice of variety grown. Increasingly, plant breeders are producing varieties with in-built resistance, or reduced susceptibility, to certain problems. Thus, it is now possible to grow antirrhinums free from rust, asters without wilt, blackcurrants and gooseberries without mildew, carrots partially resistant to carrot fly, club root-free broccoli and swede, leeks without rust, lettuce free from mildew, marrows free from mosaic virus, parsnip with no canker, potatoes without tuber blight, eelworm or virus, raspberries resistant to aphids and therefore virtually virus-free, spinach without mildew, strawberries less prone to grey mould, tomatoes without leaf mould, wilts or virus, roses with reduced susceptibility to mildew, black spot and rust and a very wide range of other plants with resistance or reduced susceptibilities to numerous other problems.

A further use of resistance in plants relates to tomato culture. The rootstock known as KNVF is resistant to corky root, nematodes (eelworms), Verticillium and Fusarium wilts. By grafting a chosen fruiting variety of tomato onto the KNVF rootstock it is possible to obtain a crop in soils infected or infested with the named pathogens.

VEGETABLES

TYPE OF VEGETABLE	VARIETY NAME	RESISTANT/LESS SUSCEPTIBLE TO
BEETROOT	'Monodet'	Bolting
	'Boltardy'	Bolting
BROCCOLI	'Trixie'	Club root
CARROT	'Ingot'	Carrot fly
	'Nandor'	Carrot fly
	'Sytan'	Carrot fly
	'Panther'	Splitting
COURGETTE	'Tarmino'	Cucumber mosaic virus
CUCUMBER	'Tyria'	Powdery mildew, leaf spot, gummosis
	'Marketmore'	Downy mildew, powdery mildew
LEEK	'Autumn Mammoth Verina'	Rust
	'King Richard'	Rust
LETTUCE	'Avondefiance'	Bolting, downy mildew, lettuce root aphid

LETTUCE cont.	'Debby'	*Downy mildew, mosaic virus, root aphid*
	'Lakeland'	*Mildew, lettuce root aphid*
PARSNIP	'Avonresister'	*Canker*
	'Bayonet'	*Canker*
	'Gladiator'	*Canker*
PEA	'Hurst Green Shaft'	*Downy mildew, fusarium*
	'Onward'	*Fusarium, mosaic virus*
	'Oregon Sugar Pod'	*Fusarium*
POTATO, SEE SEPARATE TABLE.		
SPINACH	'Medania'	*Downy mildew*
SPROUT	'Montgomery'	*Powdery mildew, ring spot, white blister*
	'Rampart'	*Powdery mildew, ringspot*
	'Widgeon'	*Powdery mildew*
	'Wellington'	*Powdery mildew*
SWEDE	'Marian'	*Club root, powdery mildew*
TOMATO	'Cyclon'	*Fusarium, leaf mould, leaf silvering, verticillium, virus*
	'Dombito'	*Tobacco mosaic virus*
	'Piranto'	*Brown root rot, fusarium, leaf mould, tomato mosaic virus*
	'Shirley'	*Fusarium, leaf mould, tomato mosaic virus*

POTATOES – the following varieties exhibit a marked degree of resistance to the problems listed:

BLIGHT (FOLIAR AND TUBER)	'Cara', 'Record', 'Romano', 'Sante' (tuber only), 'Wilja'
COMMON SCAB	'King Edward', 'Maris Peer', 'Pentland Crown', 'Pentland Javelin'
POTATO CYST NEMATODE	'Cara', 'Maris Piper', 'Pentland Crown', 'Pentland Javelin', 'Sante'

SLUG	'Kestrel', 'Pentland Dell', 'Stormont Enterprise'
SPRAING	'Bintje', 'Record', 'Romano'
VARIOUS VIRUSES	'Cara', 'Maris Bard', 'Pentland Crown', 'Pentland Dell', 'Pentland Javelin', 'Romano', 'Sante'

ROSES – In a continuing trial being conducted at St Albans, Hertfordshire by the Royal National Rose Society, the following varieties came through the first year 'relatively unscathed': 'Alexander', 'Elina' (formerly 'Peaudouce'), 'Flower Carpet', 'Gilda', 'Little Bo-Peep', 'Princess Michael of Kent', 'Red Trail', 'Telford Promise'. It was recorded that 'Freedom', 'Ingrid Bergman', 'Indian Summer', 'Hertfordshire' and 'Pink Chimo' were only slightly damaged by disease

In the tables below, also kindly supplied by the Royal National Rose Society, all the varieties listed have shown a reasonable degree of resistance to black spot, mildew and rust when growing in The Gardens of the Rose in Hertfordshire, but it must be noted that the tables can only be used as a guide and may not be reliable in all areas. Remember that resistance does break down from time to time, as growers of 'Frensham' (mildew), 'Fragrant Cloud' (black spot) and 'Super Star' (mildew) found out over the years

LARGE-FLOWERED (HYBRID TEA) ROSES	'Alec's Red', 'Alexander', 'Blessings', 'Congratulations', 'Cheshire Life', 'Elina' (formerly 'Peaudouce'), 'Felicia', 'Freedom', 'Grandpa Dickson', 'Just Joey', 'Peace', 'Pink Favourite', 'Pink Peace', 'Precious Platinum', 'Remember Me', 'Royal Romance', 'Royal William', 'Silver Jubilee', 'Simba', 'The Lady', 'Troika'
CLUSTER-FLOWERED (FLORIBUNDA) ROSES	'Amber Queen', 'Ainsley Dickson', 'Anne Harkness', 'Baby Bio', 'Beautiful Britain', 'Bonica', 'Bright Smile', 'Chanelle', 'Flower Carpet', 'City of Belfast', 'Escapade', 'Fragrant Delight', 'Invincible', 'Korresia', 'Lover's Meeting', 'Laughter Lines', 'Matangi', 'Memento', 'Princess Alice', 'Sexy Rexy', 'Sweet Magic', 'Southampton', 'The Times', 'Trumpeter'
CLIMBING ROSES	'Bobby James', 'Compassion', 'Dortmund', 'Dreaming Spires', 'Dublin Bay', 'Galway Bay', 'Golden Showers', 'Hamburger Phoenix', 'Highfield', 'Joseph's Coat', 'Maigold', 'Meg', 'Mme Gregoire Staechelin', 'New Dawn', 'Phyllis Bide', 'Rambling Rector', Rosa banksiae 'Lutea', Rosa filipes 'Kiftsgate', 'Seagull', 'Sympathie', 'Wedding Day'

FRUIT CROPS

TYPE OF FRUIT	VARIETY NAME	RESISTANT/LESS SUSCEPTIBLE TO
APPLE	'Beauty of Bath'	*Mildew*
	'Charles Ross'	*Scab*

APPLE *cont.*	'Discovery'	*Mildew, scab*
	'Greensleeves'	*Mildew*
	'Jester'	*Mildew*
	'Lord Derby'	*Mildew, scab*
	'Lord Lambourne'	*Mildew*
	'Sunset'	*Scab*
PEAR	'Beurre Hardy'	*Scab*
	'Conference'	*Scab*
BLACKCURRANT	'Ben Lomond'	*Mildew*
	'Ben More'	*Mildew*
	'Ben Sarek'	*Mildew*
GOOSEBERRY	'Greenfinch'	*Mildew, leaf spot*
	'Invicta'	*Mildew*
RASPBERRY	'Autumn Bliss'	*Aphid*
	'Glen Moy'	*Aphid*
	'Glen Prosen'	*Aphid*
	'Malling Admiral'	*Cane spot, spur blight*
	'Malling Joy'	*Aphids, grey mould*
	'Malling Leo'	*Aphids, cane spot, spur blight*
STRAWBERRY	'Bogota'	*Red core*
	'Cambridge Favourite'	*Mildew, verticillium*
	'Gerida'	*Crown rot, mildew, verticillium*
	'Honeoye'	*Mildew*
	'Pandora'	*Grey mould, mildew, verticillium*
	'Pegasus'	*Grey mould, mildew, verticillium*
	'Silver Jubilee'	*Grey mould, mildew, red core*
	'Tristar'	*Mildew, red core, verticillium*

Remember that resistances sometimes break down and that a variety which was once resistant to a particular problem may suddenly become sensitive to it.

5. PHYSICAL BARRIERS AND TRAPS

Plants attacked by flying pests, especially vegetable crops, can be covered with special, fine netting which will prevent the pests laying their eggs on or around the crop or establishing on the foliage. Such protection is of particular benefit to carrots to exclude carrot fly and brassicas to exclude cabbage white butterflies and cabbage root fly. Netting is also valuable to protect soft fruit from attack by birds, and indeed in some areas it is virtually impossible to grow a satisfactory crop of soft fruit without a permanent fruit cage. An alternative method used with some success to keep birds off outdoor crops is the use of humming or buzzing lines. A thin, tightly-stretched plastic strip held taut over a row of vegetables or soft fruit will vibrate in any wind and this is often sufficient to stop birds from damaging the crop below.

In the greenhouse and conservatory it is possible to trap quite a number of flying pests with coloured, sticky traps hung over the plants. Different pests respond to different wavelengths of light and whitefly and aphids will be attracted to yellow traps whilst thrips are more attracted to blue.

Trapping with bands of grease around tree trunks will protect apples and pears from damage by various caterpillars, including the winter moth. The female of this moth cannot fly and so has to reach the male by climbing up the trunk of the fruit tree. A band of grease would prevent this, and these are available either as a proprietary product that is applied directly on to the tree trunk or on a paper band tied tightly around the trunk. Alternatively, it may be a proprietary band purchased ready-greased or a plastic band with the sticky part hidden underneath to avoid contamination by leaves and to prevent it fouling birds, domestic animals or the gardener by accidental contact.

A grease band barrier also discourages ants from climbing up into the trees where they have been found to move greenfly around to new shoots and also to defend them from predators. The ants obtain supplies of sugary honeydew from the greenfly, and can move them to new areas of the tree when overcrowding starts to occur. A ring of barrier glue can also be applied around the tops of plant pots to stop vine weevil adults reaching the compost where they seek to lay their eggs.

A different type of physical barrier can also be used to reduce codling moth numbers. The caterpillars of codling moth of apples and pears spend the winter hiding in convenient crevices, pupate in early spring and then emerge in late spring to early summer to fly, mate, and lay their eggs. If bands of corrugated cardboard are tied quite tightly round the tree trunks in midsummer, many codling larvae will seek to hibernate there. The bands can then be removed in winter and burned, thus removing quite a proportion of the local population of that particular pest.

A further example of a useful barrier method is the use of circles of carpet underlay placed tightly around the stems of brassicas at planting-out time. These are aimed at preventing the cabbage root fly from laying eggs in the soil close to the plant stems.

Finally, earwigs can be trapped in plant pots filled with dry grass or crumpled newspapers and placed on the tops of canes. The canes are pushed into the soil between dahlias or other susceptible plants and emptied daily.

6. PHEROMONES

Pheromones are chemical substances given off by animals, including insects, for detection and response by others, usually of the same species. One example is the scent given off by female moths to guide male moths to them for mating. Man-made versions of several moth pheromones have been synthesized and used in commercial orchards in conjunction with sticky boards or water traps to catch the moths. The numbers and rate at which the moths are caught are then monitored and used as a basis on which to plan the timing of the spraying programme. When used in gardens, the pheromone traps will normally be capable of catching enough of the male moths to prevent most of the damage. For example, one trap would protect 5 apple trees within 30m (100ft) of the trap from attacks by codling moth.

An ever-increasing range of pheromones is becoming available for use in the garden, including plum fruit moth, fruit tree tortrix moth and summer fruit tortrix. A different trap, each with its own specific pheromone, is needed for each species and timing is important for maximum benefit. For codling moth the traps should be in place in late spring/early summer, no later than a week after petal fall. A pheromone for pea moth is available but this is best used as a guide to the presence of the moth in the garden, indicating that spraying is needed, as ready-mated female pea moths fly considerable distances to find the crop.

In the coming years pheromones will be used to a greater extent as more are identified and synthesized, including such substances as alarm pheromones and aggregation pheromones. Alarm pheromones for aphids, for example, cause the pests to become agitated, stop feeding, and move away or drop off the plants. Aggregation pheromones, on the other hand, cause large numbers of the insect in question to gather together in one place, where they can then be suitably controlled.

Other possible developments for the near or more distant future are the use of anti-feeding agents, synthetic versions of plant scents, insect growth regulators and virus diseases of pests. By identifying, synthesizing and applying anti-feeding chemicals, pests would be stopped from attacking the treated plants. It is also known that certain plants emit a special scent when being attacked by a pest and this scent attracts the appropriate predator.

These scents are called synomones and a possibility for the not-too-distant future is that these scents could be synthesized and applied to plants. Further into the future, it should be possible to incorporate anti-feeding substances into a range of plants by genetic engineering. An insect locates its host plant in a variety of ways, including being able to smell it. By identifying the scent given off by particular plants which the insects detect and home in on, the pests could be lured away from crops. By incorporating a sticky trap or pesticidal treatment the pests could be considerably reduced. Intercropping onions, carrots and cabbages, or planting parsley or marigolds among these crops, is sometimes recommended as a means of reducing damage by carrot fly, onion fly or cabbage root fly. The theory is to confuse the flying pests by masking the characteristic crop scent. In practice, however, when subjected to trials, this system of 'companion planting' rarely succeeds, and also mixes up the crop rotation sequence.

Insect growth regulators, also known as juvenile hormones, work in a distinctive way, normally by affecting a particular stage in the life cycle of the pest and preventing the further development to maturity. Typically, they disrupt the late larval stage and the pest dies instead of pupating. With the virus diseases, various caterpillars have been found to respond to what are known as granulosis viruses and these are being actively investigated and put on trial, prior to being released if they pass all the necessary tests.

A further possibility in the control of pests, although not for garden use, is the release of vast numbers of sterile males of a particular pest species. These would outnumber the local populations of virile males and so very few fertile eggs would be laid. This could be of value in outbreaks of forestry pests for example.

Diseases are also the subject of research and some useful beneficial fungi and bacteria have been identified which have an effect on various plant diseases. The first to become available is the fungus *Trichoderma viride*, which is supplied in both pellet and powder form. The fungus is cultured on pellets which are inserted into holes drilled into the trunks of apples, plums and related trees to prevent and to control the silver leaf fungus. The powder form of the fungus is used in diluted, liquid form as a paint to protect large pruning cuts from silver leaf infection.

7. BIOLOGICAL CONTROL

Pests have been controlled by their natural enemies in gardens since gardens were first created and there are still quite a number of helpful agents that can be encouraged to help establish and maintain the health of your garden plants in the most natural way possible. Principal among the garden friends are ladybirds and hover flies along with lacewings, which feed mainly on aphids and some other leaf-feeding pests, plus ground beetles, rove beetles and many spiders which feed on a number of ground level pests. Both ladybird adults and larvae feed on greenfly and consume around 5,500 in their lifetime. Only the larval stage of the hoverfly eat pests but each one can eat around 100 greenfly before being fully fed. Lacewing larvae are rather more effective, consuming some 1500 greenfly, but they are cannibalistic once alternative food supplies run out, so a plentiful supply of greenfly is necessary!

A strip of soil around the garden which is sown with grasses and both pollen and nectar-producing wild flowers will be of great help in supplying food and shelter to a surprising number of garden friends. Care should also be taken when using any insecticide sprays for pest infestations so that there is no over-spraying on to the wild flower strip. Where possible, spray only those parts of the plants where the pest attacks are worst, leaving other parts for the natural predators to clear up.

This kind of natural pest control is also possible in the greenhouse, where it has been practised for very many years. The first reference is probably the suggestion by J. C. Loudon in 1850 in his 'Encyclopaedia of Gardening' to keep a toad in the greenhouse to eat 'worms, ants and other insects'. On a more reliable basis, *Encarsia formosa*, a parasite of the glasshouse whitefly, was identified in 1926 and is now very widely used as a control method in commercial glasshouse crops. Biological control is now receiving considerable attention for use in both the garden and the greenhouse, and several different agents are widely available.

I **APHIDS (GREENFLY/BLACKFLY)** In the average garden, ladybirds, lacewings and hoverflies all play their part in keeping aphid populations in check, but there are also two further biological agents available for use in the greenhouse. One, *Aphidoletes aphidimyza*, is a small midge-like fly whose larvae seek out and devour up to 15 aphids per day, while the other, *Aphidius matricariae*, is a tiny wasp which lays its eggs inside the aphids, producing around 100 eggs in all. A lacewing species, *Chrysopa carnea*, has also been found to be of value against aphids in the greenhouse. The fungal parasite *Verticillium lecanii* is also effective, applied as a spray. At temperatures above 20°C (68°F) and with a relative humidity around 95% for a few hours each day, the fungus will flourish. Various strains of this fungus have been selected, and it is capable of attacking and controlling whitefly and thrips as well as aphids in the greenhouse environment.

II **CATERPILLARS** A bacterium, *Bacillus thuringiensis*, is effective against virtually all types of caterpillar. The bacterium is supplied in dried form, is mixed with water to activate it, and is then sprayed over the infested plants. Caterpillars stop feeding very quickly and die a few days later. The bacillus works equally well out of doors or under glass, although there many more caterpillar pests outside.

III **LEAF MINER** Tomato leaf miner, and in recent times some more exotic species, can cause great damage to greenhouse crops. Two biological agents are available to help in the forms of *Dacnusa sibirica* and *Diglyphus isaea*. The former lays up to 90 eggs inside leaf miner larvae over a eight to nine-day adult life span, while the adult of the latter feeds on the leaf miner larvae as well as laying eggs in the mines close to older paralysed host larvae. Each *Diglyphus* lays around 50 eggs in a three to four week life span.

IV **MEALY BUGS** Some species of mealy bug can produce as many as 500 eggs in their eight-week life cycle at 20°C (68°F). They feed on the plant sap and excrete sugary honeydew which soon becomes colonized by sooty mould fungi. Available to control these pests is an Australian ladybird relative, *Cryptolaemus montrouzieri*. This predator is active only at temperatures above 20°C(68°F) and works slowly, so control may not become evident for six weeks or so after introduction. The adult beetles live for many weeks and lay around 10 eggs each day. Another way to control mealy bug is with the parasitic wasps, *Leptomastix dactylopii* and *Leptomastidea abnormis*. *Leptomastix,* for example, lays 200 or more eggs per day at 30°C (86°F), inserting them into large nymphs and adult female mealy bugs.

V **RED SPIDER MITE (TWO-SPOTTED SPIDER MITE)** In this case the beneficial agent is a predatory mite which seeks out and eats the spider mites at up to 20 eggs or nymph stage mites per day. The predatory mite, *Phytoseiulus persimilis*, was discovered in 1960, and although widely used commercially, does need some care in the amateur greenhouse to get the best results. The main problem is that, ideally, there should be a small resident population of red spider mites at all times, sufficient to keep the predators alive, but not sufficient to cause significant plant damage. However, a programme of repeat introductions will top up the predator levels. For best results it is recommended that there should be a minimum temperature of 12°C (54°F) to ensure the predators are sufficiently active and can breed at a fast enough rate. Red spider mite can increase 100 fold in one month and 1000 fold in two months. The first introduction of the predatory mite should, therefore, be as soon as possible after the pest mite is discovered. Where there is a history of red spider mite in a greenhouse, a close check should be kept in spring for the first indications of attack (a stippling of pale spots on the foliage). To assist the predatory mites in their search for the pests, infested plants should be grouped together. A naturally occurring predatory midge, *Therodiplosis persicae*, also has potential as the adult form can fly to search out more isolated red spider infestations in the greenhouse. Between the months of May and September, temperatures outside are normally sufficiently high for the predatory mite to breed at a satisfactory rate, and the predator is used in commercial holdings on strawberries and blackcurrants.

VI SCALE INSECTS Female scale insects produce hundreds of eggs under the old scale and the young disperse widely over the infested plants as they hatch. The complete life cycle takes around three months at 20°C (68°F) and during their feeding on plant sap, vast quantities of sugary honeydew is produced.

Different species of scale insects can occur, and the soft scale types can be controlled biologically by *Metaphycus helvolus*, which is a 2mm (½in) long midge-like creature. It controls the scale

insects in two different ways as it lays up to six eggs per day which hatch out and feed on the scales, while the adults also feed actively on the pests, eating up to two dozen per day. The life cycle of the beneficial midge takes around 30 days at 20°C (68°F) but only 11 days at 30°C (86°F) so it can be an effective control, although it only feeds on the smaller scales, so for heavy attacks a number of introductions will be necessary.

VII SCIARID FLIES (FUNGUS GNATS) These annoying, small, black flies rise up from the surface of pot plant compost when disturbed. The larvae, which hatch from eggs laid in the compost, are slender, off-white creatures with small black heads and they feed on plant roots. The larvae are controlled by the vine weevil nematode, see below, but a newer control is a tiny straw-coloured mite, 1 to 1.5mm (⅙in) in size. The mite, *Hypoaspis miles*, burrows down into the compost and devours the sciarid fly larvae. The mites can live for up to up to six weeks without feeding, and so can control any subsequent invasions by sciarid flies during that period.

VIII SLUGS There can be as many as 200 slugs living and feeding in each square metre of soil, and each one is capable of laying up to 300 eggs. Their potential for damage is vast, but fortunately a useful nematode has been identified which can exert virtually complete control. Known as *Phasmarhabditis hermaphrodita*, the nematode penetrates the slug body, carrying with it masses of bacteria. The bacteria attack and kill the slug, the nematodes feed on the breakdown products and both nematode and bacteria build up and escape to seek out more prey. Slug feeding is inhibited within three to five days of the nematode attack and one treatment will normally give at least six weeks' control of slugs, provided the soil is kept moist and soil temperature is within the 5–20°C (40–68°F) band. Its use is, therefore, possible in most years from early spring to late autumn.

IX THRIPS (THUNDER FLIES) These slender black insects can be very damaging to flower crops, causing bleached spots on the petals. In recent years a particular species, western flower thrips, has become a major pest on some commercial holdings. Thrips are controlled by two related mites, *Amblyseius cucumeris* and *A. mackenziei*, which feed on the young stages of the pest. The parasitic fungi *Metarhizium anisopliae* and *Verticillium lecanii* are also known to be of use. Thrips larvae pupate in the soil to complete their development to the adult form. A control method used in commercial glasshouses is to cover the soil with plastic film coated with a sticky substance plus an insecticide. This system is valuable as it selects out one stage of the thrip life cycle, thus interrupting the continuity.

X VINE WEEVIL The adult weevils eat rounded notches out of 'hard' leaves such as rhododendrons and camellias, while the legless larvae feed on plant roots. Only female weevils occur. Attacks happen on plants growing in the garden as well as on pot plants grown in the home or greenhouse. When eggs are laid in the compost of pot plants, the resulting larvae will soon kill the plant by eating the roots. Available for pest control are the beneficial nematodes *Heterorhabditis megidis* and *Steinernema carpocapsae*, which seek out and enter the larval bodies of vine weevil larvae and some other soil pests including fungus

gnats (sciarid flies), chafers, leatherjackets and cutworms.

The nematodes carry a bacterium (*Xenorhabdus*) which kills the pest within two weeks. Nematodes and bacteria multiply within the host and then leave to seek further prey. The nematode is active at temperatures down to 12°C (54°F), so it can be used in the open garden under suitable soil temperature conditions in spring through to autumn. Under glass or in the home, vine weevil can be present in any of the life cycle stages namely egg, larva, pupa or adult, so the nematode can be used virtually throughout the year, depending on the temperature. The parasitic fungus *Metarhizium anisopliae* is known to attack vine weevil but this has now been superseded in use by the nematode control method.

XI WHITEFLY The whitefly parasite *Encarsia formosa* is probably the most commonly used beneficial insect. The parasite, which is a tiny wasp, lays eggs in the scale stages of the whitefly. The scales turn black in 10 to 14 days as the contents are eaten by the larvae of the wasp and the new adults escape about 21 days later to start the cycle over again. Each tiny wasp destroys 10 to 15 whitefly scales each day and can lay up to 300 eggs in its life span. Whitefly breed at a fast rate and can increase 100 fold in six weeks in spring, but in only three weeks in summer when the temperatures are higher. The whitefly population should, therefore, be at a low level when the *Encarsia* is introduced, and a minimum temperature of 18°C (64°F) is required. This ensures that the parasite can breed at a fast enough rate to keep up with the rate of increase of the whitefly. Where populations of the pest have reached high levels before any action has been taken, sprays of a fatty acids insecticide can be applied leaving one day, or a pyrethrum insecticide leaving a minimum of seven days, between the last spray and introducing the *Encarsia*. Strains of *Vertcillium lecanii*, a fungal parasite of various insects, has also proved of value in some situations.

XII GENERAL Two anthocorid bugs, *Anthocoris nemorum* or 'needle bug' and *Orius majusculus* the 'pirate bug', are known as a useful friends in the garden, especially on unsprayed fruit trees, feeding on a wide range of other creatures including aphids and fruit tree red spider mites. These bugs are now being used under glass where they attack a similarly wide range of insects, including western flower thrips. There is a slight snag however, as both these bugs also bite humans!

Biological control agents can be bought from specialist, mail-order suppliers. Check that you can supply the correct conditions for the control agent in terms of temperature, humidity and daylight before ordering them. When they arrive, you must read the instructions carefully before proceeding. For example, *Encarsia formosa*, the parasitic wasp that controls whitefly, is supplied on cards which are hung up in the greenhouse, but not in direct sunlight. These very specific conditions must be met or the chances are the control agent will die before it has even started its work.

Traps must be removed since they could trap the *Encarsia* as well as the whitefly and, when using any biological control, great care must be taken over the use of any pesticides, and a suitable interval must be left between the final spray and the date of introducing the predators or parasites. The aphid-specific insecticide pirimicarb can usually be used

without adverse effect, and fatty acid sprays to just the tops of plants can help to reduce an over-large whitefly population without adversely affecting the whitefly parasite. Where permethrin-containing sprays have been used it may be over two months before *Encarsia* could safely be introduced. Always seek advice from the supplier before it is introduced.

In the UK, strict controls are in place which prevent the introduction and release of exotic, as opposed to native, species in biological control programmes. This is designed to avoid adverse effects on non-target species, and extensive tests have to be undertaken before any such permissions are granted.

8. PESTICIDES

In the EU, as in many other areas of the world, powerful legislation is now in existence, covering the manufacture, sale and use of products to control pests, diseases and weeds. In the UK, for example, The Control of Pesticides Regulations 1986, part of the wide-reaching Food and Environment Act of 1985, imposes very strict rules on what is allowed to be manufactured, sold and applied and on what claims are allowed to be put on product labels. These regulations apply equally to man-made and to 'natural' or 'organic' substances and ban the use of home-made infusions. Such concoctions have never been examined for safety to the environment, to the user, or to the consumer of treated produce.

In order to use pesticides safely and effectively:

- Choose the right product. Read the label before you buy.
- If in doubt ask for help.
- Follow the instructions carefully. Use the correct rate, and note any

required interval between spraying edible crops and harvest.

- Spray thoroughly, remembering that many pests and diseases will be found underneath the leaves. Spray to wet the leaves but not so much that the spray runs off.
- Avoid spray entering ponds, ditches or streams.
- If you have surplus diluted spray left over, apply it to gravel or to unsurfaced paths or to level, bare soil.
- Wash hands and equipment after use, disposing of rinsings in the same way as surplus diluted spray.
- Store pesticides away from children and pets, in a cool, dry place.
- Always keep pesticides in the original containers; do not decant into unlabelled containers.

TIMING OF SPRAYS In the detailed sections which follow, indications are given where appropriate on the best time to apply any recommended pesticide treatment. With insecticides in particular, the timing is aimed at finding a particularly susceptible stage in the life cycle of the pest and equally at avoiding any times when the pest is likely to be in a non-susceptible stage. With control of greenfly on fruit trees and bushes, for example, a winter tar oil spray can be applied to kill the overwintering eggs. Once hatched out, however, an insecticide application at any time the pest is present (except during flowering) would be effective as adults and young nymphs are all susceptible to the treatment. On the other hand, the caterpillar of the cabbage white butterfly must be controlled before it pupates and becomes a chrysalis; eggs and chrysalis are not controlled by spraying. The best times to apply pesticides are:

- Early morning or late evening
- When bees and other insects are not on the wing
- When there is no strong sun
- When there is little wind
- When the leaves are dry
- When the treated plants are not in flower

Throughout this book, the pesticide treatments recommended are known to be effective. However, product labels are constantly being revised and amended, pests may become resistant to chemicals and certain recommendations may be withdrawn. The label must be the guide; only apply a product when the pest and the crop are listed on the label, unless there is a general recommendation such as 'controls all foliar insect pests on flowers, fruit and vegetables'. Remember, if in any doubt, seek advice from the manufacturer of the product.

9. INTEGRATED CONTROL

To obtain the best possible results, namely the maximum reduction of crop damage and losses, try to adopt an holistic approach, using as many different methods of pest or disease control as are available. This approach is known as 'Integrated Control'.

A typical example would be in the control of whitefly in the greenhouse, when the season would start off by hanging sticky, yellow traps above the plants to reduce early damage. Should an attack start to develop, the infestation could be kept under control with sprays of an insecticide based on fatty acids or pyrethrins until the average day and night temperatures were sufficiently high for the biological agent *Encarsia* to be introduced. Leave the necessary interval between the last spray and introducing the parasite.

Sticky traps would not be effective for two-spotted spider mite (red spider mite) on cucumbers, so more applications of fatty acids or pyrethrins may be necessary before conditions are favourable for the predatory mite *Phytoseiulus*. It may also be necessary to control cucumber powdery mildew and, whereas a benomyl fungicide would not upset the whitefly parasite, the mite predator would be adversely affected. In such a case, choose a cucumber variety that is resistant to mildew and therefore needs no spraying.

By combining as many cultural measures as possible, choosing as appropriate from soil treatments, crop rotations, weed control, resistant varieties, physical barriers and traps, pheromones, biological control and pesticides, it should be possible to keep damage to a minimum.

FLOWERS 1

ANNUALS, BIENNIALS, BEDDING PLANTS, OTHER FLOWERS GROWN FROM SEED

Annuals grow from seed, produce flowers and die all in a single year. Biennials grow from seed to produce vegetative plants in year one and then flower and die in the second year. Bedding plants are those raised from seed or by other means but used only for spring or summer displays then discarded.

SEEDLINGS

PESTS VISIBLE	Greenish pests clustered on young leaves and shoot tips	*aphids*
	Pale pests under leaves, making short leaping flights when disturbed, leaves bleached	*glasshouse leafhopper*
	White, moth-like pests under leaves, making short flights when disturbed, no leaf bleaching	*whitefly*
NO PESTS VISIBLE	Leaves or stems eaten, partially or completely	*millipedes, slugs, snails, woodlice, springtails*
	Seedlings collapse, roots eaten	*sciarid fly*
	Seedlings collapse, narrowing of stem at soil level	*damping off*
	Seedlings rotting away, zinnia, lobelia	*seedling blight, leaf and stem rot*

OLDER PLANTS – ROOTS

ROOTS GALLED	Cabbage family plants	*club root*
STEMS GALLED	Masses of leafy outgrowths at soil level	*leafy gall*

WITHERING ROOTS DAMAGED	Roots eaten	*chafers, cutworm, leatherjacket, sciarid fly, swift moth, vine weevil, wireworm*
	Soft rotting of tissue	*crown, foot and root rots*
WITHERING ROOTS NOT DAMAGED	Plants wilting, aster pansy grey mould present many plants any plant	*wilt, pansy sickness, grey mould, stem rot, waterlogging*

OLDER PLANTS – LEAVES

HOLES IN LEAVES PESTS VISIBLE	Green, brown or variously coloured caterpillars	*angle-shades moth, large white butterfly*
	Irregular holes, earwigs present	*earwigs*
	Irregular holes, slime trails present	*slugs, snails*
	Small holes/spots, nasturtium and cabbage family plants	*turnip flea beetle*
NO HOLES IN LEAVES PESTS VISIBLE	Greenish insects clustered under leaves and at shoot tips	*aphids*
NO PESTS VISIBLE VISIBLE FUNGAL GROWTHS	Greyish mould present and soft rotting	*grey mould*
	Greyish mould present, no rotting	*downy mildew*
	Orange, rusty spots under leaves	*rust fungus*
	Rings and spots of white fungus, cabbage family plants	*white blister*
	White, powdery coating	*powdery mildew*
LEAVES SCORCHED OR SPOTTED	Brown to black spots, many plants	*leaf spots*
	Irregular pale lines and patterns	*virus*
	Scorch marks, sweet pea any plant	*leaf scorch, frost/ low temperature*
	Silvery streaks and spots, thundery weather	*thrips*
LEAVES YELLOWING	Older leaves yellow then brown between veins	*magnesium deficiency*
	Youngest leaves yellow between the veins, or all over	*iron deficiency*

FLOWERS

SHOOTS WITH NO FLOWERS	Buds produced but drop, sweet pea and others	*bud drop*
ROTTING	Abnormal, twisted	*virus*
	Blackening of petals, cornflower	*petal blight*
	Covered with greyish mould	*grey mould*

ANGLE-SHADES MOTH The adult angle-shades moth, *Phlogophora meticulosa*, bears a number of brown markings on the wings in a series of 'V' shapes and shades, hence the name of angle-shades. Eggs are laid in spring and summer and the caterpillars feed, singly or in groups, on the foliage of a number of plants. The caterpillars grow up to 4cm (1½in) long, and are either velvet-green or brown, with slight lines and 'V'-shaped markings. Leaves, flowers and growing points may be eaten out before the caterpillars pupate in the soil over winter.

Control: Regular inspection and hand-picking of the caterpillars should be sufficient except in the case of very severe attacks. Where damage is still occurring, spray with the biological control agent *Bacillus thuringiensis* or with a contact insecticide such as permethrin, pyrethrins or fatty acids.

APHIDS (GREENFLY AND BLACKFLY)

Aphids can be very damaging, especially when attacks occur on seedlings and young plants. Many different species occur and some have the potential to spread virus diseases as they feed on the plant sap. Aphids multiply at a prodigious rate, especially when the plants are still growing under glass, and will stay on the bedding plants when they are set outside. If not controlled they will eventually fly off to alternative host plants, before flying to specific types of trees for winter egg-laying. Where aphids are feeding, leaves often curl and plants become stunted, while the sugary honeydew excreted by the pests makes the leaves sticky and often blackened due to colonisation by sooty mould fungi.

Control: While still under glass protection in the propagation and young plant stage, aphids can be kept in check by biological control agents acting both as parasites and predators. Introductions of the parasitic wasp *Aphidius* or the predatory midge-like fly *Aphidoletes* can be made as necessary (*see Biological control, pp. xvi–xxi*).

Chemically, aphids can be killed by sprays of bifenthrin, dimethoate, fatty acids, heptenophos, pirimiphos-methyl, pirimicarb or pyrethrins. After planting out, pirimicarb would be the safest chemical where ladybirds and other natural predators are present as it is almost entirely aphid specific.

Main aphid species

The following are most common:

• Black bean aphid, *Aphis fabae*, is a summer pest on nasturtium, marigold, poppy and a few other bedding plants. Leaves can be curled, plants stunted and flowering reduced. In autumn this species of aphid flies off to spindle trees (*Euonymus europaeus*) or sometimes to the guelder-rose (*Viburnum opulus*).

• Glasshouse and potato aphid, *Aulacorthum solani*, attacks most plants and can be a particular pest in unheated greenhouses during the later stages of bedding plant development. This species can overwinter in the adult form.

• Mottled arum aphid, *Aulacorthum circumflexum*, feeds on a wide range of greenhouse plants and can spread virus diseases. The adults are identified by a black horse-shoe mark on the back. Plentiful honeydew is produced by this species.

• Peach-potato aphid, *Myzus persicae*, is another species with a wide host range, and is the vector of a number of damaging virus diseases.

BLINDNESS Blindness is the term used to describe shoots that are expected to flower but which develop without a flower bud present. Various factors can be involved, including drought, waterlogging, pest damage and nutrient shortage. Blindness can also be caused by infection with the leafy gall bacterium, see below.

Control: Pinching out the shoot tip to encourage new shoots to develop will normally solve the problem of blindness, coupled with correction of any known cultural failings and control of pests (*see Earwigs, below*).

BUD DROP Bud drop can be a particular problem with sweet pea flowers, which drop off before they reach open flower stage. Soil dryness and low night temperatures are the main factors responsible.

Control: Ensure that the roots are amply supplied with water by adequate watering and mulching.

CHAFERS The adult chafer beetles are of little trouble to annuals, biennials or bedding plants but the larvae feed on plant roots, and being up to 1.5cm (½in) long can do a lot of damage.

Control: Thorough soil preparation will usually expose the large chafer grubs which can then be removed. Alternatively, treat the soil with the biological control nematode, *Steinernema carpocapsae*, or use a chlorpyrifos/diazinon soil insecticide.

CLUB ROOT The club root fungus, *Plasmodiophora brassicae*, attacks plants in the cabbage family. Annuals and biennials in this family include honesty, stocks and wallflowers. Clubbed swellings develop on the roots, growth is stunted and plants may die. The infection passes from the infected roots back into the soil and may persist for 20 years or more. To prevent, do not plant susceptible subjects into infected soil. At the first indication of attack, remove and burn infected plants, and also remove a bucketful or so of soil from around each infected plant.

Control: Club root is encouraged by acid soil conditions, so lime the soil before planting cabbage-family bedding plants. Dip the roots of transplants into a suspension of benomyl or thiophanate-methyl in water to reduce the severity of attack.

CROWN, ROOT AND FOOT ROTS Various species of fungi can be involved in the rotting of seedlings and young plants, but all have the same result. Roots, stem bases or crowns become soft and rotten, rapidly followed by wilting and death of the plants. Generally, the disease will attack plants that are growing poorly or have been injured during planting or by pests afterwards. Waterlogged conditions can also be a predisposing factor.

Control: Plant firmly, in well-drained soil, taking care not to damage the stems or roots. For plants known to be particularly at risk, water plants in after planting with a solution of copper fungicide and take measures to prevent slug damage to stems.

CUTWORM Cutworms are the larvae of various moths, like the turnip moth (*Agrotis segetum*), the heart and dart moth (*Agrotis exclamationis*), the garden dart moth (*Euxoa nigricans*), the white-line dart moth (*Euxoa tritici*) and the large yellow underwing (*Noctua pronuba*). The large caterpillars eat through plants at or around soil level and can ruin a new plant display overnight.

Control: Thorough soil cultivation before planting will expose these pests for hand removal. Where high populations are thought to be present, water the soil with the biological control nematode *Steinernema carpocapsae* in advance of planting, or incorporate a chlorpyrifos/diazinon soil insecticide.

DAMPING OFF Damping off results in seedlings and very young plants wilting and toppling over and frequently a constriction of the stems can be seen at soil level. Species of *Pythium*, *Rhyzoctonia* and *Phytophthora* fungi can be involved and these are encouraged by wet compost or over-humid conditions.
Control: Always use new compost and new, or thoroughly cleaned, pots and seed trays. Sow seed thinly and prick out as soon as possible to avoid overcrowding. Water only when necessary, and add a copper fungicide to the water once a week as a preventative.

DOWNY MILDEW Downy mildew, *Peronospora* spp., attacks a few species of bedding plant, notably alyssum, antirrhinum, clarkia, pansy, stocks and wallflower. Leaves show a yellow spotting on the upper surfaces and a growth of off-white, downy mould appears on the undersides. Plants can be severely checked or even killed by the attack.
Control: Start off with new compost and clean pots and seed trays. Should an attack appear, remove the worst plants or patches of seedlings and then water with a copper fungicide or spray with mancozeb fungicide.

EARWIG Earwigs, *Forficula auricularia*, are frequent pests of bedding plants, eating flowers, leaves and buds. Female earwigs have straight pincers at the end of

the body, whilst those of the male earwig are curved. They hide by day and feed by night, so are not often seen feeding on the plants. Damage to young buds can be one of the causes of blindness (*see above*). Being large insects, they can take a lot of killing, and are perhaps best trapped.
Control: Earwigs need to hide by day in a position where there is some pressure on both upper and lower body surfaces and so tend to squeeze into small holes or gaps. To take advantage of this fact, traps can be made by stuffing dry grass or newspaper into plant pots and putting these on canes pushed into the soil among the plants. The earwigs will move into the pots after a night's feeding and the pots can be taken off and the earwigs shaken out onto a path and squashed before the next night.

If killing the earwigs in this manner does not appeal, dust them with a bendiocarb or pirimiphos-methyl insecticide, or dust the dry grass or newspaper in the pots with the same chemical to avoid the need to shake out the earwigs each day.

FROST/LOW TEMPERATURES Various forms of leaf scorch or death follow incidences of low temperature, particularly in the early weeks after setting out, before the plants may have fully adjusted to the outside conditions. Frost can kill the entire plant, or just the existing leaves, depending on the plant and the severity of the frost, but with light damage on strong plants, recovery usually follows.
Control: Prevent damage by hardening-off the plants for a few weeks before planting, and then by covering the young plants with a woven fleece material when frost or low night temperatures are forecast. Remove the covering by day. In an

unheated greenhouse, damage can often be prevented by simply covering the trays of seedlings with newspaper.

GLASSHOUSE LEAFHOPPER Glasshouse leafhopper, *Hauptidia maroccana* (also known as *H. pallidifrons* and *H. tolosana*) is a relatively new pest in the UK, but is now well established. The adult is 3 to 4mm (⅛–⅙in) long, pale yellow with a pair of brown 'V'-shaped marks on the back. Breeding occurs throughout the year under glass, and feeding on the sap below the leaves results in a pale stippling of bleached marks on the upper surface.
Control: Sticky, yellow traps hung over the plants for whitefly control will also catch some leafhoppers. Alternatively, spray as necessary with a general insecticide, paying particular attention to the undersides of the leaves. Under cool conditions the eggs may take a month to hatch, so be prepared to repeat the sprays later on. Biological control for leafhoppers will be available to gardeners before long.

GREY MOULD Grey mould, *Botrytis cinerea*, is typically a wound parasite and can attack any form of dead or dying plant material. In a few cases it can actually start the damage. Attack causes a soft rotting, rapidly followed by a coating of greyish fungal spores over the infected area. Soft, lush growth following an excess of nitrogen fertilizer is generally more likely to be attacked, and tissue damaged by slugs is particularly susceptible. Grey mould is also encouraged by moist, humid conditions.
Control: Use only balanced fertilizers. Take action to prevent slug damage and, at the first sign of grey mould attack, remove the affected leaves or complete plants and follow with sprays of benomyl or carbendazim.

IRON DEFICIENCY Iron deficiency is evident as a yellowing of the youngest growth. In severe attacks the whole of the top of the seedling or plant turns yellow; in a less severe case the upper leaves develop a yellowing between the veins of the youngest leaves, the veins remaining green. Iron deficiency can result when the available iron in the compost or soil has been used up, or when alkalinity in the soil prevents the iron from being taken up by the roots.
Control: Apply a fertilizer containing chelated iron or use a specific chelated (or sequestered) iron product. Apply to leaves and to soil for best results.

LARGE WHITE BUTTERFLY Caterpillars of the large white butterfly, *Pieris brassicae*, can cause severe damage to nasturtiums and also to mignonette. The black-marked, white-winged adults are well known to vegetable growers, as are the yellow, white and black-marked caterpillars. Main attacks come in early summer with a second generation in late summer.
Control: Spray with the bacterial parasitic agent *Bacillus thuringiensis* (*see Biological control, pp. xvi–xxi*), or use bifenthrin, fatty acids, permethrin or pyethrins.

LEAF SCORCH Leaf scorch is the name given to a sweet pea disorder in which the leaves show pale brown blotches on the foliage. The cause of the problem is not known, although it does seem to present more of a difficulty when sweet peas are being grown as cordons rather than as branched plants. The disorder can spread upwards throughout the plant.
Control: Try removing the worst leaves and apply a few sprays of a complete foliar feed. Keep the soil well watered and mulched.

LEAF SPOTS Many different species of leaf spot fungus exist, many being virtually specific to a single group of plants. Antirrhinum, dianthus (carnation and sweet William), foxglove, pansy, primula and viola can all be attacked by leaf spot fungi. Typically, reddish or dark spots appear on the leaves, often surrounded by a dark margin, and may be followed by leaf yellowing and leaf fall. Alternatively, the spots may join together and the leaves turn brown and die, or the spots may fall out leaving a shot hole effect.

Control: Remove the worst affected leaves or plants and then spray with a fungicide based on copper or mancozeb.

LEAFY GALL Leafy gall is a form of the bacterial disease *Corynebacterium fasciens*. It shows up from time to time on a number of plants, particularly on antirrhinum and sweet pea. It takes the form of masses of flattened, stunted shoots growing from the stems at soil level, and light attacks can result in blind shoots developing.

Control: Remove and burn affected plants as well as some of the surrounding soil. Use a different site the following year, or avoid the more susceptible plants.

LEATHERJACKET Leatherjackets, *Tipula paludosa*, are the larvae of crane flies or 'daddy-longlegs'. The larvae feed in the soil on plant roots and can be quite a serious problem in bedding plant displays, particularly when a new site, previously down to grass, is being used. Larvae overwinter in the soil and resume feeding in spring so they are quite large, up to 4.5cm (1½in), by the time bedding plants are set out. Feeding is usually finished by mid- to late summer.

Control: Thorough soil preparation

will expose the leatherjackets for hand removal. Application of the nematode *Steinernema carpocapsae* for control of vine weevil or cutworm will also take care of leatherjackets (*see Biological control, pp.xvi–xxi*). Alternatively apply a chlorpyrifos/diazinon soil insecticide.

MAGNESIUM DEFICIENCY Magnesium is very soluble so frequent waterings or heavy rains can wash it from the soil or compost. Lack of magnesium shows up as a yellowing between the veins of the older leaves and progresses to a dark spotting in the yellow zones. Magnesium deficiency is common in plants fed with high levels of potassium.

Control: When feeding, use a tomato fertilizer which has magnesium included in the analysis. To correct magnesium deficiency, spray the plants with a solution of Epsom Salts (magnesium sulphate) using 100g per 5l (4oz/1gall) of water plus a wetting agent. Repeat a few times at two week intervals.

MILLIPEDE Both the spotted millipede, *Blaniulus guttulatus*, and the flat millipede, *Polydesmus angustus*, feed on seedlings, eating holes in roots, seeds and young stems. Attacked tissue is often attacked by fungi or bacteria, making the damage more severe. Millipedes can be identified by the way they curl up in a spiral when disturbed, and by the presence of two pairs of legs per segment. These features distinguish them from the beneficial centipedes which have only one pair of legs per segment, and move rapidly through the soil when disturbed.

Control: Millipedes abound in leaf litter and decaying plant tissue, so good garden hygiene is the first step in reducing numbers. Methiocarb-based slug pellets have some controlling effect on millipedes, alternatively use a gamma-HCH soil insecticide.

PANSY SICKNESS Pansy sickness is the name given to the wilting and death of pansies, generally after being grown in the same site for a number of years. The first sign is a yellowing of the leaves and stems, and plants often topple over as the roots and stem bases rot away. Several different soil-borne fungi can be involved, *Fusarium* spp. most usually .

Control: Grow pansies and violas in different parts of the garden each year. To reduce the likelihood of any disease building up if using the same beds each time, vary the plants grown, switching between pansies, double daisies, wallflowers, primroses and polyanthus from year to year.

PETAL BLIGHT Petal blight, *Itersonilia perplexans*, can be a major problem in some years on greenhouse-grown chrysanthemums, but in bedding displays it can sometimes infect cornflowers. The effect is to create small, water-soaked spots on the outer petals. Infection normally only occurs in wet seasons, but then it can spread rapidly to other cornflowers in the garden.

Control: Remove and burn infected flowers. A few fortnightly sprays with a systemic fungicide should be effective in reducing damage.

POWDERY MILDEW Various species of powdery mildew fungi can attack several types of bedding plant, resulting in a powdery white coating of spores over the leaves and flowers. Dryness at the roots and over-close planting seem to be contributory factors in the initial infection. Poppy, sweet pea, centaurea, pot marigold and many other plants can be attacked.

Control: Avoid planting too closely, and keep the soil well watered during dry weather. At the first sign of attack, spray with benomyl, bupirimate/triforine, carbendazim or propiconazole systemic fungicides or use a sulphur-based fungicide. Repeat as necessary at two week intervals.

RUST Different species of rust fungi can be found infecting annuals, biennials and other bedding plants, with antirrhinum, hollyhock, lavatera, sweet William and zonal pelargonium ('geraniums') commonly attacked. The general effect of a rust attack is the appearance on the upper leaf surfaces of bright yellow spots and, underneath the leaf, corresponding pustules with powdery yellow, orange, brown or black spores. As the infection progresses, concentric rings of spores may appear. Several of the rust fungi are relatively new to the UK, with antirrhinum rust, *Puccinia antirrhini*, first being recorded in 1933, and pelargonium rust, *Puccinia pelargonii-zonalis*, as recently as 1965. As a general rule, plants making lush growth following excessive nitrogen applications are most at risk from rust attack.

Control: Rust-resistant varieties of antirrhinums are available from seedsmen, but the rust fungus can develop new strains, so plant breeders have to keep producing new varieties to keep ahead of the disease. Should rust attack any type of plant, remove the worst affected leaves or plants and then spray two or three times at two week intervals with a propiconazole or triforine systemic fungicide. Copper fungicides and mancozeb have some controlling action, and are useful for protecting against attack. The rust fungus is, however, systemic within the plant system so a systemic-acting fungicide is required to eradicate an existing attack.

SCIARID FLY Sciarid fly adults, *Bradysia* spp., can be seen on the surface of the compost as small, black, midge-like insects. They lay eggs in the compost and the larvae feed on both the organic matter in the compost and on the seedling roots. In severe attacks, the larvae bore into stems of seedlings and cuttings. The larvae are virtually transparent with tiny, black, biting mouthparts at the head end.

Control: Hang sticky, yellow plastic traps above the plants to catch the adult flies, and to monitor their numbers. In severe cases, the use of the vine weevil-controlling nematodes (*see below*), will also control sciarid fly larvae. A recent addition to the armoury for sciarid larvae control is the mite, *Hypoaspis miles*, which burrows into the compost in search of the sciarid larvae.

SEEDLING BLIGHT Seedling blight, *Alternaria zinniae*, attacks seedling zinnia plants, resulting in grey spots with red margins on the leaves and dark, cankered areas on the stems. Affected plants usually collapse and die.

Control: Protect from attack by adding a copper fungicide to the water at weekly intervals. Where an attack has occurred, remove and burn affected seedlings and spray the remaining seedlings with a copper fungicide.

SLUGS Slugs feed mainly at night, grazing on leaves and young stems and leaving irregular holes as well as the characteristic slime trails. Soft rots often follow slug damage, especially when the plants are growing under humid, greenhouse conditions. By day, slugs will hide under pots, seed trays and in other cool, damp places, or burrow into the soil.

Control: Keep the greenhouse area tidy and free from hiding places for slugs. Prevent attacks by a light scattering of metaldehyde or methiocarb slug pellets over the trays and benches, or by watering the plants and the surrounding areas with a metaldehyde solution. If it is known that the slugs are hiding mainly in the soil, use the beneficial nematode *Phasmarhabditis hermaphrodita* but keep the soil well watered for best effect (*see Biological control, pp. xvi–xxi*).

SNAILS Snails cause the same kind of damage as slugs, but hide by day above ground, rarely under the soil.

Control: Remove slugs by hand when seen. Otherwise treat with pellets or liquid as for slugs, above. As snails stay mainly above the soil surface, the nematode treatment for slugs is not effective against them.

SPRINGTAILS Springtails, *Bourletiella hortensis* and *Onychiurus* spp., can cause severe damage to seedlings, especially when the plants are being grown under rather wet conditions. Seed leaves and stems can be pitted by the feeding, and valuable roots and root hairs are eaten. Attacked seedlings may collapse and die. Older seedlings may have leaves skeletonised where they touch the soil or compost.

Control: Keep the pots and seed trays off old soil to avoid spread of the springtails up into the compost. Always use new, high quality compost for seeds and young plants, and avoid overwatering. These measures will normally be sufficient to prevent damage.

STEM ROT Stem rot can be due to specific fungal attack or to a general rotting, often a rotting of tissue damaged by other agencies. On antirrhinum, clarkia, godetia and on wallflower, a brown spotting spreads round the stems which are then killed. The disease may pass up into the leaves causing spotting.

Control: Remove and burn affected plants to prevent further spread. Regular addition of a copper fungicide to the water should prevent initial attacks. Where attack does occur, spray with a copper fungicide after removing the affected plants.

SWIFT MOTH Caterpillars of the garden swift moth, *Hepialus lupulinus*, can be common pests of bedding plants once they are set out in the garden. The adult moths fly in early evening in late spring to early summer, dropping 300 or so eggs at random during flight. The caterpillars have off-white, translucent bodies and brown heads, and feed on plant roots. They favour plants with fleshy roots and tunnel into them. Bedding dahlias grown from seed, as well as those grown from tubers, are a favourite food plant, but many weeds are also attacked.

Control: Regular soil cultivations and good weed control will do much to control attacks. Where a problem is suspected, application of a chlorpyrifos/diazinon soil insecticide would be effective.

THRIPS Thrips of various species attack a number of bedding plants, causing silvery spots or streaks on the leaves and a white spotting of the flowers. The adult thrips are slender, black insects around 2mm (½in) long and are present in vast numbers during close, thundery weather. The larvae are normally pink or cream in colour and feed on the outer tissue of leaves and flowers.

Control: Spray with a general insecticide when damage is first seen.

TURNIP FLEA BEETLE Turnip flea beetle, *Phyllotreta cruciferae*, attacks nasturtium as well as the more usual host plants in the cabbage family, namely alyssum, honesty, stock and wallflower. The adult beetles eat small holes in the seed leaves, forming little pits, and considerable stunting can result in extreme cases. The larvae feed on the outside tissue of plant roots.

Control: Treat the seedlings and the soil with a rotenone dust and repeat at weekly intervals as necessary.

VINE WEEVIL Vine weevil, *Otiorhynchus sulcatus*, can be a problem with bedding plants, especially with the different types of primula although, in general, perennials and pot plants are more at risk. Eggs are laid in the soil or in pots of compost, and the white, legless larvae hatch out to feed on the plant roots before pupating. Severe wilting is the first sign of attack and plants can be killed by the root loss.

Control: The best form of control is to use one of two nematodes: *Heterorhabditis megidis* or *Steinernema carpocapsae*. The nematodes are applied to the compost as a suspension in water and actively seek out and enter the weevil larvae. Death follows rapidly as bacteria, carried by the nematodes, attack the tissue of the larvae.

VIRUS Several different virus types attack annuals, biennials and other bedding plants. The general effects include yellow or white spotting or striping of the foliage, leaf distortion, poor flowering and growth, and flecking or mottling of the flowers. Most viruses are spread by aphids as they feed on the sap, but others can be spread by different agencies.

Control: There is no control for virus attack. Try to prevent damage by keeping the aphid population well in check, and by removing any suspect plants at an early stage to avoid possible further spread.

WATERLOGGING Waterlogging kills plant roots, resulting in wilting, and in death in prolonged cases. Early symptoms include wilting and pale foliage, often followed by soft rots at soil level. Wetness also encourages damping off diseases, grey mould, and springtail activity.

Control: Adequate preparation of garden beds prior to sowing or planting out, by correcting drainage problems and by incorporating plentiful organic matter, can help to prevent waterlogging. Plants in pots should not be left standing in water that has drained down through the compost after watering.

WHITE BLISTER White blister, *Albugo candida*, attacks cabbage family plants, so potentially could be found on alyssum, honesty, stock and wallflower. The fungus appears as raised, white spots and as the infection develops the spots often grow out to form rings of white pustules. The pustules become powdery as spores are produced to spread the infection still further.

Control: Dig up and burn infected plants, ideally before the powdery spores are produced. Applications of a copper fungicide should protect plants from attack, but the fungus is unpredictable and may crop up after many years' absence, and then not occur again for several years.

WHITEFLY Glasshouse whitefly, *Trialeurodes vaporariorum*, can be troublesome during the greenhouse stage of bedding plant production. Attacks can build up rapidly and weaken the plants and deposits of sugary honeydew will soon turn black on the leaves, following colonisation with sooty moulds. Premature leaf fall can follow damage.

Control: Catch early attacks on strips of sticky, yellow plastic, hung just over the tops of the seedlings. Temperatures during bedding plant production will be too low for the parasitic wasp *Encarsia formosa* to be effective, so watch for the wasps and spray as necessary with bifenthrin, fatty acids or permethrin.

WILT Wilt fungi can attack various plants, but aster wilt, caused by *Fusarium oxysporum* f. sp. *callistephi* is the most serious with regard to bedding plants. Attack occurs on China asters which wilt and turn brown when just on the point of flowering. Stems can be seen to be brown or black and develop a pinkish colour.

Control: Prevent attack by growing varieties of aster listed in seed catalogues as being resistant to aster wilt. Should an attack occur, dig up and burn affected plants and avoid growing asters on the same spot for a few years or restrict those grown to resistant varieties only.

WIREWORM Wireworm, *Agriotes lineatus*, can be an occasional pest of bedding plants, particularly in new gardens or new beds where grass grew previously. Seedlings or plants are attacked at the roots by the stiff, orange or yellow larvae and may be killed. The wireworms can take as long as five years to complete their development to the adult click beetle form, so a lot of damage can be done in that time. More damage occurs in the moister conditions of spring and autumn than in summer or winter.

Control: Thorough soil cultivations, hand removal, and good weed control will all help to reduce wireworm numbers. If numbers are known to be high, apply a chrorpyrifos/diazinon soil insecticide a few weeks before planting.

WOODLICE Two main types of woodlouse occur in gardens and greenhouses, pill bugs *Armadillidium* spp., that roll into tight balls when disturbed and *Oniscus* and *Porcellio* spp., that remain flat. They all feed on young stems and on leaves that are touching the soil or compost surface, producing ragged holes.

Control: Strict hygiene to remove debris, old wood and piles of pots or seed trays will reduce hiding places of woodlice. Methiocarb-based slug pellets will normally also control woodlice; alternatively apply a bendiocarb, gamma-HCH or pirimiphos-methyl insecticide dust around likely hiding places and around plants.

FLOWERS 2

HERBACEOUS PERENNIALS

Herbaceous perennials grow from a permanent root and shoot system, produce flowers, and then die down, all within the span of one year.

ROOTS

EATEN	Soil pests	*chafer grubs, cutworm, leatherjacket, swift moth, vine weevil, wireworm*
ROTTED	Roots and crowns, becoming discoloured and rotting	*root and foot rots*

STEMS AND LEAVES

NO HOLES IN LEAVES PESTS *VISIBLE*	Bleached spots on leaves, pale pests under leaves which take short leaping flights when disturbed	*leafhoppers*
	Blotchy or winding mines in leaves	*leaf miner*
	Cuckoo spit at leaf/stem junctions	*froghopper*
	Green, brown or pinkish pests clustered under leaves and at shoot tips	*aphids*
	Violet leaves rolled tightly, white larvae inside	*violet leaf midge*

NO HOLES IN LEAVES	Leaves with silvery streaks or spots	thrips
NO PESTS VISIBLE	Pale stippling and some distortion of foliage	mites
	Stems with outgrowths of leafy shoots at soil level	leafy gall
HOLES IN LEAVES PESTS VISIBLE	Brown, green or variously coloured caterpillars present	caterpillars
	Leaves with small holes and tattered appearance. Active green or brown pests sometimes seen	capsid bugs
HOLES IN LEAVES PESTS NOT VISIBLE	Ragged holes in leaves (and flowers), no slime trails	earwigs
	Ragged holes in leaves, slime trails present	slugs/snails
	Variously distorted and twisted foliage and stems, poor flowering	eelworm, mycoplasma, virus
LEAVES DISCOLOURED	Brown or black spots on leaves	leaf spot
	Dark spotting and blotching of delphinium leaves and stems	black blotch
	Older leaves yellowing between the veins	magnesium deficiency
LEAVES WITH VISIBLE FUNGAL GROWTHS	Black, powdery spores produced from swollen areas	smut
	Yellow, orange, brown or black powdery spots on leaves	rust
	White, powdery coating	powdery mildew
STEMS/LEAVES ROTTING	Dianthus plants rotting and some leaf spotting	leaf and stem rot
	Leaves and stems (and flowers) rotting and coated with grey fungus	grey mould
	Rotting in crowns of rosette-forming plants	crown rot
STEMS FLATTENED	Wide, flattened stems as if several fused together	fasciation
PLANTS WILTING	Firm soil, brown discolouration in centre of stem tissue	wilt diseases
	Loose soil under plants, ants present	ants
	Peony, young stems turn brown, wilt and die	peony blight

FLOWERS

Black spotting of outer petals of chrysanthemums	petal blight
Flower stems blacken and topple, flowers fail to open	pedicel necrosis
Peony flowers fail to open	peony wilt
Petals and other flower parts eaten	caterpillars
Petals with bleached spots	thrips
Ragged holes in petals, no slime trails	earwigs
Ragged holes in petals, slime trails present	slugs/snails

ANTS Ants are not major pests, but their nest-building activities in the soil can undermine plants and result in roots being left without adequate contact with the soil. Such plants wilt and may die unless the soil is re-firmed and the ants removed. Ants also move aphids around on plants and help to spread those infestations.

Control: Treat soil, and/or exposed

nests, with bendiocarb, bioallethrin, cypermethrin or permethrin in spray or dust form.

APHIDS (GREENFLY AND BLACK-FLY) Virtually all herbaceous perennials can be attacked by at least one species of aphid. They feeding on the sap, which can weaken the plants, leaves may be curled, and they can also spread virus diseases. Aphids excrete sugary honeydew as they feed, which makes leaves sticky and, as sooty moulds colonize the honeydew, the leaves and stems turn black. Ants are attracted to the honeydew and to the aphids which they stimulate to exude more honeydew. Ants can also move the aphids to new leaves and defend them from predators. Aphid infestations build up very rapidly as the females produce living young without needing to mate.

Control: Natural predators, including ladybird larvae and adults, lacewing and hover fly larvae and a number of other beneficial insects help to keep aphid numbers in check. Where such biological control agents are late to arrive, or are inadequate for the size of the aphid infestation, spray with the aphid-specific pirimicarb to avoid damage to the predators. Alternatively, where no predators are present, spray with bifenthrin, dimethoate, fatty acids, heptenophos or pirimiphos-methyl, or use pirimicarb.

Main aphid species:
- Black bean aphid, *Aphis fabae*, feeds on a number of herbaceous plants during summer, before returning to spindle trees *(Euonymus europaeus)* or the guelder rose *(Viburnum opulus)* for winter egg-laying.
- Leaf-curling plum aphid,

Brachycaudus helichrysi, moves on to aster, chrysanthemum, and other herbaceous and bedding plants after starting life on plum trees. A return to plum occurs in autumn.
- Lupin aphid, *Macrosiphum albifrons*, is worthy of mention in view of the extreme damage it can cause to lupins. The species only came to the UK and Europe from North America in 1981, but it is already well established and widely distributed. The lupin aphid attacks flowers, stems, leaves and roots. It is host-specific and, with each female capable of producing 80 nymphs in 16 days, virtually all attacks are severe and plant death frequently follows. Winged forms appear in summer to spread the infestation to other lupin plants.

BLACK BLOTCH Black blotch, *Pseudomonas delphinii*, is a bacterial disease affecting delphinium leaves. Attack results in large black blotches appearing, and these can spread to stems and flower stalks.

Control: There is no real control although a programme of copper sprays to soil and plants from an early growth stage may help.

CAPSID BUGS Common green capsid, *Lygocoris pabulinus*, and the tarnished plant bug, *Lygus rugulipennis*, feed on a wide range of herbaceous plants, both garden plants and weeds, during late spring and summer. Where the pests insert their feeding tubes the leaf tissue dies, resulting in a series of small dead, brown spots. As the leaves expand, the spots develop into holes and the leaves take on a tattered appearance. Flowers can also be distorted by bugs and may abort.

In autumn, common green capsids move to woody host plants for winter egg-laying, whilst the tarnished plant bugs overwinter in plant debris.

Control: Spray with a contact insecticide at the first sign of damage and repeat if necessary two weeks later. As the capsids tend to drop to the soil at the first sign of danger or disturbance, spray the ground under the plants and then up into the plant itself for best results. Insecticides containing fatty acids, permethrin or pyrethrins would be appropriate.

CATERPILLARS Many different species of caterpillar can attack a range of herbaceous plants, mainly feeding on the leaves and sometimes on, or in, stems and on flowers. There may be one or two generations of the pests per year. Most of the caterpillars will be greenish or brownish in colour, and are often very well camouflaged.

Control: Caterpillars are well controlled by sprays of the agent *Bacillus thuringiensis* (*see Biological control, pp. xvi–xxi*). Alternatively, spray with bifenthrin, permethrin, fatty acids or pyrethrins.

Main caterpillar species:
- Angle-shades moth, *Phlogophora meticulosa*. Caterpillars of the angle-shades moth attack a wide range of herbaceous and greenhouse-grown plants, including scabious, geranium, anemone, chrysanthemum and primula. The caterpillars can be a velvety green or brownish in colour and feed mainly from late summer to early autumn.
- Allied shade moth, *Cnephasia incertana*, and the flat tortrix moth, *Cnephasia asseclana*, lay eggs in summer and the caterpillars feed in late summer and autumn and then again

in the following spring, having spent the winter in cocoons. Quite a wide range of herbaceous plants can be attacked, including chrysanthemum, geranium, golden rod, helenium, phlox, primula and rudbeckia.
- Rosy rustic moth, *Hydraecia micacea*, can be a real problem from time to time on chrysanthemum, sunflower and a few other strongly-growing subjects. The pinkish caterpillars tunnel into the stems of suitable plants in mid- to late spring and then bore down to the crown where they may kill the plant by their feeding.

CHAFERS The adult garden chafer, *Phyllopertha horticola*, feeds on leaves and flowers in late spring and early summer and the chafer grubs feed on plant roots from late summer through to the following spring. Chafers are commonly a problem in gardens or flower beds recently reclaimed from grassland or from lawn.

Control: Good soil cultivations will generally expose the grubs for hand removal. Alternatively, use the biological control nematode, *Steinernema carpocapsae* as for vine weevil (*see Biological control, pp. xvi–xxi*), or apply a chlorpyrifos/diazinon soil insecticide.

CROWN ROT Crown rot can be due to attack by the fungus *Phyophthora cactorum*, but is found mainly among rosette-forming plants where it is due not to disease but to waterlogging or excess wetness in the crown. Lewisia, sempervivum, sedum and similar plants can succumb, particularly during wet winter weather.

Control: Improve drainage around the roots and crowns of susceptible plants. In winter, protect the crowns from rain with cloches or with sheets of glass or plastic propped up securely over the plants. Where an attack has occurred, remove the affected plants and prepare the soil well before replanting with a different type of plant.

CUTWORM Cutworm caterpillars feed at or around soil level, eating through stems. They can even kill quite large plants. The main species of cutworm are turnip moth (*Agrotis segetum*), heart and dart moth (*Agrotis exclamationis*), white-line dart moth (*Euxoa tritici*), garden dart moth (*Euxoa nigricans*) and the large yellow underwing (*Noctua pronuba*).
Control: Thorough soil cultivations will often give sufficient control. Regular watering is also helpful as the caterpillars tend to be attacked by disease in wet soil. Otherwise, watering the soil with the biological control nematode, *Steinernema carpocapsae*, or applying a chlorpyrifos/diazinon soil insecticide would give control.

EARWIG Earwigs, *Forficula auricularia*, feed on leaves, flowers and flower buds, and can cause quite serious damage in some years. Feeding takes place at night, but by day the earwigs hide away and so are rarely seen at work.
Control: Trapping is perhaps the best way to control earwigs. Fill plant pots with dry grass or crumpled newspaper and put these on canes amongst the plants. In the morning, shake out the earwigs which have collected in them on a path or other hard surface and kill them. An alternative strategy would be to dust the grass or newspaper with bendiocarb or pirimiphos-methyl insecticide dust, which would avoid the necessity of shaking out the catch each day. (*See also Earwig, p.76.*)

EELWORM Stem eelworm, *Ditylenchus dipsaci*, is the main nematode species damaging herbaceous plants. Various biological races of this eelworm occur, each specific to a particular group of plants. The phlox race is the one causing damage to a number of herbaceous plants including aubrieta, evening primrose, golden rod and helenium, as well as phlox plus a number of common weeds. Affected phlox plants develop thickened and cracked stems while the foliage becomes twisted and deformed, and often narrowed to just the main vein. Flowering is gradually reduced to virtually nil.

Leaf nematodes, *Aphelenchoides ritzemabosi* and *A. fragariae*, spread in the film of moisture that covers damp plant foliage and crowns, and attack various herbaceous plants, resulting in the leaves turning brown or black, often in zones bounded by the leaf veins. Chrysanthemum are particularly damaged, along with aster, delphinium, doronicum, peony, pyrethrum and others.
Control: No chemicals are effective, so infested plants should be removed and burned. Take care when accepting plants from friends and make sure that they appear to be healthy with no suspect symptoms. Keeping weeds under control will deny eelworms a second home.

FASCIATION Fasciation is the name given to the phenomenon in which a number of shoots appear to fuse together to produce a wide, flattened shoot. Leaves sprout from the stems and flowers may develop, although in an atypical form. Foxgloves and delphiniums are quite often subject to this condition. The exact cause of fasciation is not known, but it is thought to result from damage to the growing point by some agency, which could be insect or other pest, or weather – including frost, drought or waterlogging.

Control: The condition is not catching, so no treatment is necessary (or possible).

FROGHOPPERS Common froghoppers, *Philaenus spumarius*, are responsible for the frothy blobs known as cuckoo spit which can be found on many plants in late spring to early summer. Young shoots and flowers may be distorted by the feeding, but generally no great harm is done.

Control: Spraying the froth with a jet of water from a hose will normally dislodge the creamy pests and some may fail to re-establish on the plants. For severe attacks, a general insecticide could be used.

GREY MOULD Grey mould, *Botrytis cinerea*, will attack any dead or dying plant tissue, so it frequently follows physical injury inflicted by pests, adverse weather or by the gardener. Attacked tissue turns soft and rots, and has a grey, fluffy coating of spores over the surface. Moist, humid conditions encourage grey mould.

Control: Take care when hoeing not to damage the stems or leaves, and thin out any over-dense plantings. Should grey mould attack, remove the diseased parts and apply a few sprays of benomyl or carbendazim fungicide.

LEAF AND STEM ROT Leaf and stem rot is a general description covering a number of different fungal species, including leaf rot of carnations (*Heteropatella valtellinensis*), stem rot of pansies (*Myrothecium roridum*) and crown rot and associated stem and leaf stalk lesions of delphinium (*Diplodena*).

Control: Remove and burn affected

plants and only propagate from healthy stock. A few sprays with a copper fungicide may help to protect unaffected plants growing close to where the outbreak occurred.

LEAFHOPPER The chrysanthemum leafhopper, *Eupteryx melissae*, will also attack a number of other plants, resulting in bleached spots on the upper surfaces of the leaves. The adults take short, leaping flights when disturbed, leaving behind the wingless nymph stages, generally to be found alongside the main veins where they feed on the sap. Also present will be the white, cast skins of the insects.

Control: Where control is needed, spray with dimethoate, pirimiphos-methyl, permethrin or pyrethrins.

LEAF MINER Leaf miner larvae create winding mines or blotches within the leaves. Chrysanthemums have two leaf miner species, *Phytomyza syngenesiae*, which favours chrysanthemums under glass but does attack outdoor ones as well, and *Phytomyza horticola*, which is found on outdoor chrysanthemums as well as on poppy, tobacco plant, sweet pea, phlox and various other ornamental species.

In addition to the damage caused by the larvae within the leaves, the adults cause small spots where they probe the tissue, either to feed or to test for egg-laying sites. Other leaf miner species attack dianthus, gypsophila, golden rod, helianthus, columbine and other herbaceous plants. Most of the leaf miners create the characteristic winding mines, but in a few species the larvae make large blotch mines that look like hollow, brown blisters.

Control: Pick off severely mined leaves. Smaller infestations can be dealt with by regularly inspecting the leaves and squashing any larvae or pupae within the mines while the leaves are still on the plants. Insecticides are of limited use, and are mainly aimed at killing the tiny adult flies as they lay their eggs. Permethrin would be a suitable insecticide to use.

LEAF SPOT Many different species of leaf spot fungus can attack herbaceous plants, although few cause severe damage. Chrysanthemum, carnation and other dianthus types, foxglove, hollyhock, lupin, primula and viola are among those commonly subject to leaf spot damage. Perhaps the most severe is the hellebore leaf spot, *Coniothyrium hellebori*, which attacks most types of hellebore, but is particularly damaging on Christmas rose, *Helleborus niger*. On this plant, brown to black spots develop and these grow and can join together. Concentric darker rings appear, the leaf tissue dies and often falls from the leaves, resulting in large holes appearing. Attacks also occur on the stems and plants can be killed if the infection girdles the stems. Spots can also appear on the white flowers, ruining their appearance.
Control: Pick off and burn, or otherwise dispose of safely, all badly spotted foliage and stems. A few fortnightly applications of a mancozeb or copper fungicide should protect from attack. Where attack has previously occurred on Christmas rose or other prized plants, it would be worth applying protective sprays in advance of any visible signs of the spotting.

LEAFY GALL Leafy gall, caused by the bacterium *Corynebacterium fasciens*, can attack quite a few herbaceous plants including chrysanthemum, marguerite, heuchera and geranium, resulting in a proliferation of flattened and stunted

shoots at or around soil level. The infection is soil-borne.
Control: No chemical control measures exist. Remove and destroy affected plants, and grow non-susceptible plants in the infected area. Disinfect hands and tools after digging up and handling infected plant material.

LEATHERJACKET Leatherjacket is the name given to the larva of the crane fly, *Tipula pallidosa* and other species. The greyish, legless larvae feed on the roots of garden plants and weeds from summer through to late spring, growing to 4.5cm (1½in) in length in the process.
Control: Good soil preparation should expose most of the leatherjackets for hand removal. Where large numbers are present, apply the nematode *Steinernema carpocapsae* to seek out and kill the pests. Alternatively, dust the soil with a chlorpyrifos/diazinon insecticide.

MAGNESIUM DEFICIENCY Magnesium is quickly washed out of the soil by heavy rain but is essential for healthy plant growth. A shortage of magnesium in the plant results in the mobilisation of available reserves and the plant moves magnesium from the older to the younger leaves. The end result is a deficiency in the older foliage, showing up as a yellowing between the veins. Magnesium deficiency is also associated with over-generous applications of potassium fertilizers.
Control: To correct magnesium deficiency, water the plants and the soil with a solution of magnesium sulphate (Epsom Salts) using 100g per 5l (4oz/1gall) of water. A few fortnightly treatments should be sufficient under normal conditions. When feeding herbaceous plants, use a tomato or rose

fertilizer either in dry or liquid form, selecting a product that lists magnesium amongst its contents.

MITES The main mite found to be troublesome in herbaceous borders is the cyclamen mite, *Phytonemus (Tarsonemus) pallidus*. A distinct race of this mite attacks Michaelmas daisy, particularly the *Aster novi–belgii* varieties, resulting in a scarring of the flower stems on which rosettes of small, green leaves appear instead of normal flowers. *Aster amellus* and *Aster novae–angliae* are less severely damaged.

Control: Remove and burn infested and suspect plants. No chemicals are available so in gardens where the problem has occurred avoid planting Michaelmas daisy, or stick to the *A. amellus* and *A. novae angliae* types.

MYCOPLASMA A mycoplasma is an organism somewhere between a virus and a bacterium, rather like a bacterium but without a cell wall, while the damage it causes resembles that caused by a virus. Mycoplasma attacks on certain herbaceous have a similar effect to the strawberry green petal mycoplasma, in that the flowers appear green rather than the normal colours.

Control: No control methods are available other than removal and destruction of affected plants.

PEDICEL NECROSIS Pedicel necrosis is a physiological disorder in which the area of the flower stalk (pedicel) just below the bud turns black and usually shrivels, and the developing flower bud fails to open. The bud will then turn brown and the stem may droop. The problem is usually related to very dry soil conditions, to lack of adequate nutrients, or to other factors that prevent uptake of adequate water and nutrients to sustain the bud development.

Control: In spring, apply a balanced fertilizer (a rose food would be ideal), water as necessary in dry weather and mulch the soil with compost or bark to help even out water availability to the plants. Where the condition occurs, cut out affected shoots; subsequent ones should develop normally if the causal agents are corrected.

PEONY BLIGHT Peony blight is due to attack by the fungus *Botrytis paeoniae* and usually occurs in spring as new growth is being made. The stems turn brown around soil level, the shoots wilt and then die. Where the attack occurs later in the season, brown patches appear on the leaves, and the flower buds may fail to develop. As with pedicel necrosis, above, the flower buds then turn brown, but with peony blight a grey, furry growth of fungus develops on the flower stalk.

Control: For spring attacks, cut out the affected shoots below ground level and collect for safe disposal. For summer attacks, cut out the failed flowering stems and thin out any crowded shoots. Follow with a few sprays using a benomyl or carbendazim fungicide. To prevent attacks, avoid excess applications of nitrogen, thin out crowded shoots and spray with one of the above fungicides two or three times at two week intervals, starting as the shoots first appear in spring.

PETAL BLIGHT Petal blight, *Itersonilia perplexans*, is chiefly a problem with greenhouse-grown chrysanthemum flowers, but it does occur outside in wet weather. The first signs of infection are small, pinkish-brown spots towards the tips of the outer petals, overlaid with a dull white bloom. The browning spreads towards the centre of the flower and the whole blossom can turn brown and soggy. The grey mould fungus, *Botrytis cinerea*, frequently occurs as a secondary infection to compound the problem.

Control: Pick off the damaged petals as soon as seen, or remove the whole flower if damage is advanced. A few sprays with a sulphur or a systemic fungicide applied for mildew control may have a slight effect in reducing petal blight at the same time.

POWDERY MILDEW Large numbers of different powdery mildew species occur, each with a fairly restricted host range. Some, such as pea mildew, *Erysiphe pisi*, can be damaging on agricultural crops but also attack herbaceous plants in the same botanical family, for example, lupin is affected by pea mildew. Affected plants become coated with a white, powdery coating of disease spores, and in severe cases the leaves can turn brown and die. General growth and flowering can be reduced. Powdery mildew tends to be most serious during spells of dry weather, with evening dews to moisten the foliage.

Control: Keep plants well watered in dry weather. Cut out badly infected growths, first enclosing them in a plastic bag to prevent masses of infective spores being spread around. Spraying with a systemic fungicide based on benomyl, carbendazim, propiconazole or triforine will eradicate an existing attack and protect against new infections. Sulphur could be used as an alternative for protective purposes.

ROOT AND FOOT ROTS Various rotting fungi can attack roots and stem bases of herbaceous plants, resulting in a soft or hard rot and the loss of the flowering stems. Among the most common rots are species of *Thielaviopsis*, *Corticium* and *Rhizoctonia* (some of which are now grouped together as *Thanatephorus*). When young or weak plants are attacked they may be killed.

Control: If the rotting has not gone too far, plants can be dug up, damaged parts removed, and the plants put into a new area with careful attention to watering. Otherwise, just dig up and burn.

RUST Numerous species of rust fungi can attack herbaceous plants, but most are very specific with regard to their favoured host plant. Chrysanthemum, carnation, aquilegia, centaurea, geranium and others develop yellow, orange or brown to black, powdery spores in pustules under the leaves. The upper leaf surfaces normally show a yellow spotting. Leaves then turn yellow and die, and in severe cases most of the leaves can be lost.

Control: Pick off the worst of the infected leaves and burn. Follow with a few sprays at fortnightly intervals with propiconazole or triforine fungicide. To guard susceptible plants against attack, spray on a regular basis with one of these fungicides, or use copper or mancozeb. To keep severe hollyhock rust, *Puccinia malvacearum*, in check without constant spraying, raise new seedlings every year, grow on for a year to flower in year two, and then replace with fresh, one-year-old plants.

SLUGS Slugs can be extremely damaging in spring on tender new shoots, with delphiniums being particularly affected. Leaf damage can also be extensive, with hosta foliage apparently being singled out for attention. The main damaging species in gardens are the field slug, *Deroceras reticulatum*, and the garden slug,

Arion hortensis, while various keeled slugs, *Milax* spp., will attack underground systems. Slugs feed mainly at night and are most troublesome in wet weather or when heavy dews fall at night. By day they hide under boxes, stones and in similar places. The rough edges left by slugs to the areas they graze are prone to attack by *Botrytis* fungus.

Control: Scatter metaldehyde or methiocarb pellets thinly over the infested areas, or water plants and soil with a metaldehyde solution. Best results are achieved by application during damp weather, followed by a dry day which assists in desiccating the slugs. Alternatively, apply the beneficial nematode *Phasmarhabditis hermaphrodita* to the soil. Keep the soil moist for a few weeks afterwards (*see Biological control, pp. xvi–xxi*).

SMUT Smut fungi, mainly *Entyloma* and *Urocystis* species, are close relatives of the rusts, but normally produce swellings on various parts of infected plants. The swellings erupt in due course to liberate vast quantities of black, powdery spores. Calendula, carnation, gaillardia, trollius and viola can be affected.

Control: No control measures exist, other than removing and destroying all infected plants as soon as any damage can be seen.

SNAILS Like slugs, snails are active in damp conditions, feeding on plant leaves, stems and flowers and are more common in calcareous regions. The garden snail *Helix aspersa*, the strawberry snail *Trichia striolata* and banded snails *Cepaea* spp. are the most troublesome to herbaceous plants.

Control: A light scattering of metaldehyde or methiocarb pellets over the border or close to particularly attractive plants should prevent damage. Alternatively, the soil and the plants can be watered with a metaldehyde solution.

SWIFT MOTH The ghost swift moth, *Hepialus humuli*, and the garden swift moth, *H. lupulinus*, can both be serious pests of herbaceous plants. The translucent larvae feed on roots and also bore into rootstocks of plants. Ghost swift moth larvae feed for two and sometimes three years before pupating, whilst the garden swift moth larvae complete their development in two years.

Control: Apply a chlorpyrifos/diazinon soil insecticide around plants when damage is suspected, or in early summer to protect from attack.

THRIPS Thrips, commonly referred to as 'thunder flies' are most active in humid and thundery weather conditions. The onion thrips, *Thrips tabaci*, is the most damaging species to herbaceous plants, and the cream to orange larvae feed on the leaf surfaces, resulting in silvery streaks and spots. The adults are slender, black creatures around 2mm (⅒in) long. Grain thrips, *Limothrips cerealium*, often move into country gardens when nearby cereal crops are harvested.

Control: Spray with permethrin or pyrethrins and repeat as necessary.

VINE WEEVIL Vine weevil, *Otiorhynchus sulcatus*, feeds as an adult on leaves of rhododendron, camellia and similar 'hard' leaves, but the larvae eat plant roots. Most types of herbaceous plant are potential hosts, but saxifrage, sedum, sempervivum, Michaelmas daisy, peony, phlox and primula are favoured. The larvae eat the smaller roots and burrow into larger fleshy ones causing wilting, and death in severe attacks.

Control: Treat the soil with one of the beneficial nematodes *Heterorhabditis megidis* or *Steinernema carpocapsae*. The nematodes seek out and penetrate the vine weevil larvae, and a bacterium carried by them completes the work (*see Biological control, pp. xvi–xxi*).

VIOLET LEAF MIDGE Violet leaf midge, *Dasyneura affinis*, attacks wild and cultivated violas. The adult midge lays eggs in the rolled leaf edges of young foliage, which then become swollen and fail to unroll. Plants can be severely stunted, flowering may cease and plants may die. Inside the galled leaves can be found numerous white or orange larvae, around 2mm (⅒in) long, which feed on the leaf tissue. There are normally four overlapping generations per year, so considerable damage can be done by this pest.

Control: Hand-picking of the infested and swollen leaves will give good control if done thoroughly. Sprays with dimethoate or pirimiphos-methyl systemic insecticides may also be effective.

VIRUS Various types of virus can attack herbaceous plants, resulting in spotting, streaking and distortion of flowers and leaves. Infected plants are rarely vigorous, and may die. Chrysanthemums can be affected by a number of viruses and fifteen different ones have been identified in the UK. Some varieties of chrysanthemum act as carriers, in that they have the virus within their systems, but show no symptoms. The two most serious viruses of the chrysanthemum are aspermy and stunt.

With aspermy, little effect is seen in the foliage, but flowers show severe twisting or rolling, with petals developing to uneven lengths while darker-coloured varieties show paler streaks and flecks. Damage is particularly severe in the second year after the initial infection.

With stunt, the plants are reduced to around a half to two-thirds of their usual height, with leaf and flower size being reduced in proportion. Flower colours are paler, but there is no spotting or flecking. Flowering is, however, a week or more earlier than in healthy plants of the same variety. Leaf mottle viruses, spotted wilt, mosaic and sundry other less common problems can also be found.

Arabis mosaic, cucumber mosaic and tomato spotted wilt can all be found on occasions, causing a stunting or leaf damage on delphinium, lupin and other plants. Virus infection can be spread by various agencies, some (but not all) by aphids, by leaf contact or by hand when taking cuttings or removing side shoots, for example. Strict hygiene is necessary to avoid transmission.

Control: Remove and burn suspect plants. Wash hands after handling and disinfect knives and other hand tools used in dealing with infected plants, particularly when such plants are being grown under glass.

WILT DISEASES Michaelmas daisy can be attacked by the wilt fungus, *Phialophora asteris*, which attacks all but *Aster novae-angliae* varieties. Stems will wilt and leaves turn brown but stay firmly affixed to the stems. Most infected plants die within a year or two. Chrysanthemum and phlox plants are attacked by the wilt fungus *Verticillium*, and this has much the same effect; if stems are split open lengthways a brown staining can be seen in the central, water-conducting tissue. Dianthus is attacked by the related wilt fungus *Fusarium*, and delphiniums by *Diplodina*. All these wilt fungi are carried in the soil.

Control: Remove and burn infected subjects and do not replace with the same type of plant. When taking cuttings or dividing, take every care to propagate only from healthy plants.

WIREWORM The garden click beetle, *Athous haemorrhoidalis*, and the common click beetle, *Agriotes lineatus*, lay eggs in the soil and these hatch out into the yellow to orange larvae known as wireworms. The wireworms feed on plant roots and can take up to five years to be fully fed and reach pupation stage. During this time extensive damage can be done to plants in herbaceous borders as the pests feed on plant roots and bore into fleshy roots, stem bases and even up into the stems.

Control: Thorough soil preparations before original plantings, and regular hoeing of established borders, will help to reduce wireworm numbers. For existing attacks, apply a chlorpyrifos/diazinon soil insecticide.

FLOWERS 3

BULBS, CORMS, RHIZOMES, TUBERS

Bulbs are swollen leaf bases, corms are developed from thickened stem bases, tubers resemble swollen roots, but unlike true roots they are complete with buds and are more akin to stems, and rhizomes are surface or underground modified stems with the ability to spread over or through the soil.

DAMAGE TO BULBS, CORMS, RHIZOMES, TUBERS IN STORE OR IN THE GROUND	Dug up	*mice, squirrels, voles*
	Eaten in the soil	*cutworm, millipedes, narcissus flies, slugs, swift moths, wireworm*
	Pests present in store, brown insects clustered on many bulbs and corms and on any young shoots	*tulip bulb aphid*
	Pests present in store, small black insects on gladiolus	*thrips*
	Rotting in the soil, no pests present	*bacterial soft rot*
	Rotting in the soil, small, shiny mites present	*bulb mite*
	Rotting in the soil, violet fungal strands visible	*violet root rot*
	Spotted or rotting before planting	*basal rot, blue mould, bulb scale mite*

DAMAGE TO BULBS, CORMS, RHIZOMES, TUBERS IN STORE OR IN THE GROUND *cont.*		*chalkiness, core rot, dry rot, grey bulb rot, hard rot, ink disease, rhizome rot, scab, smoulder, white rot*
	Tulip bulbs produce swollen white, downward-pointing growths	*'droppers'*
GROWTH STUNTED	Growth distorted, flower colours breaking	*stem eelworm*
	Hyacinth leaves spotted, flowers die, growth stunted	*yellows*
	Plants stunted with distorted and discoloured leaves	*virus*

STEMS AND LEAVES

STEMS AND LEAVES ROTTING	Gladiolus leaves show yellow striping, plants die back	*yellows*
	Gladiolus leaves turn brown, stems rot at soil level	*dry rot*
	Hyacinth plants turn yellow and collapse after flowering	*black slime*
	Iris leaves collapse	*rhizome rot*
	Lily-of-the-valley stems turn brown and rot	*peony blight*
SOIL LEVEL GROWTHS	Galls growing out	*crown gall*
	Outgrowths of flattened stems	*leafy gall*
HOLES IN LEAVES PESTS PRESENT	Bright red beetles and slimy larvae feeding on leaves and flowers of lily, fritillary and Solomon's seal	*lily beetle*
	Grey caterpillars feeding on iris	*iris sawfly*
	Grey caterpillars feeding on Solomon's seal	*Solomon's seal sawfly*
	Leaves of dahlia with small holes and tattered appearance	*capsid bugs*
	Water lily leaves with brown beetles/black caterpillars	*Water-lily beetle*
HOLES IN LEAVES NO PESTS PRESENT	Irregular holes in leaves, no slime trails present	*earwigs*
	Irregular holes in leaves, slime trails present	*slugs, snails*
NO HOLES IN LEAVES PESTS PRESENT	Black or green pests clustered on shoot tips, leaves and flowers	*aphids*
	Iris leaves with blotchy mines, pests visible inside	*iris leaf miner*
	Pale stippling of foliage, tiny green to red mites present	*two-spotted mite*
	Small, shiny beetles eating strips of surface tissue from iris leaves	*iris flea beetle*
HOLES IN LEAVES NO PESTS PRESENT	Brown scorch marks on tulip leaves and flowers	*tulip fire*
	Crocus leaves wrinkled	*drought*
	Iris leaves become reddish-brown and die	*iris scorch*
	Leaves of begonia and dahlia wilt, brown staining inside stems	*wilt*

HOLES IN LEAVES	Lily leaves develop oval spots	*leaf blight*
NO PESTS PRESENT	Narcissus leaves appear scorched at tips	*leaf scorch*
	Silvery streaks and spots on leaves and flowers	*thrips*
VISIBLE FUNGAL	Brown or black spots on leaves	*leaf spot*
GROWTHS	Dahlia stems rot, become coated with fluffy white mould	*sclerotinia disease*
	Leaves and flower stalks rot, with grey fungal coating	*grey mould*
	Narcissus leaves turn yellow and brown and then wilt and die, becoming coated with grey spores	*smoulder*
	Off-white mould under upwardly-rolled anemone leaves	*downy mildew*
	Orange, brown or black powdery spores under leaves	*rust*
	Swollen pustules on leaves and stems, erupting into black spores	*smut*

FLOWERS

	Flowers lacking	*blindness*
	Petals blackened	*smut*
	Petals distorted	*capsid bugs, stem eelworm*
	Petals eaten, no slime trails	*earwigs*
	Petals eaten, slime trails present	*slugs and snails*
	Petals rotted	*grey mould, smoulder*
	Petals torn	*sparrows*
	Petals with bleached spots	*thrips*
	Petals with dark spots	*petal blight, tulip fire*

A PHIDS (GREENFLY AND BLACKFLY) Various species of aphid are found on plants growing from bulbs, corms, tubers and rhizomes, starting while they are still in store. Numbers can build up even before planting and the pests then multiply at an increased rate after planting. Other species fly in to the plants when they are in full growth, and many spread virus diseases to the host plant.

All the aphid species feed on the plant sap, and this frequently results in distorted growth and honeydew deposits. As with other aphid types, the honeydew is soon colonized by sooty mould fungi, causing a blackening of the leaves. With some species, ants are attracted to the aphids or the honeydew, and can spread the infestation.

Control: In store, application of a contact aphid killer such as bifenthrin or fatty acids would be sufficient for control. Once growing in the open, it may be better to use a systemic insecticide such as dimethoate or heptenophos.

If beneficial insects such as ladybirds, lacewings or hover flies are already present and feeding on the aphids, leave well alone. Should this control not be adequate, however, spray with pirimcarb which is virtually aphid-specific. The iris aphid, *Aphis newtoni*, attacks waterside iris plants and these would best be controlled by strong jets of water from a hosepipe rather than by insecticide, which could harm fish and other pond-life. The water-lily aphid, *Rhopalosiphum nymphaeae*, can be also be controlled by jets of water or, in some ponds, by raising the height of the water to submerge the leaves and the aphids. The winter host of the water-lily aphid is blackthorn, *Prunus spinosa*, and winter washing with a tar oil spray would kill the overwintering eggs.

Main aphid species:

- Bulb and potato aphid, *Rhopalosiphoninus latysiphon*, and mangold aphid, *R. staphyleae*, attack tulip, gladiolus, crocus, lily and other bulbs and corms. When the attack spreads to the developing leaves they may blacken or shrivel.

- Peach–potato aphid, *Myzus persicae*, attacks growing plants of dahlia, calla lily, hyacinth and a wide range of other plant types. It is an important carrier and spreader of several virus diseases. Severe attacks can prevent the production of bulbs or corms for the following year.

- Potato aphid, *Macrosiphum euphorbiae*, also attacks a range of plants growing from bulbs, corms and tubers, as well as other types of plant. Some viruses are spread and plants can be distorted or stunted.

- Tulip bulb aphid, *Dysaphis tulipae*, is a common pest of bulbs, corms and tubers in store, including crocus, lily, snowdrop, gladiolus and tulip. When infested bulbs, corms or tubers are planted, the pests build up rapidly on stems, leaves, flowers and even on

seed pods later in the season. This species also attracts ants.

BACTERIAL SOFT ROT Bacterial soft rot, caused by *Erwinia carotovora* and other bacteria, is quite often found on bulbs and other storage organs, particularly following damage by slugs or other pests. Attacked tissue rapidly rots and the infection spreads to give a foul-smelling, rotten mass. The bacterium is favoured by wet, poorly drained soil, over application of organic matter, and plants made soft by the application of excess nitrogen and inadequate potassium.

Control: Avoid the factors above that encourage attack. If found on tubers and other storage organs when being lifted, cut out the diseased and discoloured tissue and treat the remainder with a sulphur dust.

BASAL ROT Basal rot, *Fusarium oxysporum* f. sp. *narcissi*, is a fairly widespread problem attacking crocus and narcissus, and has also been found on lachenalia. The disease attacks after the foliage has died down, and can occur in store or on bulbs left in the ground. The base of narcissus bulbs becomes soft and gradually the whole bulb rots, generally accompanied by a pinkish-white mould. On crocus, growing plants can be attacked, leaves turn yellow and the plants die. The corms show rings of brown sunken spots. Attacks of basal rot are most common following hot summers.

Control: Discard any soft or discoloured bulbs or corms after lifting and dip the rest in a benomyl suspension. If there is a problem with narcissus, try to improve drainage, and plant only narcissus from the groups that show resistance to the disease, namely the triandrus, tazetta and jonquil groups.

BLACK SLIME Black slime, *Sclerotinia bulborum*, can affect hyacinth, scilla, fritillary and crocus. Plants turn yellow and die and, as the infection spreads, large dead areas can develop. The bulbs rot to produce a black mass. The infection can persist in the soil.
Control: Remove a layer of soil from any beds which need to be replanted with hyacinths each year. Otherwise, plant narcissi instead of hyacinths.

BLINDNESS Blindness is the term used to describe a plant or shoot that fails to produce a flower. With bulbs, it can be due to lack of nutrients or a shortage of water, or to the bulb not yet being large and strong enough to produce a flower. Blindness can also result from storing the bulbs, corms or tubers at too high a temperature.
Control: Prevent blindness by growing in good soil, by adequate watering in dry weather and by cool storage of the bulbs after lifting.

BLUE MOULD Blue mould rots are due to attack by *Penicillium gladioli* and other penicillium species. A wide range of corms, and sometimes bulbs, can be attacked, resulting in a series of sunken lesions, and general rotting. A growth of blue or brown mould follows. Attacks can occur in the soil, generally following slug or other damage.
Control: When buying, avoid any bulbs or corms with blue moulds or brown markings, and avoid planting any home-produced subjects with the same damage symptoms. Use the biological control nematode, *Phasmarhabditis hermaphrodita*, to reduce slug damage in the soil.

BULB MITE Bulb mite, *Rhizoglyphus callae*, attacks damaged tissue of bulbs, corms and tubers and can then extend the damage quite extensively. Dahlia, freesia, gladiolus, hyacinth, lily, narcissus and tulip are the most frequently attacked. The actual pests are quite large for mites, being almost 1mm (¹⁄₂₄in) in size, and are conspicuous by being very shiny. Attacked plants develop distorted and ragged leaves and plants may be killed. The related bulb mite, *Rhizoglyphus robini*, causes similar damage, but will attack healthy plants rather than ones already damaged by other causes.
Control: Control slugs and other soil pests to prevent most bulb mite attacks. Check any stored plants for signs of mites and discard any found to be infested.

BULB SCALE MITE Bulb scale mite, *Steneotarsonemus laticeps*, can be an important pest on amaryllis and narcissus, particularly when they are being forced into flower. Amaryllis leaves are streaked with red, and flowers are distorted. Narcissus leaves are bright green and lack the normal greyish bloom, later they become yellow-streaked and scarred. Vigour and flowering are greatly reduced. If an infested bulb is cut across, angular brown markings can be seen, particularly near to the neck of the bulb.
Control: It is probably best simply to discard any suspect bulbs, but if any really choice varieties are infested it is possible to clear up the infestation by soaking in water maintained at 44.4°C (112°F) for three hours. This treatment will also control stem eelworm (*see below*).

CAPSID BUGS Both the common green capsid, *Lygocoris pabulinus*, and tarnished capsid bug, *Lygus rugulipennis*, attack dahlia plants. Leaves become tattered by tiny holes which enlarge as the leaves expand; buds may be damaged and flowers distorted or killed. Most damage is done from late spring, when the capsid bugs emerge from hibernation or move on to other plants from woody winter and spring hosts, through to summer.

Control: Spray with fatty acids, permethrin or pyrethrins, directing the spray onto the ground and then up into the plant itself. Repeat as necessary. Weed control is also important as capsids can feed on a wide range of weeds.

CHALKINESS Chalkiness occurs mainly with tulips, and can be recognized by a hardening of the bulb and a chalky white appearance of the hard tissue. Such bulbs will not grow and flower normally. Chalkiness follows lifting too early, before the foliage has had sufficient time to die back.

Control: If bulbs have to be lifted early, heel them into another part of the garden and keep well watered to assist continued growth for a few more weeks.

CORE ROT Core rot, *Sclerotinia draytonii*, occurs mainly on gladiolus, but also to a lesser extent on acidanthera, crocus and freesia. The disease is most common in cool, wet years when the foliage turns yellow and then brown and a rot starts at soil level. Rotting tissue is coated with greyish mould. In store, infected corms develop a rot of the central part, and the entire centre of the corm may drop out.

Control: Do not replant corms with any signs of rotting. Dip healthy corms after lifting and drying in a suspension of benomyl to protect from attack.

CUTWORM Cutworm is the name given to the caterpillars of certain moths. The caterpillars feed in the surface layer of the soil, and can eat their way through numerous plants from late spring to early autumn, depending on the species involved. Bulbs can be eaten or plants eaten off at soil level, the damage occurring during the night. The main cutworm species include turnip moth (*Agrotis segetum*), heart and dart moth (*Agrotis exclamationis*) and large yellow underwing (*Noctua pronuba*). The names come from the markings or colour of the adult moths' wings.

Control: Regular hoeing will disturb and expose the caterpillars or the pupae for hand removal. Where damage is severe, apply a chlorpyrifos/diazinon soil insecticide or use the biological control nematode as for slugs (*see below*).

DOWNY MILDEW Anemone downy mildew, *Peronospora ficariae*, causes an upward rolling of anemone leaves which become coated on the underside with an off-white mould. Leaf discolouration may follow. Attacks are more likely in wet years.

Control: Remove badly affected leaves or plants and spray with a mancozeb or copper fungicide.

DROPPERS Droppers is the name given to the thick, white growths that sometimes appear growing downwards from tulip bulbs. Droppers appear when the original bulb is planted insufficiently deeply in the soil or when the soil is particularly dry. The swollen growths will eventually produce a bulb but it will take several years for a bulb of flowering size to develop.

Control: Ensure that tulip bulbs are planted at the correct depth, with 15 to 20cm (6–8in) of soil above the tip of the bulb, and water the soil in dry weather. If the soil is very light and prone to drying out, incorporate organic matter when preparing the bed each year.

DROUGHT Drought affects all plants and can cause blindness or death in extreme conditions. With tulip it can cause 'droppers' to develop, while with crocus the leaves become wrinkled.
Control: Incorporate organic matter into the soil to conserve moisture and apply water as necessary in dry weather.

DRY ROT Dry rot, *Sclerotinia gladioli*, is mainly found attacking gladiolus, but has also been found on crocus and freesia. Attack causes the leaves to turn brown, the stems to rot at soil level, and the plants may collapse. On the corm, the disease is evident as rings of small, sunken spots.
Control: Dip new corms in a benomyl suspension before planting, and then again each year after lifting and drying.

EARWIGS Earwigs, *Forficula auricularia*, can eat irregular holes in dahlia leaves and flowers. The damage is done at night, and as the earwigs hide away by day the pests are rarely seen feeding on the plants. Damaged petals may turn brown and the earwig droppings spoil the blooms.
Control: Earwigs can be trapped in plant pots filled with dry grass or newspaper. The earwigs will hide in the pots after feeding at night, and the pots can be shaken out each day and the pests killed. Alternatively use a bendiocarb or pirimiphos-methyl dust on the grass or paper in the pots.

GREY BULB ROT Grey bulb rot, *Rhizoctonia tuliparum*, can be a serious disease on tulip, but is less severe on bulbous iris, hyacinth, narcissus, lily and colchicum. A dry rot occurs at the tip of the bulb and if any shoots do emerge they will quickly die. Bulbs and soil may be coated with a white growth and in the soil will be found dense white fungal bodies up to 8cm (3¼in) across. These sclerotia (resting stage of the fungus) soon turn black and can persist in the soil for several years.
Control: When bulbs fail to emerge, or die shortly after emergence, dig them up and remove them together with a bucketful or so of soil from the site of each bulb. There is no effective chemical control for garden use.

GREY MOULD Grey mould, *Botrytis cinerea*, can cause a rotting of flowers or foliage in wet weather, or following damage by slugs or snails. Petals falling on to leaves and remaining there may start an attack. Snowdrops have their own grey mould species, known as *Botrytis galanthina*.
Control: Remove all dead or dying flowers and foliage. Where grey mould is particularly serious, as can sometimes occur on dahlia and anemone, spray a few times with a sulphur fungicide or with benomyl or carbendazim.

HARD ROT Hard rot of gladioli, crocus, freesia and acidanthera is due to the fungus *Septoria gladioli*. It shows on the foliage as a series of small dark spots and on the corms as a brown spotting at the base. The corm spots gradually enlarge and become sunken, and may join together or carry small black fungal bodies.
Control: Discard any diseased corms, and dip the remainder in a benomyl suspension before planting or after lifting each year.

INK DISEASE Ink disease, *Drechslera iridis*, affects bulbous iris and can be found occasionally on montbretia (and on lachenalia in the greenhouse). The leaves of diseased plants develop numerous yellow streaks and black spots and the upper portions will then wither and die. The bulbs rot away to leave shells of outer scales full of black powder. Damage is most serious in wet years and the infection can pass from plant to plant.

Control: Removal of infected plants, bulbs and some adjacent soil is the only treatment possible. When leaf-spotting first starts, or in gardens where the disease has occurred in the previous year, it may be worth trying a few fortnightly applications of mancozeb fungicide.

IRIS FLEA BEETLE Iris flea beetle, *Aphthona nonstriata*, attacks yellow flag iris but is also to be found on cultivated garden forms. The shiny blue beetles, up to 3mm (⅛in) long, feed on the upper leaf surface creating long pale stripes.

Control: Spray with fatty acids, permethrin or pyrethrins or dust with rotenone. Squash the pests by hand as far as possible when the plants are close to water rather than using chemical control.

IRIS LEAF MINER Iris leaf miner, *Cerodontha ireos*, is another insect that attacks both wild and cultivated flag iris. Conspicuous blotchy mines are formed in which the larvae or the pupae can be clearly seen.

Control: Squash the pests within the mines.

IRIS SAWFLY Iris sawfly, *Rhadinoceraea micans*, is mainly a pest of wild, waterside iris, but can be found in the southern parts of the UK on *Iris laevigata*. The bluish-grey larvae, up to 2cm (¾in) long, feed in summer and eat the leaves from the tops downwards.

Control: Spray with fatty acids, permethrin or pyrethrins, but do remove the pests by hand if the attacked plants are growing close to water.

IRIS SCORCH Iris scorch is thought to be due to adverse soil conditions in winter and spring. Foliage becomes rust-coloured and falls over. Rhizomes are unaffected but the roots die and become hollow.

Control: Prepare the soil well before initial planting. At the first sign of damage, lift and replant in better soil after taking off dead roots and leaves.

L**EAF BLIGHT** Lily leaf blight, also known as lily disease, is caused by the fungus, *Botrytis elliptica*. The disease is encouraged by damp weather and attack results in a series of reddish-brown elliptical, water-soaked spots on the foliage. Spotting spreads to stems and flower buds, infected buds fail or produce distorted flowers. *Lilium candidum* is most severely attacked, but *L. regale* and *L.* x *testaceum* are also subject to attack.

Control: Remove any leaves showing signs of the spotting as soon as seen, and in wet seasons spray a few times at two week intervals with benomyl, carbendazim or copper fungicide.

LEAF SCORCH Leaf scorch, due to *Stagonospora curtisii*, attacks narcissus, amaryllis, crinum, snowdrop and sternbergia. Affected leaves develop a scorched appearance at their tips shortly after emerging, and may then shrivel and die. Flowers show black blotches on the petals. With amaryllis, brownish-red spots appear on leaves and flower stems and when any part of the affected tissue is cut, a red stain appears. As the new leaves push up through the old bulb scales they pick up the infection.

Control: Destroy badly-infected bulbs. With lighter attacks, particularly on amaryllis, it may be worth trying to cut away the old leaf bases at the neck of the bulb. With narcissus, spray protectively in spring as the foliage appears and repeat a few times at fortnightly intervals. Use benomyl, carbendazim or mancozeb.

LEAF SPOT Leaf spot of iris, *Mycosphaerella macrospora*, produces oval brown spots which may join together and kill the leaf. Wet weather encourages attack. Anemone has two leaf spot fungi, *Septoria anemones* var. *coronariae* and a *Phillosticta* species. Attacks result in spotting and complete browning of the foliage.
Control: Remove the worst spotted leaves and then apply a few sprays of mancozeb or copper fungicide.

LEAFY GALL Leafy gall describes the outgrowths produced in response to attack by the bacterial disease, *Corynebacterium fasciens*. Dahlias can be infected and produce masses of flattened leafy shoots at soil level. Such shoots are blind and fail to grow to any extent.
Control: Remove and destroy infected plants.

LILY BEETLE Lily beetle, *Lilioceris lilii*, is a major pest in clearly defined parts of the UK. The beetles attack fritillary, and Solomon's seal in addition to lilies. The bright red beetles have black legs and head and feed on all above-ground parts of the plant. The larvae are basically orange-red in colour with black head and markings, but the coating is slimy and the larvae cover themselves in their own droppings. In the UK, lily beetles are localized; they are found in Surrey and in all, or virtually all, the counties adjoining.

Control: Hand pick all the beetles and larvae seen. If damage continues, spray with bifenthrin or permethrin.

MICE Mice dig out and eat newly-planted bulbs and corms, and crocus species often seem to be preferred to the less choice, large-flowered crocus hybrids.
Control: Firm the soil after planting, and water with an aluminium ammonium sulphate repellent. Trapping or baiting can be carried out provided the bait or traps are suitably protected against non-target species.

MILLIPEDES Spotted millipedes, *Blaniulus guttulatus*, feed on the bulbs during the year, often following initial damage by some other agency. In severe attacks the entire bulb or corm can be destroyed. Tulips are frequently attacked in this way.
Control: Good garden hygiene will help to reduce millipede numbers, as will methiocarb slug pellets. In severe cases, apply a gamma-HCH dust in advance of planting.

NARCISSUS FLIES The large narcissus fly, *Meredon equestris*, is a damaging pest of narcissus as well as attacking amaryllis, galtonia, hyacinth, iris, snowdrop, scilla, snowflake and vallota. The adult fly looks rather like a bumblebee, being pale brown in colour, hairy and 1.4cm (½in) long. Adults are on the wing in late spring, or even earlier in commercial bulb-forcing glasshouses, and lay eggs in the necks of bulbs as the foliage dies down. There is normally one larva per bulb, and feeding hollows out the centre. Small bulbs will be killed, while larger, or less damaged, bulbs will produce some leaves but they will not flower.

The small narcissus fly, *Eumerus* spp., is largely a scavenger, eggs being laid in bulbs that are already rotting from disease. Similar in appearance to the large narcissus fly but half the size, the adult fly lays many eggs in each bulb and at least five, and often many more, larvae will be found per bulb.

Control: Raking soil over the withering foliage as the bulbs die down will help prevent infection, as will examination of lifted bulbs for any softness, and removal if necessary. Hot water treatment, as recommended for bulb scale mite, above, will also kill any larvae in the bulbs.

PEONY BLIGHT Peony blight, *Botrytis paeoniae*, attacks lily of the valley as well as peonies, causing a brown rotting at soil level.

Control: Remove diseased shoots and spray with benomyl or carbendazim. In autumn, scrape away a few centimetres of soil and replace with new. When growth starts the next spring, apply further sprays of benomyl or carbendazim.

PETAL BLIGHT Petal blight, *Itersonilia perplexans*, can attack anemone and dahlia and causes a dark spotting on the outer petals. In severe cases the whole flower may be affected by a brownish rot.

Control: Pick off affected petals or flowers. A few sprays with carbendazim, benomyl or sulphur should be effective.

RHIZOME ROT Rhizome rot, *Erwinia carotovora* var. *carotovora*, is a bacterial problem which causes a foul-smelling rot of iris rhizomes. Related rots attack hyacinth, muscari and zantedeschia. Plants rot and fall over. These bacterial diseases are more severe in wet years.

Control: If the rot is found early enough, cut out the affected areas and dust the wound with sulphur fungicide. When planting up new beds, ensure that the soil is well drained, plant shallowly and take appropriate measures to prevent slugs damaging the plants (*see below*).

RUST Different rust species attack a wide range of plants, and virtually every bulb, corm, rhizome and tuber plant has its own rust species. In general, attack by rust fungi results in pustules of fungal spores on the foliage, releasing yellow, orange, brown or black spores to spread the infection.

Control: Remove badly infected plants and follow with a few sprays of propiconazole or triforine.

SCAB Scab, *Pseudomonas gladioli*, attacks crocus, freesia and related subjects as well as gladiolus. Infection starts as a reddish-brown leaf spotting and spreads down to the corms. There, round yellow spots develop into golden-yellow depressions from which masses of bacteria exude.

Control: Destroy infected corms and rest infected soil from susceptible plants.

SCLEROTINIA DISEASE *Sclerotinia sclerotiorum* is found on dahlia stems which become coated with a cotton wool-like growth of fungus. Beneath, the stems become brown and rotted, and plants wilt and die. Black resting bodies of the fungus pass into the soil where they can persist for several years.

Control: Remove and burn affected plants, and also remove some soil which will hopefully contain the resting bodies. Plant dahlias in a different position the next year.

SLUGS Various keeled slugs, *Milax* spp., live in the soil and feed on underground storage organs. Most bulbs, corms, rhizomes and tubers are, therefore, at risk. Other slug species feed at the soil surface or on the higher foliage.

Control: For soil-inhabiting species, and other species which hide in the soil by day, apply the biological control nematode *Phasmarhabditis hermaphrodita* (*see Biological control, pp. xvi–xxi*). For surface control, apply methiocarb or metaldehyde slug pellets thinly over the soil, or water plants and soil with a solution of metaldehyde.

SMOULDER Smoulder, *Sclerotinia narcissicola*, attacks narcissus leaves and flowers in wet years, and also causes a rotting of the bulbs in store. On the foliage and flowers the affected tissue dies and is coated with a mass of fungal spores.

Control: Spray at the first sign of attack with benomyl or carbendazim. Dip bulbs after lifting and drying off in a suspension of one of these fungicides.

SMUT Smut diseases are related to the rust fungi, but generally have a more drastic effect on the plant. Large, swollen blisters often develop on the affected parts and these erupt to produce masses of fungal spores. The smut species attacking anemone, *Urocystis anemones*, is a typical example.

Control: Destruction of infected plants is the only feasible treatment.

SNAILS Snails are most active during damp weather, and graze on leaves and flowers. The ragged edges left are often infected by the grey mould fungus. The garden snail, *Helix aspersa*, is one of the most damaging species, but banded snails, *Cepaea* spp., and the strawberry snail, *Trichia striolata*, can also be troublesome.

Control: Apply a light scattering of metaldehyde or methiocarb pellets over the infested area or water the plants and soil with a metaldehyde solution.

SOLOMON'S SEAL SAWFLY Solomon's seal sawfly, *Phymatocera aterrima*, rapidly defoliates Solomon's seal plants. The greyish larvae appear in numbers following summer egg-laying, and feed together underneath the leaves. When fully fed the larvae drop to the soil where they spend the winter in silken cocoons and pupate the following spring.

Control: Look out for the first signs of damage in early to midsummer and squash or remove the larvae by hand. Alternatively, spray with a contact insecticide. Bifenthrin, fatty acids, permethrin or pyrethrins would be suitable.

SPARROWS The house sparrow, *Passer domesticus*, can completely ruin crocus displays by tearing the petals to shreds. The damage appears to be motiveless.

Control: Place small sticks amongst the flowers and criss-cross with black cotton thread. Alternative methods which sometimes work are to place life-size toy cats among the flowers and to move them around from time to time, or to place lengths of brightly-painted hosepipe on the ground, the theory being that they resemble snakes. Lengths of 'humming lines' (thin, tightly-stretched plastic strips) could be used, but would be generally difficult to use over wide areas of crocus in flower.

SQUIRRELS Grey squirrels will dig up and eat newly-planted bulbs and corms.

Control: Firm the soil after planting and water with aluminium ammonium sulphate deterrent. Prickly shoots of hawthorn or holly may help until the soil has become partially compacted by rain.

STEM EELWORM Stem eelworm, *Ditylenchus dipsaci*, exists in a number of distinct races, such as the narcissus race and the tulip race, although nematodes of one race can infest plants of a different type. The eelworms feed and breed constantly at suitable temperatures, and can survive in wet soil in the absence of a suitable host plant for a year. Under unfavourable conditions, the eelworms gather together in vast numbers and form what is known as 'eelworm wool'. In this state they are resistant to unfavourable conditions. Twisted and distorted foliage and flowers, and colour breaking of petals are typical symptoms of attack.

Control: Bulbs showing any suspect symptoms should be dug up and burned and the soil kept free of susceptible plants for a year or more. Keep weeds under control as they can harbour the pests.

SWIFT MOTHS Caterpillars of the garden swift moth, *Hepialus lupulinus*, and the ghost swift moth, *Hepialus humuli*, feed on plant roots and bore into underground storage organs. Growth can be retarded and plants killed. The caterpillar is white and semi-transparent, with a brown head. The gut canal can be seen clearly, and the caterpillar wriggles quickly backwards when disturbed. Garden swift moth larvae complete their development in two years while the ghost swift moth can take three years.

Control: Regular soil cultivations and good weed control will do much to control attacks. Where a problem is suspected, application of a chlorpyrifos/diazinon soil insecticide would be effective.

THRIPS Gladiolus thrips, *Thrips simplex*, and iris thrips, *Frankliniella iridis*, between them can attack most plants in the bulb, corm, rhizome and tuber group. Attacks are particularly prevalent during close, thundery weather, and damage is most severe on gladiolus where the foliage develops red, yellow or silvery stripes and flowers show innumerable white spots where the pests have fed. In severe attacks the whole flower turns brown and dies. Attacks also occur on the gladiolus and other corms in store, and growth from damaged corms is of poor quality.

Control: Dust corms in store with malathion or gamma-HCH dust. To control thrips on the plants, spray with fatty acids, permethrin, pirimiphos-methyl or pyrethrins.

TWO-SPOTTED MITE The two-spotted mite, *Tetranychus urticae*, is a pest of dahlia in hot, dry seasons. Infested foliage shows a pale stippling where the mites have fed and in severe cases there may be a fine webbing over the leaves and flowers. Considerable stunting can result from a heavy infestation. Attack may start in the greenhouse where plants are started as cuttings from overwintered tubers.

Control: Keep plants well watered in dry weather. To control an existing attack, spray upper and lower leaf surfaces with bifenthrin, fatty acids, or pyrethrins. Repeat a few times at weekly or fortnightly intervals.

TULIP FIRE Tulip fire is caused by attack of *Botrytis tulipae*. Elongated pale brown patches appear on leaves, stems and flowers, and the buds develop a spotting and white coating of mould and the infection spreads rapidly to other plants. Plants usually die and infected bulbs produce shoots that are distorted and soon wither. Whole beds of tulips can be killed by this devastating disease.

Control: Remove and dispose of any infected tulips as soon as seen and spray the remainder with benomyl. After lifting apparently healthy bulbs from the beds, and before replanting for the following year's display, check them carefully for small black fungal bodies under the scales and discard any found, then dip the remainder in a suspension of benomyl. Spray the new season's shoots as they come through the soil and again a few weeks later.

VIOLET ROOT ROT Violet root rot, *Helicobasidium purpureum*, attacks storage organs in the soil. Infected bulbs, tubers, corms and rhizomes rot and become covered with purplish fungal growths.
Control: Destroy infected plant material and keep weeds under control. The infection persists in the soil, so if possible confine planting in infected sites to annuals or plants with small root systems.

VIRUS Several different virus types can be found on bulbs, corms, rhizomes and tubers. Arabis mosaic, cucumber mosaic, iris mosaic, dahlia virus, tomato spotted wilt, lily mottle and lily rosette viruses cause leaf mottling, growth stunting and distortion, streaks and dwarfing, and a breaking of flower colours giving stripes of different shades.
Control: No control exists for virus diseases. Many are spread by aphids or by hands and tools, so good pest control and care to wash or disinfect hands and tools are helpful. Infected and suspect plants should be destroyed.

VOLES Voles may prove to be a nuisance in some areas by digging up and eating newly-planted bulbs and corms.
Control: Firming the soil after planting,

and watering the area with an aluminium ammonium sulphate deterrent may be enough to prevent losses. As an extra precaution, cover the soil for a few weeks after planting with thorny shoots of hawthorn or some prickly holly.

WATER–LILY BEETLES The water-lily beetle, *Galerucella nymphaeae*, is sometimes a serious pest. The black larvae eat off patches of the upper leaf surface, feeding in groups, and then bite completely through the foliage.
Control: A strong jet of water from a hose will dislodge the larvae. In pools and ponds where it is possible to raise the water level, this would submerge both leaves and larvae.

WHITE MOULD White mould, *Ramularia vallisumbrosae*, attacks narcissus and results in dark patches on the foliage, followed by a white covering of fungal spores.
Control: Where the disease has been troublesome before, protective spraying with mancozeb, benomyl or carbendazim, starting when the shoots have grown a few centimetres through the soil, should be helpful. Repeat the spraying every few weeks.

WHITE ROT White rot, *Sclerotium cepivorum*, is a serious disease of onions and leeks. In the flower garden it can attack ornamental onion relatives, namely *Allium* species. The bulbs are subject to a smelly rot and become covered with a white, fluffy mould. Black resting bodies are produced in the white mould and these pass into the soil.
Control: Destroy infected bulbs, and rest the site from alliums for a few years.

WILT Wilt fungi can attack begonia and dahlia. Mature plants wilt and die and when the stems are cut open lengthwise a brown discolouration will be seen in the water-conducting tissue.

Control: Removal of infected plants together with some of the soil from the rooting area is the only treatment, although sprays of benomyl or carbendazim may protect plants from attack.

WIREWORM Wireworms, larvae of the click beetles *Agriotes haemorrhoidalis* and *A. lineatus*, feed on various underground storage organs.

Control: It is unusual for severe damage to result, but where control is needed, thorough soil preparation before planting will help, and an application of a chlorpyrifos/diazinon soil insecticide may be justified.

YELLOWS Yellows is a term used to describe the bright yellow striping on gladioli leaves due to attack by *Fusarium oxysporum* f. sp. *gladioli* and also the yellow discolouration of hyacinth leaves following attack by *Xanthomonas hyacinthi*.

Control: There is no really effective control for either disease. Removing infected plants plus the surrounding soil may help.

FLOWERS 4

TREES AND SHRUBS, INCLUDING ROSES AND CONIFERS

This section includes all those plants which have permanent woody systems of stems and branches.

TRUNKS AND BRANCHES

ROTTING	Die back and rotting of heart wood	*heart rot*
STEMS EATEN	Bark eaten from trunks, young shoots grazed off	*deer, rabbit, hare, squirrel, vole*
PESTS PRESENT	Green to red or purple stationary insects clustered round growing points and on leaves	*aphids*
	Scab-like insects on bark	*scale insects*
	White, woolly-covered pests on bark or stems	*adelges, beech aphid, woolly aphid*
VISIBLE FUNGAL GROWTHS	Fungal bodies growing out of trunks of trees	*bracket fungi*
	Pinkish pustules, mainly on dead or dying wood	*coral spot*
	Pustules producing yellow, orange, red or brown, dusty spores	*rust fungi*
	Stems dying, furry grey mould coating	*grey mould*

GALLED	Knobbly outgrowths on stems	*broom gall mite, crown gall*
	Pineapple-like swellings on spruce shoots	*spruce pineapple-gall adelges*
CANKERED	Black, oval spots on willow stems and leaves	*anthracnose*
	Brown cankers at base of rose stems	*rose canker*
	Conifer stems develop cankers (and may die back)	*larch canker, stem canker, Phomopsis*
	Long cankers on wood, amber gum on bark, and leaf shotholing	*bacterial canker*
	Rough, cankered areas on branches	*apple canker*
DYING BACK	Clematis plants wilt, and may regrow, only to wilt again	*clematis wilt*
	Die back of shoots preceded by silvery sheen of leaves and followed by small, purple bracket fungi on dead wood	*silver leaf*
	Elm tree leaves turn yellow and trees die	*Dutch elm disease*
	Heather and conifers, but also other plants, develop yellow leaves down one side of the plant. Die back and death usually follows	*Phytophthora*
	Lavender shoots wilt and bushes may die	*Lavender shab disease*
	Plants wilt and die back, no obvious pest or disease	*faulty root action*
	Rhododendrons die back from silver leaf attack, but without the expected silvering of the foliage	*silver leaf*
	Roses, and certain other shrubs and trees, fail to establish well on re-used sites	*soil sickness*
	Shrubs and trees killed, followed by masses of honey-coloured toadstools	*honey fungus*
	Shrub shoots die and become covered with a furry, grey fungus – grey mould	*grey mould*
	Various trees and shrubs die back, small cankers and bacterial ooze occur	*fireblight*
	Young lilac shoots turn brown and wither, usually just before flowering	*lilac blight*
WITH GREY GROWTHS	Greyish growths appear on shoots and branches	*lichen*
DISTORTED	Clusters of tightly packed twigs	*witches' brooms*
	Shoots appear in wide, flattened forms	*fasciation*
WITH PEELING BARK	Bark peeling from stems	*papery bark*
	Sycamore bark peels off revealing masses of black spores	*sooty bark*
SPLITTING	Trunks split vertically	*frost, drought*
SLIMY PATCHES	Foul-smelling liquid oozing from cracks	*slime flux*

NO FLOWERS PRODUCED	Shoots fail to produce flowers when expected	*blindness*

LEAVES

VISIBLE PESTS	Flat, scab-like insects underneath leaves	*scale insects*
	Green to red or purple pests mainly clustered underneath leaves	*aphids*
	Thin, pale insects under leaves, making short, leaping flights when disturbed	*leafhopper*
	White, waxy pests plus leaf curling or swelling	*suckers*
	White, woolly pests on needle bases of conifers	*adelges*
LEAVES SKELETONIZED	Rose and some other leaves reduced to network of veins	*sawfly*
LEAVES HOLED	Green, brown or variously-coloured caterpillars eating leaf tissue	*caterpillars*
	Larvae and adult beetles eating away or grazing on various leaves	*leaf beetles*
	Leaf edges of rhododendron and similar 'hard' leaves notched	*weevils*
	Irregular holes eaten in leaves of clematis and other 'soft' leaves	*earwig*
	Leaves develop round, brown spots which fall out	*shothole*
	Rounded pieces eaten from rose and some other leaves	*leaf-cutter bee*
DISCOLOURED	Conifer needles turn yellow and may fall prematurely	*conifer spinning mite*
	Leaf edges or tips scorched	*frost*
	Leaves develop a silvery sheen	*silver leaf*
	Leaves discoloured for no apparent reason	*faulty root action*
	Leaves of acers turn brown at the edges in spring, then shrivel and dry up	*cold winds*
	Older leaves develop yellow then brown areas and patches between veins	*magnesium deficiency, manganese deficiency*
	Small bleached spots on upper leaf surface, leaping pests below	*leafhopper*
	Thuja needles turn brown and develop dark fruiting bodies	*Thuja blight*
	Various spottings, mottlings and distortions	*virus*
	Yellowing between veins of youngest leaves	*iron deficiency*
	Yellow mottling of upper leaf surfaces of rhododendron leaves, rusty brown below	*rhododendron bug*
SPOTTED	Black marks and spots on willow stems and leaves	*anthracnose*
	Dark spotting of rose leaves, followed by leaf yellowing and fall	*black spot*

SPOTTED *cont.*	Dark spotting on leaves and fruit of malus and pyracantha	*scab*
	Large black spots with pale surrounds on sycamore	*tar spot*
	Various small to large dark spots on foliage	*leaf spot*
	Yellow spots, changing through red to black on rowan leaves	*pear leaf blister mite*
VISIBLE FUNGAL GROWTHS	Black, powdery deposit where sap-sucking pests have been feeding	*sooty mould*
	Grey fungal growths underneath leaves, pale spotting above	*downy mildew*
	Powdery, white fungal deposit on foliage	*powdery mildew*
	Yellow, orange, red or black powdery spots mainly under leaves	*rust fungi*
DISTORTED	Hawthorn and yew tree tips produce rosettes of leaves which fail to grow out	*gall midge*
	Holed and tattered leaves often distorted	*capsid bugs*
	Leaves reduced to narrow structures with wavy and tendril-like edges, stems twisted	*hormone weed-killer damage*
	Rhododendron leaves reduced in width and twisted	*frost*
ROLLED	Rose leaves rolled tightly downwards	*leaf-rolling rose sawfly*
MINED	Blotch or winding mines in leaves	*leaf miner*
FROTHY MASSES	Froth in joints between leaves and stem	*froghopper*
GALLED	Azalea leaves become bloated then develop white 'bloom'	*azalea leaf gall*
	Flowering peach and relatives develop swollen and discoloured foliage	*peach leaf curl*
	Hollow swelling appears on poplar leaf stalks, grey insects inside	*lettuce root aphid*
	Large or small galls of varying shapes on leaves	*gall wasps*
	Variously-shaped galls on leaves	*gall mites*
	Yellow blisters appear on lower surfaces of poplar leaves	*yellow leaf blister*
CORKY PATCHES	Camellia leaves develop corky lines and patches	*oedema*
WEBBED	Juniper foliage webbed together by brown caterpillars	*juniper webber moth (see caterpillars)*
FALLING OFF	Conifer needles turn brown and fall off	*needle cast*

FLOWERS

WITHERING	Flower stalks of roses blacken and dry, buds fail	*pedicel necrosis*
	Malus and prunus flowers wither but stay on tree	*blossom wilt*
	Rose buds fail to open, outer petals turn brown and rot	*capping*

ROTTING	Failed buds rot and become coated with grey, furry fungal growths	*grey mould*
	Rhododendron petals become spotted and rot into soggy masses	*petal blight*
EATEN	Buds and petals eaten in mid summer	*chafer*
	Dormant flower buds eaten	*birds*
	Ragged holes eaten in soft petals of clematis, etc	*earwigs*
	Rose and other flowers bored into or eaten, often in bud stage	*caterpillar*
DISCOLOURED	White or brown spots and streaks on petals	*thrips*
DISTORTED	Rose buds grow out from centres of other rose flowers	*proliferation*
FAILING TO OPEN	Flower buds turn brown, shoot tips die back	*blossom wilt*
	Rhododendron buds turn brown and produce black pinhead-like growths	*bud blast*
	Stems turn brown and shrivel behind partly-opened flowers	*lilac blight*
DROPPING	Camellia, and some other buds, turn brown and drop before opening	*bud drop*

FRUIT

SPOTTED	Malus and pyracantha fruits develop black spots and cracks	*scab*

ADELGES (*SEE ALSO SPRUCE GALL ADELGES, BELOW*) Adelges are very similar insects to aphids and feed on conifers. Unlike aphids, they do not produce living young. Scots pine adelges, *Adelges pini*, feeds on Scots pine and other two-needled pine species, Douglas fir adelges, *A. cooleyi*, alternates between Douglas fir and spruce, and larch adelges, *A. laricis* feeds on larch. Autumn-laid eggs hatch in spring and the nymphs coat themselves with waxy threads, rather like woolly aphids of apple trees. Winged forms are produced in late spring and fly off to spread the infestation.
Control: Spray with bifenthrin, dimethoate, fatty acids, heptenophos, pirimicarb or pirimiphos-methyl.

ANTHACNOSE Anthracnose is a disease caused by the fungus *Marssonina salicicola*, which attacks willow trees, particularly the weeping willow, *Salix babylonica*. Oval black spots appear on the young stems and leaves and small cankers may develop on the stems. Leaves become twisted and yellow, and fall prematurely.
Control: Gather up and burn fallen leaves. On smaller trees, prune out the spotted growths as soon as seen, but especially in spring when new growth is starting, and follow with a spray using a copper fungicide. Repeat the cutting out and spraying in mid- to late summer. On larger trees there is little that can be done other than gathering up fallen leaves. Tree surgery may be necessary to remove infected shoots or branches and to start again to build up a new branch framework.

APHIDS (GREENFLY AND BLACKFLY) (SEE ALSO LETTUCE ROOT APHID, BELOW) Many different species of aphid attack trees and shrubs, generally resulting in some degree of leaf curling. Very few species of tree or shrub could be claimed to be free of a potential aphid attack. Blackening of the leaves follows attack as sooty moulds grow on the honeydew excreted by aphids as they feed. Some species produce vast quantities of honeydew which falls on to whatever is beneath the tree at the time, making surfaces sticky. Beech aphid and woolly aphid produce waxy threads to protect themselves, and this can interfere with insecticide penetration.

Control: Spray as soon as the infestation is noticed using pirimicarb, which is virtually aphid-specific. Once an infestation has developed it is more difficult to control, probably needing a fully systemic insecticide such as dimethoate or heptenophos. On flowering counterparts of fruit trees, ornamental *Malus* and *Prunus* species for example, application of a tar oil winter wash would kill any overwintering aphid eggs and so prevent early damage the following spring.

Main aphid species:
- Beech aphid, *Phyllaphis fagi*, occurs both on beech and parrotia. It coats itself with white, waxy threads which protect the insect from predators, and also from sprays unless well wetted. The beech aphid is a particular nuisance on beech hedges, spoiling their appearance.
- Honeysuckle aphid, *Hyadaphis passerinii*, is a particularly damaging species. It spends virtually the whole year on honeysuckle, all attacks seem to be severe ones, and flowering can be completely ruined. Early and

repeated treatment is usually essential.
- Lime leaf aphid, *Eucallipterous tiliae*, and sycamore aphid, *Drepanosiphum platanoidis*, are not particularly damaging to their host trees, but are unwelcome as they are among the most copious producers of honeydew, as many car owners discover to their cost, after parking under trees infested with them.
- Roses can be attacked by several different species of aphid, with the rose aphid, *Macrosiphum rosae*, being among the most numerous. Some of the winged forms can fly off to feed on holly, scabious and teasel, but others stay on roses for the whole year, even during the winter egg stage.
- Viburnum aphid, *Aphis viburni*, overwinters in the egg stage on viburnum and early spring attack causes the terminal leaf clusters to curl over, in which state they remain all year. Viburnums are also attacked by the black bean aphid, *Aphis fabae*, which prolongs the damage.
- Woolly aphid, *Eriosoma lanigerum*, is mainly a pest of fruiting apples but also attacks crab apples, cotoneaster, (especially *C. horizontalis*), pyracantha, Japanese quince (*Chaenomeles*), and rowan.

APPLE CANKER Apple canker, *Nectria galligena*, attacks crab apples but also ash, beech, poplar and rowan trees. Rough cankered areas develop on the branches, usually centred on a bud or spur, and the branch will die if it becomes completely girdled. Dark red spore-producing bodies, known as perithecia, develop in the diseased tissue.

Control: Cut away the infected tissue or brush thoroughly with a wire brush and then paint with a proprietary wound paint. Smaller shoots can be pruned out and burned. Autumn sprays with a copper fungicide at the start of leaf fall and again half way through leaf fall will protect the leaf scars from infection.

AZALEA LEAF GALL Azalea leaf gall is the result of infection by the fungus *Exobasidium vaccinii*. Attack causes the terminal leaves to become pale, swollen and puckered into galls. As the infection develops the galls are coated with white, somewhat waxy-looking spores.
Control: Pick off and burn affected leaf clusters, and follow with a spray using a copper fungicide. Repeat the copper spray the following spring when new growth starts.

BACTERIAL **CANKER** Bacterial canker, *Pseudomonas mors-prunorum*, attacks flowering plum and cherry trees. Attacks on the trunk or branches result in cankers, often in the crotch region where the branches break out from the trunk. The cankered tissue oozes amber-coloured gum which sets in hard lumps. The leaves develop rounded brown spots which soon fall out, resulting in a shot-hole effect.
Control: Where the tree is still small enough to spray, three applications of copper fungicide in late summer to early autumn will protect the leaf scars, which are the main point of entry for the bacterium. Resistant rootstocks for new trees should greatly reduce damage.

BEECH APHID (SEE *APHIDS, ABOVE*)

BIRDS Several types of bird, but bullfinches, *Pyrrhula pyrrhula*, in particular, eat buds and flowers of a number of trees and shrubs during the winter and spring months. Crab apples, cherry,

plum, almond and forsythia are amongst those regular damaged. Poorer flowering is the end result. In one series of observations, bullfinches were seen to destroy around 12,000 buds per bird in two months, and with only 15 minutes of feeding per day. Buds were pecked off, rolled in the beak to remove the outer scales, and then eaten.
Control: Netting can be used to protect shrubs from attack, and some reduction in damage on trees can be obtained by repeatedly throwing reels of cotton over the trees to spread a number of strands over the branches. Bird repellents based on aluminium ammonium sulphate can be sprayed over the trees, but do need to be repeated after rain. Regular feeding of the birds during the critical months works for some gardeners, but not for all.

BLACK SPOT Black spot of roses, *Diplocarpon rosae*, first appears as a dark, rounded or diffuse spotting of the foliage of roses. The leaf turns yellow shortly after the initial attack and premature defoliation follows. Bushes can be seriously weakened by a severe, untreated, black spot attack. The disease caries over from year to year on infected leaves and on fungal spots on the stems. Various strains of the black spot fungus exist, and breeding for resistance is a very tricky operation (*see Resistant varieties, pp. x–xiii*).
Control: Pick up and burn all fallen leaves, and during winter prune out any stems with the characteristic black spotting on the wood. To protect from attack, or eradicate an existing infection, spray several times at fortnightly intervals using myclobutanil, propiconazole, or triforine/bupirimate.

BLINDNESS Blindness is the failure of shoots to produce flowers as expected. It occurs quite frequently with roses, and can be due to lack of water or nutrients, or to root damage that prevents uptake of sufficient nutrients in solution. Blindness can also be induced by late frosts.

Control: Water and feed as necessary in dry spells and take action to control any soil pests. Should blind shoots appear, cut them back to strong buds, which should then flower in due course.

BLOSSOM WILT Blossom wilt is due to attack by species of the *Monilinia* fungus. Blossom and leaf trusses on ornamental *Malus* and *Prunus* varieties (crab apples and flowering cherries, etc) fail to develop and hang on the tree through winter. The fungus develops as a grey spore mass in wet weather which spreads the infection, and the disease passes down into the spur to cause similar damage in subsequent seasons.

Control: Prune out as many of the dead trusses as possible together with the infected spurs. A winter wash of tar oil applied for aphid egg control will also help in controlling blossom wilt. Spring sprays of benomyl or carbendazim, applied for disease control, would also be of benefit.

BRACKET FUNGI Trees can be attacked by a number of wood-rotting diseases and many of these have bracket fungi as their fruiting bodies. One of the most common is the birch polypore, *Piptoporus betulinus*. The fruiting bodies are somewhat hoof-shaped, pale buff on top and lighter below. Birch trees snap off around 3m (10ft) from the ground and the fungi appear on the main trunk and the detached top. Older, hardened specimens of this fungus were once used to strop razors, giving it the alternative common name of razor strop fungus.

Attack kills the tree in a year or so. Other bracket fungi produce heart rots or brown rots of the wood and attacks occur mainly on ash, beech, birch, oak and on spruce.

Control: If the tree is still living, remove the brackets and cut off any smaller branches with the fruiting bodies. Where large trees are involved, consult a qualified tree surgeon who can determine whether the tree is in danger of falling over or if any remedial action is feasible.

BROOM GALL MITE Broom gall mite, *Eriophyes genistae*, occurs on both *Genista* and *Cytisus* plants. The mites invade young buds in spring and the buds then develop into clusters of pale knobbly growths, each up to 3cm (1¼in) across. Badly infested bushes are unsightly and can be stunted.

Control: Cut out and burn infected shoots as soon as the damage is seen. Severely damaged bushes are best dug up and replaced.

BUD BLAST Bud blast of rhododendrons is due to the fungus *Pycnostysanus azaleae*. Infected buds turn brown in winter and fail to open in spring, but remain on the bush. Small black fungal bodies, known as coremia but looking like minute pinheads, appear and spores from these spread the infection. Such spread is by a unique route, as the rhododendron leafhopper is involved. Spores of the bud blast disease are thought to gain entry into the bud through the slits made by the female rhododendron leafhopper as she lays her eggs.

Control: Remove and safely dispose of all buds that fail to open in spring. Controlling the leafhopper by sprays of fatty acids, permethrin, pirimiphos-methyl or pyrethrins during late summer to mid-autumn should effectively prevent spread of any bud blast spores. Some rhododendron varieties are more susceptible than others and if damage is always severe, look around the locality to spot and note the names of any that appear to have some resistance to attack. These could be used to replace the more susceptible sorts.

BUD DROP Bud drop is principally a problem with camellia, hibiscus and wisteria. Buds look healthy, but fail to open in spring and fall off the bushes. Some may just start to open, but the petal tips turn brown and the bud then drops off. Bud drop of camellia is due to a shortage of water in the previous autumn, while with hibiscus and wisteria it is more usually associated with cold, drying winds and spring drought.
Control: Keep the soil well watered in late summer and autumn and mulch well to help conserve the moisture. With camellias in tubs, daily watering may be required. Where the plants are growing close to walls, extra watering will be needed.

CAPPING Capping is the term used to describe the way that roses and some other blooms swell but then fail to open, apparently at the last minute. The cause is heavy rain at the critical stage which damages the petals and seals the outer layers together. Rose varieties differ widely in their susceptibility to the disorder and multi-petalled roses, including many old varieties, suffer most from this affliction. Grey mould frequently attacks the capped blooms resulting in a wet, mouldy mass.
Control: Prune out the affected shoots, cutting them back to strong buds to encourage good replacement flowering

stems. If roses are being grown for a flower show or other particular occasion it is possible to protect the blooms from adverse weather conditions with special conical covers.

CAPSID BUGS Both the common green capsid, *Lygocoris pabulinus*, and the tarnished plant bug, *Lygus rugulipennis*, attack a range of trees and shrubs. Feeding is mainly carried out in the late spring to early summer period, after which the pests tend to move on to attack herbaceous plants. In autumn, *Lygocoris* returns to woody plants for winter egg-laying while *Lygus* spends the winter under leaf litter and similar material. Where the capsids insert their feeding tubes the tissue dies out leaving a series of tiny brown spots, but as the leaves develop the spots enlarge into tattered holes. Fuchsia and caryopteris are often singled out for severe attacks, but most trees and shrubs are potential hosts at some stage in their development.
Control: Spray with dimethoate, fatty acids, permethrin or pyrethrins as necessary. Capsids tend to drop off plants when danger threatens, so spray first over the soil and then direct the sprayer up into the foliage.

CATERPILLARS Caterpillars of various moths and sawflies can be found eating holes in the leaves of many trees and shrubs. Some species tend to form large colonies and feed together, sometimes causing very severe damage although, in general, most trees and shrubs can tolerate quite a lot of caterpillar feeding. Among the species found feeding in colonies are several sawflies including the gregarious spruce sawfly, *Pristiphora abietina*, on fir and spruce, poplar sawfly, *Trichiocampus viminalis*, on poplar and willow, and

Hemichroa crocea, on birch and alder. On young trees the damage can be unsightly and quite important. Caterpillars of certain moths also feed in company on a wide range of woody hosts, with the buff-tip moth, *Phalera bucephala*, being particularly widespread on beech, birch, hazel, lime, hornbeam, oak, prunus, rose, viburnum and others. The orange and black caterpillars can defoliate a large tree in a very short time. Other moth caterpillars feed under the cover of a woven 'tent' and so are protected from birds and other natural enemies.

Such caterpillars include those of the lackey moth (*Malacosoma neustria*), common small ermine moth (*Yponomeuta padella*), brown-tail moth (*Euproctis chrysorrhoea*), yellow-tail moth (*E. similis*) and juniper webber moth (*Dichomeris marginella*), which can be found on juniper and cryptomeria.

Control: Hand-pick the caterpillars from small trees, or prune out and burn shoots with 'tents' of caterpillars. Wear rubber gloves when dealing with the brown-tail moth as the hairs can be an irritant to some skins. Where hand-removal or pruning out is not possible or desirable, for example on young plants where a branch framework is being established or with juniper 'Skyrocket' where the central growing point must not be removed, spray with the biological control agent *Bacillus thuringiensis* or with a contact insecticide such as bifenthrin, fatty acids, permethrin or pyrethrins.

CHAFER Rose buds and flowers are sometimes eaten by adult chafer beetles. Being large insects, the damage they do can be extensive with only a few chafers present. The chafers fly around to find food plants so are not often found at work.
Control: If large pieces are being eaten

from rose or other flowers in summer, an application of bifenthrim or permethrin should reduce damage from chafers landing on the blooms in the following couple of weeks.

CLEMATIS WILT Clematis wilt is normally due to attack by the *Ascochyta clematidina* fungus. Attack causes the stems to wilt and die back to soil level in summer. New stems are generally produced but these may also wilt and die shortly afterwards.
Control: Avoid damaging the stem bases during hoeing. Cut out all wilted shoots back to clean wood and spray the bases and later the regrowth with benomyl or carbendazim systemic fungicide.

COLD WINDS Cold drying winds can cause a scorching of the leaf edges on young spring growths. Acers are particularly susceptible to this kind of damage. Similar damage can result from lack of water uptake after planting and before new root activity starts up.
Control: Where wind damage is responsible, some form of temporary protection during the critical spring months will normally be sufficient. A semi-permeable barrier, such as fine netting would be better than a solid wind barrier as it will reduce wind speed without any buffeting effect being produced. A solid barrier creates eddy currents which can still damage the leaves.

CONIFER SPINNING MITE Conifer spinning mite, *Oligonychus ununguis*, can be damaging on young spruce trees, causing needles to turn mottled yellow and then brown. Needles may fall early and shoot growth can be checked.
Control: Spray in late spring with bifenthrin, fatty acids or pyrethrins.

CORAL SPOT Coral spot, caused by the fungus *Nectria cinnabarina*, attacks dead and dying twigs on a range of trees and shrubs and appears as pinkish pustules over the wood. Elaeagnus is particularly susceptible to infection and the whole shrub can be killed as the attack spreads into the previously healthy wood. On most other shrubs, only dead wood is attacked in the normal course of events, but spread into sound wood from spurs and pruning cuts is fairly normal.
Control: Cut out all infected wood and when pruning try not to leave any snags. Paint any large cuts with a wound paint. Check the garden for pea sticks or other possible sources of infection.

CROWN GALL Crown gall is caused by the bacterium *Agrobacterium tumefasciens*, and can be found on daphne and viburnum, manifested as a series of small galls along the stems.
Control: Cut out and burn infected shoots and then apply a copper fungicide as a precaution. Badly infected shrubs are best dug up and burned. Remove a bucketful of soil from the rooting area.

DEER Deer graze on shoots and leaves in spring and summer and on tree bark in winter. Trees can be killed by excessive removal of bark.
Control: A 2m (6ft 6in) high fence is the only complete control. Individual trees can be protected in the early years by proprietary tree guards and sleeves. Rags soaked in bone oil or creosote can be effective as deterrents, while human hair or sheep wool and sheep droppings are claimed by some to have kept deer out.

DOWNY MILDEW Downy mildew is a minor problem of trees or shrubs, but hebe can be attacked in wet season by *Peronospora grisea*. The fungus can be seen as a velvety, grey growth underneath the leaves with corresponding pale spots above.
Control: Spray with mancozeb or with a copper fungicide.

DROUGHT Lack of water is damaging to all plant growth, but particularly so on newly planted trees and shrubs. Established trees can suddenly develop quite deep vertical cracks through the bark.
Control: Incorporate plenty of organic matter into the soil when planting, ensure that the soil is really well firmed around the roots and water as necessary.

DUTCH ELM DISEASE Dutch elm disease, *Ceratocystis ulmi*, is spread by scolytus bark beetles as they feed below the bark of elm trees. The water-conducting tissues are rapidly blocked by the effects of the disease and a toxin is also produced in the tree; mature trees can die in a few weeks. In the UK the disease has wiped out vast numbers of mature elm trees since a new, virulent strain arrived on some logs from Canada in the late 1960. Elms in hedges will regrow to around 5m (15ft) or so and then yellow and die back. This may be because, at that height and stem diameter, the bark beetles fly to them, or because the root connections link up to infection in other roots.
Control: There is no feasible treatment for the virulent strain although some success did follow injections of special formulations of benomyl when used on valuable specimen trees.

EARWIG Earwig, *Forficula auricularia*, attacks soft leaves and flowers and can be a major problem on clematis in some years.

Control: Spray the plants with a permethrin insecticide or trap in pots stuffed with dry grass or newspaper (*see also Earwig, p.37*).

FASCIATION Fasciation is a growth disorder frequently seen on forsythia, birch, holly, prunus, ash and on conifers. Stems develop in a flattened form, as though a number of stems has become fused together. Some fasciations of conifers have been propagated and introduced as novelties, for example *Cryptomeria japonica* 'Cristata'. The exact cause is unknown but suggestions include insect damage, drought or waterlogging and frost. The fact that at least some fasciated shoots can be propagated by cutting suggests that a genetic mutation may be involved.

Control: Cut out unwanted fasciated shoots.

FAULTY ROOT ACTION Faulty root action generally results in plants showing severe nutrient deficiency symptoms, wilting and dying back, and in death in severe, untreated, cases.

Control: If found in time, lifting the plant, improving the soil conditions with compost or bark and replanting at the correct depth, suitably firmed-in, should solve the problem. Some cutting back of the stems will help, and application of a transplant spray to cut down water loss through the leaves will also be of benefit.

FIREBLIGHT Fireblight is a bacterial disease caused by *Erwinia amylovora*. It was first confirmed in Europe in 1957 when it was discovered in a Kent pear orchard. Fireblight attacks trees and shrubs in the rose family, and in addition to attacking ornamental apple, pear and quince trees it has been widely found on hawthorn, larger cotoneasters, whitebeam, pyracantha and *Photinia*. Shoots appear as if scorched by fire with the foliage turning bright orange and brown. Leaves stay on the trees and under suitable conditions trees can be killed in a single year. Cankers develop on the bark and bacterial slime oozes out under wet conditions to spread the infection, often aided by pollinating insects visiting flowers.

Control: No control exists other than cutting out all suspect tissue or felling the entire tree in severe cases.

FROGHOPPER Various trees and shrubs support nymphs of froghoppers feeding on the sap. The cream-coloured insects produce masses of froth by forcing air from a special canal into a liquid secretion produced from the hind end of their bodies. The resultant froth, known as 'cuckoo spit', protects the nymphs from predators and from drying out. The species with the widest host range of woody and semi-woody plants is *Philaenus spumarius*, the common froghopper. No serious harm is done except perhaps to young trees and shrubs which can be distorted by the feeding.

Control: Spraying with a forceful jet of water from a hose will dislodge most of the froghopper nymphs. For severe attacks on young and valuable specimen plants a spray with permethrin would be effective.

FROST Frost affects most growing plants in some way. A late spring frost will turn leaf tips brown, kill flower buds, and adversely affect growth. Rhododendrons produce wavy-edged and curled leaves of a reduced size following a severe frost as the new foliage starts to grow. Softer growths, of roses for example, may wither back almost to soil level.

Camellias and young trees and shrubs can have the bark split by severe frost in winter.

Control: When frost is forecast, valuable plants can be covered by a woven fleece to keep out a few degrees of frost. In the morning following a frost, training a lawn sprinkler on to the plants will slow down the thawing process and will reduce, if not prevent, actual damage. Leaving the sprinkler on at night when frost is forecast would also be effective, although inexpensive where water is on metered supply.

GALL MIDGE Gall midges are very small, delicate-looking flies which mainly attack leaves or growing points, depending on the species, resulting in rolling or other distortions to growth. Amongst the most common are the hawthorn button-top midge, *Dasyneura crataegi*, and the yew gall midge, *Taxomyia taxi*. The hawthorn type feeds in the growing point and the tips develop into a rosette form rather than growing out as new shoots. The yew gall midge causes much the same type of damage, the resulting growths being known as artichoke galls.

Control: Cut out and burn the affected shoot tips as soon as seen.

GALL MITES Dozens of different gall mite species exist causing a variety of leaf galls, spots and distortions. Among the more commonly found galls are maple bead-gall mite, which causes the small red pimples on field maple and some other acers, and various sycamore gall mites resulting in similar damage, particularly evident on *Acer pseudoplatanus* 'Brilliantissimum', alder bead-gall mite, causing green pimples on alder, broom gall mite on cytissus and genista, pear leaf blister mite on rowans and nail-gall mite of lime, seen as small upright red growths on lime leaves.

Control: No chemical control exists and if the growths are too unsightly all that can be done is to remove and burn the worst-affected leaves as soon as the attack is noticed.

GALL WASPS As with the gall mites above, dozens of different gall wasps exist, causing numerous swellings and galls on a wide range of plants. Several have different hosts for different stages in the life cycle. The oak tree has more than its fair share of gall wasps, including those causing the various spangle galls on oak leaves, evident as round, yellow or brown discs under the oak leaves, oak marble gall (often wrongly called oak apples), true oak apples which are soft and spongy, and the acorn cup gall which consists of cristate ridges of tissue growing over and round the acorn.

More common in the average garden are the smooth pea-gall and the spiked pea-gall of roses plus the rose bedeguar gall. The bedeguar gall is composed of a mass of branched, moss-like growths surrounding a harder centre in which several cells are to be found, each one containing a single gall wasp larva. It has been found that, as well as the original bedeguar gall wasp larvae, there can be at least one other gall wasp acting as a 'lodger' plus five or more parasites and predators feeding on the gall wasps and on each other. In bygone times the bedeguar galls were used in herbal medicine and were referred to as 'Robin's pincushions' after Robin Goodfellow, the woodland sprite.

Control: Except in the case of the acorn cup gall, no real harm is done to the host plant and no control measures are needed. Acorns affected by the cup gall growths fail to germinate and on some trees all the acorns can be attacked, which has repercussions in terms of regeneration of oaks from seed. Removal of such acorns from small trees would help a little.

GREY MOULD Grey mould, *Botrytis cinerea*, is perhaps the most common fungus to be found in gardens, feeding as it does on all manner of dead and dying material. Unfortunately it also spreads into previously healthy tissue, making the disease a major problem, especially under warm and humid conditions. On roses and some other shrubby plants the fungus gains entry through pruning cuts and snags and causes a die-back.
Control: Prune out diseased stems to 5cm (2in) or so below the visible signs of die back. Take care when pruning not to leave any lengths of stem between the cut and the bud below.

HARES Hares tear strips of bark off tree and shrub stems in winter and graze on the leaves and young shoots in spring and summer. They are less common, but more damaging, than rabbits.
Control: Use spiral tree guards or netting protection to deny access to the tree or shrub. Bear in mind that when a deep layer of snow covers the ground the hares will then be able to reach higher up the trunks.

HEART ROT Heart rot affects a number of large trees including alder, ash, beech and birch, and is mainly due attack by various toadstool-forming fungi. The wood in the centre of the trunks goes brown or white and is generally soft. With several conifers there is a dark rot and then the wood breaks up into small cubes. Depending on the fungus involved there may be bracket fungi developing on the trunks or toadstools around soil level.
Control: Many heart rot fungi attack through wounds so care when pruning is helpful. When a rot is discovered it is usually a matter for a qualified tree surgeon, as extensive branch thinning or tree felling may be necessary.

HONEY FUNGUS Honey fungus, *Armillaria mellea*, can attack a wide range of trees and shrubs including conifers, although experience suggests that some species are less commonly attacked and others are more frequently attacked. Shoots wilt and turn brown and death may follow in the same year that the first symptoms appear. Under the bark at the base of the dead or dying plant will be found a web of white fungal threads, the mycelium, and in the soil around there will be found black, bootlace-like growths known as rhizomorphs. It is these that give the fungus its alternative name of bootlace fungus. The rhizomorphs spread through the soil to infect other host plants. The old, dead plant will continue to rot and large clumps of honey-coloured toadstools then appear around the base.
Control: Claims are made for the successful use of phenolic drenches around both lightly-infected and healthy trees, and may be worth trying. The only alternative is to dig up and burn infected plants and leave the soil unplanted except for annuals, for some years, or to remove up to $1m^3$ ($1yd^3$) of soil and replace with new. Ensure that all traces of rhizomorphs are also removed.

HORMONE WEEDKILLER DAMAGE Some trees and shrubs are particularly susceptible to traces of weedkillers used to kill nettles or weeds on lawns, and of these roses are the most severely affected. Shoots twist, often curling through 360°, and fail to flower, while the leaves twist and become thinned down to little more than the mid-vein together with frilly edges of tissue. Other trees and shrubs behave in similar fashion, but are less severely affected.

Control: Cut out all affected shoots to well below the damaged area. Recovery may take place, although in severe cases, and depending on the weedkiller concerned, more long-term effects may be caused. Prevent by taking care to confine weedkiller application to the weeds concerned, or to the lawn, and use different cans or sprayers for applying weedkillers and for watering plants. Do not rely on washing out weedkillers, because it is practically impossible to remove all traces.

IRON DEFICIENCY Iron deficiency is typically seen in the leaves of acid-loving plants when they are grown on an alkaline soil. The young leaves become yellow between the veins and gradually the whole leaf turns yellow or white. Plants lack vigour and gradually die. Iron is not mobile within the plant so any that is in the plant stays in the older leaves (unlike magnesium, *see below*).

Control: Apply a chelated or sequestered iron preparation to the soil and foliage to supply iron in an available form. The chelating process makes the iron available to plant roots but not available to the soil to lock up into insoluble salts. Special fertilizers are now sold which supply the necessary iron and other elements and which also contain sulphur to make the soil more acid.

LAVENDER SHAB Lavender shab disease is the name given to attack by *Phomopsis lavandulae*. Infected shoots wilt suddenly in early summer and the plant may die.

Control: Remove dead plants and burn. When taking cuttings use only very young shoots of healthy plants. Where attack has occurred, it is probably safest to purchase new plants and to propagate from those.

LARCH CANKER Larch canker is caused by *Trichoscyphella willkommii* and is evident as a cankering of stems and branches, Die-back is common where the canker girdles the branch. Small white and yellow spore-producing fungal bodies appear in the cankered tissue. Winter damage and canker attack are frequently inter-related.

Control: Cut out and burn cankered tissue. Avoid planting larch trees in known frost pockets, and prepare the soil well before planting in suitable sites.

LEAF BEETLES Leaf beetles, also called chrysomelid beetles, are mainly small and brightly coloured and both the larvae and the adults feed on plant foliage. Poplar and willow are both attacked by numerous species and there are leaf beetles to be found on viburnum, heather, potentilla and other trees and shrubs. Normally the leaf-biting or skeletonizing that is done is not significant in terms of serious damage to the host plants.

Control: There is normally no need to take any action. For severe attacks on young plants, spray with fatty acids, permethrin or pyrethrins.

LEAF–CUTTER BEE The common leaf-cutter bee, *Megachile centuncularis*, cuts rounded portions from leaves of rose, and several other shrubs and trees, including laburnum, lilac, privet and *Amelanchier*. The leaf sections are rolled into cigar-like tubes and inserted into holes in the soil, in rotting wood and quite frequently in pots of compost in the greenhouse. Each cell receives pollen, nectar and an egg and the cells are then closed with a cap of leaf tissue. Six or so such cells are usually constructed in a line and then the hole is closed over with wood, soil or compost as appropriate.

Control: Not recommended as bees are useful pollinators of garden crops.

LEAFHOPPER Many species of leafhopper feed on the leaves of trees and shrubs resulting in pale or silvery spots appearing on the upper leaf surfaces. The pests feed underneath the leaves and take short, leaping flights when disturbed, The nymphs, being without fully developed wings, stay on the leaves and also present will be numbers of cast skins of the insects. Particularly damaging are the rose leafhopper, *Edwardsiana rosae*, which can render the entire leaf surface a pale creamy-yellow colour, and rhododendron leafhopper, *Graphocephala fennahi*, which is involved in spreading bud blast disease (*see above*).

Control: Spray as necessary with dimethoate, pirimiphos-methyl, permethrin or pyrethrins.

LEAF MINER Various trees and shrubs have their leaves mined by small moth caterpillars or by the larvae of small flies. Mines can be winding or blotchy and are are unsightly, but except on specimen plants or severe attacks on young trees or shrubs, damage is not normally critical. Azalea leaf miner, *Caloptilia azaleella*, and lilac leaf miner, *Caloptilia syringella*, both make blotchy mines but then surface and complete their development under leaf tips which they roll over and tie with silken threads. While some leaf miners attack only one or two different types of plant, apple leaf miner, *Lyonetia clerkella*, has a very wide host range including birch, cherry, laurel, cotoneaster, hawthorn, and rowan as well as apples.

Control: Pick off and burn infested leaves as soon as seen. Sprays are not particularly effective as the pests are protected inside the mines, but for severe attacks dimethoate or pirimiphos-methyl would be worth trying.

LEAF SPOT Numerous leaf spotting fungi exist and cause light or dark spots, often with dark concentric rings and followed by small black fungal bodies in the dead tissue. Azalea leaf spot, *Septoria azaleae*, is particularly damaging, often resulting in considerable leaf drop. Most other leaf spots are unsightly, especially on specimen trees or shrubs.

Control: Remove and burn spotted leaves. For severe attacks, spray with a copper or mancozeb fungicide.

LETTUCE ROOT APHID Lettuce root aphid, *Pemphigus bursarius*, has a winter and early spring stage on Lombardy poplar. Eggs are laid on the bark of the poplar trees and hatch in spring. The young aphids feed on the leaf stalks and this results in hollow galls developing. Further multiplication occurs inside the galls until midsummer, when winged forms develop and fly off to attack lettuce and sowthistle, and a few other related plants. There they feed on the plant roots until autumn when winged forms fly back to the poplars.

Control: No control is practicable on the poplar. (For control on lettuce roots, *see Lettuce root aphid, p.126.*).

LICHEN Lichens grow on the bark of trees and shrubs particularly in moister regions. Rhododendrons and azaleas seem more prone than most other shrubs to lichen growths on the leaves and a dense cover will interfere with normal leaf functioning. Poorly-growing plants appear to be more at risk.
Control: Feed the plants and remove the worst affected branches or leaves. Thin out other branches, or remove whole plants, to provide more air movement around the leaves and remaining bushes.

LILAC BLIGHT Lilac blight, *Pseudomonas syringae*, attacks leaves and young shoots, often just before the flowers open. Shoots blacken and wither and flowers shrivel.
Control: Prune out affected shoots to a few centimetres below the visible signs of damage and apply a copper fungicide. Spray during the following spring in advance of symptoms appearing.

MAGNESIUM DEFICIENCY Magnesium shortage is evident as a yellowing between the veins of the older leaves, as the available magnesium is moved by the plant up to the newest growths. In time, there is a brown spotting among the yellow areas, and early leaf fall can follow. Magnesium shortage occurs in wet years and is more of a problem where the plants are receiving too much potassium.
Control: For rapid correction of the deficiency, spray leaves and soil with magnesium sulphate (Epsom Salts) using 100g per 5l (4oz/1gall) of water plus a wetting agent. When feeding, use a fertilizer which also contains magnesium (as found in many rose foods).

MANGANESE DEFICIENCY Manganese shortage often looks very similar to magnesium deficiency but is usually a problem in alkaline soils with a high organic content.
Control: Spray when the symptoms are evident using manganese sulphate at 15g per 5l (½oz/1gall) of water.

NEEDLE CAST Needle cast is a condition affecting many species of conifer. Needles become discoloured and fall off, often in considerable numbers. Some of the damage can be due to cultural or weather factors including water shortage or waterlogging and can also follow extreme wind buffeting. Other needle casts are due to attack by fungal diseases.
Control: Good pre-planting soil preparation and watering young conifers in dry weather will help to reduce any cultural problems. For disease-induced needle drops on valuable specimens, a few sprays of copper or sulphur fungicide in spring may help.

OEDEMA Oedema is a common problem with camellia leaves on which lines of rough, corky tissue appear. Oedema, also known as dropsy, is the result of more water being taken up by the roots than can evaporate through the leaves. Cells rupture, leaving corky patches.
Control: Good soil preparation should normally prevent trouble with waterlogging. If the problem does occur regularly, consider lifting the affected plants, improving the soil conditions, including drainage, and replanting, perhaps raised by good soil under the root ball a little higher than before.

PAPERY BARK Papery bark is a physiological disorder which is related to waterlogging or other adverse root conditions. The bark becomes paper thin and peels off in horizontal strips or in patches. In severe cases the shoots may be killed.

Control: Thorough soil preparation before planting will help to avoid papery bark later on. Where attacks are occurring, replanting in better conditions is the only remedy, after removing the affected shoots.

PEACH LEAF CURL Peach leaf curl disease, caused by *Taphrina deformans*, attacks the ornamental, flowering counterparts of fruiting almonds and peaches. Affected leaves become bloated and twisted and change from green to yellow, red or purple. Early leaf-fall follows and a severe attack can completely defoliate a tree. The fungus spends the winter between the bud scales and then becomes active in early spring rains to infect the new leaves.

Control: If the tree is sufficiently small to cover over with plastic sheeting, the lack of moisture would prevent the spores from germinating in spring. Ideally the cover should be in place from late winter to mid-spring. Where this is impracticable, spray with a copper fungicide at the first sign of buds breaking in spring and repeat in autumn as the leaves start to fall.

PEAR LEAF BLISTER MITE Pear leaf blister mite, *Phytoptus pyri*, is a pest of pear trees which also attacks the leaves of mountain ash (*Sorbus*). As with pears, attack results in a pimpling of the foliage with spots that start green and age through yellow and red to brown or black. The damage is unsightly and can lead to early leaf-fall, but except on small trees the overall effect is not serious.

Control: Pirimiphos-methyl applied for aphid control may help to reduce blister mite attacks, but control is rarely essential.

PEDICEL NECROSIS Pedicel necrosis is the name given to the blackening of the flower stem, and damage is followed by a failure of the flower to open. It is common with certain varieties of rose and is encouraged by lack of water or nutrients.

Control: Cut off the affected flower, pruning back to a sound-looking bud. Water and feed as necessary, using a fertilizer with a good level of potassium. Should a variety continually be affected, consider replacing it with a more strongly-growing variety.

PETAL BLIGHT Petal blight is a disease of azaleas caused by the fungus *Ovulinia azaleae*. Spots appear on the petals, generally after periods of heavy rain, and gradually the whole bloom becomes water-soaked and finally degenerates into a brown, soggy mass. Infected blooms hang on the bushes until the following year.

Control: No control measures are feasible, but remove affected blooms as soon as seen, feed to encourage strong growth and thin out any overcrowded plants to assist in more rapid drying of the flowers after rain.

PHOMOPSIS Phomopsis disease of conifers normally starts as a die back of tips of the main shoot or the laterals when the terminal 30cm (1ft) or so turns brown and looses all the needles. A cankering of smaller shoots can then follow, and characteristically there is a marked difference in diameter of healthy and diseased wood. Finally, sunken cankers develop on larger branches. Different species of the *Phomopsis* fungus attack different conifer host plants.

Control: Cut out and burn all diseased shoots and cut out cankers from larger branches. Protect cuts with a wound paint.

PHYTOPHTHORA Phytophthora foot rot, caused by the fungus *Phytophthora cinnamomi*, is a relatively recent problem that has become particularly trouble-some to growers of heathers and conifers. Other species of *Phytophthora* can be involved, and young broad-leaved plants are also susceptible. Typically one side of the attacked plant turns yellow following infection of the root, but whole plants can suddenly die when the infection spreads rapidly to all the root system. Cutting through the stem base usually shows a brown, dis-eased area below the upper, healthy tissue. The disease spreads in infected soil and can be carried on boots, tools, seed trays, etc. In wet soil conditions, the dis-ease produces swimming spores which move in the moisture to infect the plant roots.

Control: Remove and burn infected plants together with some of the soil from round the rooting area. Use disin-fectant to wash the tools used. As the disease spreads in soil water, good drainage will be of help, so prepare the site well before planting. No chemicals are available for garden use.

POWDERY MILDEW Various species of powdery mildew can be found attacking trees and shrubs. Leaves are coated with a white, powdery coating of disease spores, leaf death often follows and shoots may be killed. Crab apples are attacked by the same disease that affects fruiting varieties and other species can be found on hawthorn, rose, cotinus, oak, hazel, and many other host plants.

Control: Cut out and burn the affected shoots, especially during the winter months when the white to brown fungal coating, or silvery shoots can be seen; this will remove the primary infection. During the growing season, prevent or cure powdery mildew attacks by regular sprays using benomyl, carbendazim, propiconazole or triforine or, on roses only, using myclobutanil. Alternatively, as a protectant, spray with a sulphur fungicide. Rose varieties vary consider-ably in their resistance or susceptibility to mildew attack (*see Resistant varieties, pp. x–xiii*).

PROLIFERATION Proliferation is the term used to describe production by some roses of small vestigial blooms growing from the centre of an older flower. The condition is normally the result of some injury by frost or pest during an early stage of the bud development.

Control: Cut off the affected flower to encourage the production of a normal replacement. Should the condition be repeated throughout the season it would be best to replace the bush with a new plant of a different variety (but *see Soil sickness, below*).

RABBITS Rabbits strip bark off trees and shrubs in severe winter condi-tions, and generally 'sample' the bark, stems and leaves of new planting in the garden. In lighter soils, rabbits can also be a great nuisance when they attempt to dig burrows in lawns and under hedges. Considerable differences exist amongst trees and shrubs relative to their palata-bility to rabbits.

Control: Protect very new trees and shrubs with proprietary plastic tubes and older ones with spiral tree guards or wire surrounds. For severe rabbit damage where high local populations exist, some professional help in clearing the rabbits may be necessary in the absence of a suitable perimeter fence. Current recommendations for fencing are that it should be 31mm (1¼in) mesh, 1.25mm (½in) wire, 1m (3¼ft) wide, with the bottom 15cm (6in) turned at right angles away from the garden and covered by turf. The wire should be suitably supported by braced struts. Approved designs of traps are also available, but must be visited at regular intervals, no less than once a day.

RHODODENDRON BUG The rhododendron bug, *Stephanitis rhododendri*, is also called lacebug because of the lacelike veins of the wings. Despite being winged, however, the insect does not fly, so populations build up on infested plants. The pests feed on the sap and cause a yellow mottling to appear on the upper leaf surfaces with a rusty-brown discolouration below. Leaf wilting is a common problem and damage is most severe in dry years or on plants in dry situations.

Control: Egg-laying takes place in autumn, so removal of badly infested leaves or shoots in spring or summer will give good control. Where attacks warrant spraying, apply a thorough application to wet the undersides of the leaves well. Use fatty acids, permethrin or pyrethrins in early summer and repeat the application a couple of times at three week intervals.

ROSE CANKER Various fungi can be involved in the cankering of rose stems but *Leptosphaera coniothyrium* is usually the most prevalent. Attack by this species results in a canker developing on the stem (other fungi cause cankers which

may be at soil level). Leaves turn yellow and, if the canker girdles the entire stem, it will die.

Control: When pruning, cut back to sound buds taking care not to leave stubs or torn stems to act as infection points. Should attack occur, cut out all cankered shoots to below the damaged area and then protect the cuts by applying a wound paint.

RUST FUNGI Many trees and shrubs are susceptible to attack by different species of rust fungi. Typically, attack results in small yellow spots appearing on the upper surfaces of the leaves with pustules of the fungus on the undersides. The pustules erupt to release yellow, orange, red or black spores depending on the disease concerned and the stage of the life cycle of the particular rust fungus. Roses are commonly attacked by species of *Phragmidium*, hypericum and willow by *Melampsora*, rhododendrons by *Chrysomyxa*, and conifers by *Gymnosporangium* and *Cronartium*. In virtually all cases the damage is to the leaves, thus affecting general health and growth, but on pines the damage is to the stems and can result in die-back.

Control: Where the plants are small enough to be sprayed, applications of propiconazole or triforine, or of myclobutanil to roses only, should eradicate the infection and prevent further attacks. Many rust fungi have alternating generations on different hosts, some of which include garden weeds, so good weed control can also be of help.

SAWFLY Some sawfly caterpillars eat holes in the leaves of different plants and these are discussed in the section on caterpillars (*above*). Other sawfly caterpillars graze on the leaf surface leaving behind only the vein network and these are included here. Among the most common in gardens is the rose slug sawfly *Endelomya aethiops*. The yellowish larvae, known as slugworms, feed on the upper leaf surface and normally leave the lower surface untouched. Attacked leaves appear bleached and soon turn brown. Other sawfly slugworms often found damaging garden trees or shrubs include pear and cherry slugworm, *Caliroa cerasi*, on hawthorn and rowan as well as pear and cherry, and various species on oak, willow and poplar. The leaf-rolling rose sawfly, *Blennocampa pusilla* probes rose leaves with her ovipositor and this causes the leaf edges to roll downwards. The sawfly does not always lay eggs at each site, but the eggs that are laid hatch into white larvae that feed inside the rolled leaves.

Control: Light slugworm attacks can be controlled by removing the caterpillars by hand. For more extensive attacks, spray with dimethoate, permethrin or pirimiphos-methyl. For leaf-rolling sawfly, spraying in advance of attack using permethrin may be of help.

SCAB Scab fungi attack crab apples and pyracantha causing brown spotting of the foliage and a cracking and dark spotting of the fruits. On crab apples the disease is the same as that attacking fruiting apples, namely *Venturia inaequalis*, while the disease on pyracantha is *Spilocaea pyracanthae*. Attack spoils the attractiveness of the fruits and also results in early leaf fall.

Control: Collect up fallen leaves and prune out any shoots bearing scab lesions. As the buds start to open in spring, spray with benomyl, carbendazim or mancozeb or use a copper fungicide. Repeat a few times at fortnightly intervals, continuing to spray for a longer period if wet weather prevails.

SCALE INSECTS Scale insects of varying species can be found on trees and shrubs, mainly on the bark, but sometimes also on the leaves. The pests feed on the sap and weaken the plants but also excrete sugary honeydew which falls on to the leaves below, soon to be colonized by sooty mould fungi. Many scale species are named according to their appearance, so the mussel scale, *Lepidosaphes ulmi*, has the general shape of a mussel, the brown scale, *Parthenolecanium corni*, is brown and the scurfy scale, *Aulacaspis rosae*, is rather scurfy-looking. Others, such as juniper scale, euonymous scale, and yew scale are named after the tree or shrub they most commonly attack.

Control: On flowering counterparts of fruit trees and bushes such as *Malus*, *Pyrus* or *Ribes* species, a winter spray with tar oil is effective. On other subjects, spray during the growing season with dimethoate, fatty acids, permethrin, pirimiphos-methyl or pyrethrins.

SHOTHOLE Shothole occurs on flowering cherries and other *Prunus* species. Attack by the fungus *Stigmina carpophila* causes small rounded brown spots to appear on the leaves. The spots then fall from the leaves giving them the appearance of having been peppered by shotgun pellets.

Control: Feed and water as necessary as the disease is more damaging on weak-growing plants. Spraying the leaves with a complete foliar feed is also worth while, and with severe attacks apply a copper fungicide at the start of leaf-fall.

SILVER LEAF The silver leaf fungus, *Chondrostereum* (formerly *Stereum*) *purpureum*, attacks a wide range of trees and some shrubs, mainly entering through pruning cuts and other wounds. With many plants, attack causes the upper leaf surface to separate from the central leaf tissue, thus altering the light-reflecting properties and giving the foliage a silvery look. On rhododendrons and some other hosts, this typical silver leaf symptom does not appear. The silvered leaves are not a source of infection, but the affected branches will soon die back and later produce the small, purplish, bracket-like fungal bodies on the surface. These produce spores to spread the infection.

Control: Cut out and burn all dead and dying wood, preferably by midsummer to avoid the main spore-producing period. The antagonistic fungus, *Trichoderma viride*, can be used to combat infection (*see Top fruit, p.172*).

SLIME FLUX Slime flux is the name given to describe the nasty-smelling liquids that can flow from wounds and cracks in the bark of various trees. The liquid can kill the bark and any plants under the trees. Poplar, horse chestnut and willow are especially prone to attack. Various fungi and bacteria are involved but the underlying cause is a build up of water and gas pressure within the tree.

Control: The treatment would normally be a matter for a qualified tree surgeon, but where smaller garden trees are concerned, cutting out all discoloured wood from the site of the liquid exit point could attempted. Large areas of exposed tissue can be painted over with a wound paint, although current policy appears to be to leave them open to the air.

SOIL SICKNESS As far as trees and shrubs are concerned, soil sickness is the term used to account for the lack of growth and difficulty in establishing trees or shrubs where specimens of the same type have grown before. In apple orchards, for example, the sickness is known as 'S A R D' which is short for 'specific apple replant disorder'. Roses suffer from the same sort of problem, and often grow very weakly if planted in soil where roses have been grown previously. The exact cause is not fully understood, but soil nematodes (eelworms) may be involved along with root exudates.

Control: The best way to prevent the problem in gardens is to avoid following like with like. If it is necessary to replace an old rose bed, for example, with a new one in the same position, exchange the soil in the site to a depth of 60cm (2ft) or so with soil from elsewhere in the garden. The addition of plenty of well rotted manure is also of benefit.

SOOTY BARK Sooty bark disease is due to attack by *Cryptostroma corticale* and affects sycamore trees and occasionally other acer species. Leaves and shoots of infected trees wilt and the bark develops small blisters. Soon the blistered areas open up as the bark peels, revealing small pillars of fungal tissue and masses of dark brown, powdery spores. One estimate of the number of spores ranged from 30 million to 170 million per cm^2.

Control: Diseased trees are best felled and burned.

SOOTY MOULD Sooty mould develops on the sugary honeydew excreted by aphids, scale insects, suckers and certain other pests as they feed on sap. The actual moulds, *Cladosporium* and other species, do no direct harm to the plant tissue, but by blocking or reducing the amount of sunlight reaching the leaf they also reduce the ability of the leaf to make foodstuffs. Sooty moulds are also very unsightly.

Control: Controlling the pests that produce the honeydew will also control the sooty moulds. Otherwise, the moulds can be gently sponged off the leaves of smaller plants with luke-warm water plus a little detergent. Rinse with clear water afterwards.

SPRUCE PINEAPPLE-GALL ADELGES
Attacks by the spruce pineapple-gall adelges, *Adelges abietis*, result in the growing points of Christmas trees and other spruces swelling up into pineapple-like galls. The growing points then continue normally, and a further generation of the adelgids develops inside the galls. Green at first, the galls become brown and woody by late summer, and stay permanently on the tree. No great harm is done to the tree itself but its appearance and its potential sale value as a Christmas tree are impaired.
Control: Spray in mild weather during winter or early spring using an insecticide recommended for aphid control. Bifenthrin, dimethoate, fatty acids, heptenophos, pirimicarb, pirimiphos-methyl or pyrethrins should be effective.

SQUIRRELS The grey squirrel can be an occasional pest in gardens, eating bark off trunks and grazing on leaves, cones and young shoots (as well as digging up bulbs).
Control: There is not a lot that can be done easily in a garden apart from protecting young bark with tubes or spiral guards.

STEM CANKER Stem canker due to *Nectria cucurbitula* attacks spruce branches and can result in a die-back. The fungus mainly, or possibly always, attacks wounded tissue, and can also be found on dead branches.
Control: On normal garden conifers, stem canker is unlikely to be much of a

problem but should any die-back occur, cutting the dead part back to sound, healthy tissue would be the correct action.

SUCKERS Bay sucker, *Trioza alacris*, box sucker, *Psylla buxi*, and hawthorn sucker, *Psylla melanoneura*, feed on the young shoots in the spring. Honeydew and white, waxy threads are produced. Bay sucker attack causes the leaf edges to roll, swell and become pale yellow in colour whilst sttack by box sucker results in the terminal growths becoming cupped into small cabbage-like galls.
Control: Apply a drenching spray using fatty acids or pyrethrins or apply the systemic insecicides dimethoate or heptenophos.

TAR SPOT Tar spot of sycamore appears as large, rounded marks each with a paler surround. The fungal disease responsible, *Rhytisma acerinum*, infects the young leaves in spring, having spent the winter in the spots on fallen leaves. Early leaf-fall may follow a severe attack.
Control: Gather up and burn the fallen leaves in autumn.

THRIPS Various species of thrips can attack leaves and flowers of trees and shrubs, but damage is normally only a major problem on roses. Feeding on the petals by rose thrips, *Thrips fuscipennis*, takes the colour out and damaged spots then turn brown and may rot. Damage can occur from late spring to autumn and with early attacks the thrips feed between the petals causing blooms to distort or fail to open fully. Thrips are particularly active in hot, thundery weather.
Control: Spray with dimethoate, permethrin, pirimiphos-methyl or pyrethrins and repeat as necessary.

THUJA BLIGHT Thuja blight, *Didymascella* (formerly *Keithia*) *thujina*, can be found attacking needles of the western red cedar, *Thuja plicata*. Bright brown, cushion-like fungal bodies appear on individual needles and gradually the bodies turn black before falling out, leaving small holes in the needles. The needles turn brown and the holes can be seen on close examination.

Control: Prune out the affected shoots as soon as any browning is seen, ideally before the fungal bodies fall out of the needles.

VOLES Voles feed on the bark at the bases of trees and shrubs, sometimes causing considerable damage.

Control: Voles are less likely to cause problems where the area around the trunks is kept free of grass and weeds. It would also be worth using spiral tree guards or netting where voles are usually a problem.

VIRUS Different types of virus infect trees and shrubs resulting in varying degrees of spotting, mottling, vein-banding and vein-clearing, mosaic, line patterns and distortion. Virus may be spread by aphids and some other pests, on the hands and on garden tools.

Control: No effective treatments other than plant destruction are available for garden use. Always purchase plants from reputable suppliers, particularly in the case of roses, daphne, passion flower, privet and clematis which could otherwise carry some virus infection. Good aphid control would help to slow down attack by some virus types.

WEEVILS Rhododendron, camellia, photinia, laurel and other 'hard' leaves can frequently be seen with rounded notches eaten from the leaf edges where vine weevil, *Otiorhynchus sulcatus*, and clay-coloured weevil, *O. singularis*, adults have been feeding. Clay-coloured weevils also scrape away the stem tissue and young plants may be ring-barked in the process. The larvae of weevils also cause harm to plant roots.

Control: To prevent damage in the long term, water the soil with a suspension of either of the beneficial nematodes *Heterorhabditis megadis* or *Steinernema carpocapsae*. These seek out and kill the weevil larvae in the soil and in time should prevent the adult stage from being reached (*see Biological control, pp. xvi–xxi*). In the shorter term, damaged leaves, and the soil around, can be sprayed with permethrin to kill the adult weevils as they feed.

WITCHES' BROOMS Tangled growths composed of numerous small branches and known as witches' brooms occur on a wide range of trees, but are particularly common on birch, silver fir and prunus species. The cause of the outgrowth can be a fungus, as with *Taphrina cerasi* on cherry, *T. insititiae* on plum and *Melampsorella caryophyllacearum* on fir, a virus as on *Robinia*, or a bud mutation (which has given rise to a some dwarf conifer forms).

Control: If the growths are too unsightly, and are within reach, they can be cut out to a few centimetres below their point of origin. With conifers, consider taking cuttings from any witches' broom which appears to be different from those already in commerce.

WOOLLY APHID (*SEE APHIDS, ABOVE*)

YELLOW LEAF BLISTER Yellow leaf blister fungus, *Taphrina aurea* (syn. *populina*), is a relative of peach leaf curl which causes large yellow blisters on the leaves of poplars. The concave side of the blister faces downwards and is bright yellow in colour.

Control: If the tree is small enough, remove and burn affected leaves. One or two copper sprays in the early months of the year may prevent attacks on trees normally subject to the fungus.

LAWNS

SOIL

HEAPS OF SOIL PRESENT	Large heaps 10cm (4in) or more high	*moles*
	Medium heaps, ants running around	*ants*
	Small heaps, no obvious entry or exit hole	*earthworms*
	Small heaps, clear entry hole	*mining bees*

TURF

DEAD PATCHES OF TURF	Irregular shape or in lines	*fertilizer scorch*
	Pale grass, tops pull off roots, grey, legless grubs found	*leatherjackets*
	White grubs with pale brown head	*chafer grubs*
	Small yellow patches, increasing in size and joining together	*Fusarium patch*
	Signs of bird activity, legless grubs with dark heads found under turf	*bibionid flies*
	Yellow patches, not increasing in size	*urine*
DISCOLOURED PATCHES OF TURF	Pinkish colouration visible	*red thread*
	Small straw-coloured patches	*dollar spot*
RINGS OF DISCOLOURED TURF	Small, pale rings	*Ophiobolus patch*
	Large and expanding rings of lush grass, dead areas inside	*fairy rings*

OTHER GROWTHS PRESENT

	Fungal fruiting bodies	*mushrooms or toadstools*
	Flat, leaf-like bodies, brown above, pale below	*lichen*
	Rounded, gelatinous greenish blobs	*blue-green algae*

ANTS Ants, various species but particularly *Lasius flavus,* construct their nests in turf, particularly in sandy areas. The ant hills interfere with mowing, the ants are likely to become a pest in the house, and can give small children nasty bites. Ants can also 'farm' aphids and protect them from predatory insects.

Control: Exposing the nest with a spade and dusting with an insecticidal dust is quite effective. Alternatively, water with a carbaryl suspension.

BEES (*SEE MINING BEES, BELOW*)

BLUE–GREEN ALGAE Blue-green algae, *Nostoc* spp., appear in wet years, particularly on turf that is shaded and compacted. The overall effect is to create a blackish-coloured, greasy-looking and slippery area.

Control: Improvements in drainage and air movement will often prevent blue-green algae. However, where it does develop, applictions of a dichlorophen moss killer should be effective. Otherwise apply copper sulphate or iron sulphate in solution.

BIBIONID FLIES Bibionid flies, or St Mark's flies, *Bibio* spp., can be a nuisance in some years. The larvae feed on the turf, and the medium to large, slow-flying adult flies can appear in vast swarms. *Bibio marci* adults appear in spring and *B. johannis* in early summer.

Control: Applications of a carbaryl drench for other soil pests will also kill bibionid flies.

CHAFER GRUBS Chafer grubs, are the larvae of various chafer beetles, the usual one found in lawns being the garden chafer, *Phyllopertha horticola*. The larvae are usually found curled in a 'C' shape but are up to 1.5cm (⅝in) long with off-white bodies and pale brown heads. They can cause considerable

damage to turf in their short feeding period from early or midsummer to autumn.

Control: Watering the lawn with a carbaryl lawn pest killer in summer should be effective.

DOLLAR SPOT Dollar spot, caused by the fungus *Sclerotinia homeocarpa*, is mainly a problem on the finer fescue grasses. Attack causes pale, roughly circular spots 2.5–5cm (1–2in) across to appear on the turf. The spots may join up to give larger patches.

Control: Treat with benomyl, carbendazim or dichlorophen as necessary.

EARTHWORMS Casting species of earthworms, principally *Allolobophora longa* and *A. nocturna*, deposit ingested soil on the surface of the lawn. These worm casts get flattened by the feet or by mower rollers, provide sites for weeds to grow and prove a nuisance when the lawn is regularly used for croquet, putting or bowls. A high population of earthworms may also encourage moles to tunnel in the lawn. On the credit side, earthworms do create large numbers of channels under the lawn, thereby improving drainage.

Control: Worms can be discouraged by using acid fertilizers rather than an alkaline material such as nitro chalk, and by applying acid soil top-dressings. Where population levels of worms are such that control is needed, apply a carbaryl lawn pest killer in spring or autumn, when the worms are most active. Worms are killed below ground by this chemical, and it is unlikely to penetrate too deeply into the soil, so the non-casting species may not be adversely affected.

FAIRY RINGS Fairy rings appear as a result of fungal activity in the soil.

Circles of toadstools appear, and the rings gradually expand outwards towards the edges of the grass area. Various fungi can be involved, but the species most damaging to grass is *Marasmius oreades*. This fungus feeds on dead organic matter in the soil, not being parasitic upon the grass, and sends dense growths of water-repellent mycelium under the turf. By-products of the fungal activity stimulate the grass, creating a dense green ring, but inside that is an area of brown grass due to the lack of water penetration. As the ring expands, the brown area slowly recovers, and in summer and autumn the toadstools appear. On large lawns there may be a number of different fairy rings.

Control: There are no chemicals for use by the gardener on lawns for the control of fairy rings. If there is a major problem, a contractor can be brought in to treat the lawn. The best treatment for amateur use is to make a number of crowbar holes in the brown area of the ring and to squirt washing-up liquid into them. A thorough hosing of the area should then result in much better water penetration. The treatment will need to be repeated as the ring expands.

FERTILIZER SCORCH Incorrect application of lawn fertilizer can result in scorch marks appearing, although with most products there would need to be quite a gross overdosing before serious damage was caused. The grass turns brown or straw-coloured and may die. Over-application may also result in very dark strips, where a fertilizer distributor is putting on too much, and particularly when the application is overlapped so a double dose is applied. Except with gross overdosing, the lawn will recover in a few weeks.

Control: Flooding the area with water may quicken the recovery by diluting the excess nutrients. Otherwise, avoid the problem by reading and following the application details, and by using a spreader approved by the fertilizer manufacturer for the product to be applied.

FUSARIUM PATCH Fusarium patch is the result of damage by the fungus *Fusarium nivale*, also known as *Monographella nivalis*. Attacks occur mainly in autumn and again in spring. The disease is also known as snow mould as it can develop on grass under a covering of snow, which creates the damp conditions required for infection. The disease starts as small pale spots on the grass and, as the attack develops, the spots enlarge and coalesce. Fusarium is encouraged by excessive applications of nitrogen, particularly in autumn, by compaction and by a lack of air circulation which creates humid conditions.

Control: Avoid excessive applications of nitrogen fertilizer in late summer or autumn, try to encourage air movement by careful pruning of overhanging trees, and by aerating the lawn well in autumn and spring. On very fine turf, professional greenkeepers disperse morning dews with long bamboo canes or birch besoms; this may be worth imitating on a high-quality garden lawn. For chemical control, apply benomyl, carbendazim or dichlorophen in autumn and spring, or as directed on the product label.

LEATHERJACKETS Leatherjackets are the larvae of the crane fly, *Tipula paludosa*, which is also known as 'daddy-longlegs'. Eggs are laid in the soil of lawns and beside many other types of plant in late summer and early autumn, and the larvae feed in autumn, rest in winter, and resume feeding in spring. Whole patches of turf may die out following root destruction, and damage is also caused by rooks, starlings and other birds pecking into the turf to find the leatherjackets. Population densities can be monitored by watering the lawn heavily in the evening and then covering it over with a black plastic sheet. In the morning most of the leatherjackets will be up at the surface of the lawn.

Control: For small areas, the heavy watering and covering system can be used, with the leatherjackets being gathered up by hand in the morning. Alternatively, a carbaryl lawn-pest killer solution in autumn should prove successful, and better than spring application, as the pests will have had little time to damage the turf.

LICHEN Lichen can be a nuisance on lawns. The usual species is *Peltigera canina*, the dog lichen. It appears as flat, leaf-like growths on the grass, brown above and pale grey below. It is pliable when damp, but becomes brittle when dry conditions prevail. Dog lichen is mainly a problem on grass growing on sandy soils, particularly when they are low in nutrients.

Control: Treatment of the lawn for moss control, using a dichlorophen lawn moss killer, is usually effective against the lichen also. To prevent attacks, feed the grass regularly in spring and summer, and keep up soil moisture on light, sandy soils.

MINING BEES The tawny burrowing bee, *Andrena fulva*, nests in soil and is sometimes found in lawns, particularly on sandy sites. Although a solitary bee, with only one adult laying eggs in each hole, large numbers can be present in a small area. The soil is excavated to create a series of underground cells and the outside appearance is like a tiny volcano with a mound of soil and a central hole.

Control: Mining bees are very useful pollinators in the garden and measures to kill them in lawns are not really justified. If they are being a real nuisance, for example where young children are playing, a wasp-nest powder based on carbaryl or rotenone could be used, but it would be better to disperse the mounds before mowing, and to keep children away for a month or so while the nests are being provisioned.

MOLES The mole, *Talpa europaea*, is a troublesome pest of fine turf and lawns. The animal burrows through the soil under the turf searching for earthworms, slugs and other food, and pushes up piles of earth and stones on to the surface at intervals. At times, the mole will burrow along just under the surface, creating ridges, and the grass often dies after the resulting root disturbance. Soil levels are upset both by the hills and by the soil dropping down into the tunnels. Moles are very competitive animals and, with a poor food supply, there may be only one mole present in half a hectare (an acre) of land. In land where food is more plentiful, the numbers of moles may reach five or six, or even more.

Control: Mole smokes are available, and can be effective, but really the best control is by trapping although it takes some time to learn, by trial and error, how to go about using the traps successfully. In some areas there are still professional mole catchers, very often retired gamekeepers or estate workers, who can be hired. Reduction of earthworm populations by carbaryl application (*see above*) may also deter the moles from invading any particular lawn.

OPHIOBOLUS PATCH Ophiobolus patch, caused by the fungus *Ophiobolus graminis* var. *avanae*, can be found occasionally on lawns. Fescues are not attacked, but the bent grasses, *(Agrostis* spp.) are susceptible. When the bents are killed by the disease, weeds and weed grasses tend to fill in. The disease is encouraged by wet weather, and over-application of lime, used perhaps to correct an over-acid turf. Lime is best applied in a number of small doses until the correct level of acidity or alkalinity (pH level) is reached.

Control: There is no chemical control, so avoid excessive lime application, and reseed quickly any bare patches of lawn to help keep out weeds and unwelcome coarse grasses.

RED THREAD Red thread, or Corticium disease, is due to infection by *Corticium fuciforme*. It mainly attacks fine grasses and shows up in late summer as a pale bleaching of the grass in patches. An examination of the patch will reveal small pink outgrowths on the grass.

Control: Feeding the turf with nitrogen in spring and summer will often prevent the condition appearing later on in summer, but when it does occur, applications of benomyl or carbendazim will be effective.

TOADSTOOLS Various fungi appear on lawns in the form of toadstools, particularly in spring and in autumn. In general, they are not harmful to the turf, since they live on dead organic matter in the soil. Edible mushrooms may appear, but are the exception not the rule. Often the appearance of toadstools indicates that there is some buried organic matter such as dead tree roots below the turf.

Control: In such a case, the only short-term answer is to roll back the turf, dig out the roots, fill any holes and replace the turf. The alternative is to do nothing; the fungi will, sooner or later, break down all the organic matter and then die out. Injection of a liquid nitrogen feed or a lawn food in liquid form may help to accelerate the rotting process. Where there is a worry that children may have access to the toadstools and may be harmed, a daily brushing would remove them from harm's way.

URINE Where a dog, and particularly a bitch, has regular access to the lawn, bright brown or yellow patches will develop where the animal relieves itself. If the dog is always accompanied, and the owner carries a can of water to dilute the urine, most of the damage should be prevented. Where damage has already occurred, it may help to dust the areas lightly with lime to neutralize any acidity. After a light scarifying of any dead grass, grass seed can be sown to make good the damage.

Control: The best solution is to take the dog on more walks so the lawn receives less attention. It is also possible to train a dog to use a particular area of the garden, but no doubt this does depend to some extent on the willingness of the dog in question to learn.

INDOORS 1

GREENHOUSE AND CONSERVATORY FLOWERING PLANTS AND HOUSEPLANTS

ROOTS

EATEN	Crescent-shaped, brown-headed grubs found in compost	*vine weevil*
	Small, colourless maggots with small black head end	*sciarid fly*
NOT EATEN	Mealy-covered, stationary pests feeding on roots	*root mealybug*
PESTS PRESENT	Powdery, mobile insects feeding on roots	*root aphids*
DEAD OR DYING	Shrivelled and/or brown	*waterlogging*
ROTTING	Soft rotting of root tissue	*root rots*

STEMS

EATEN	Slime trails present	*slugs/snails*
	No slime trails present	*woodlice*
ROTTING	Black rot at base of zonal pelargonium stems	*blackleg*
	General soft rotting	*crown rot*
	Tissue covered in furry fungus	*grey mould*
GALLED	Corky patches on cacti and succulents	*faulty growing conditions*
	Outgrowths of stunted, leafy shoots	*leafy gall*
WILTING	Begonias wilt and leaves develop spotting	*bacterial wilt*
	Carnations wilt and may die	*wilt*
	Compost heavy and wet	*waterlogging*
	Compost light and dry	*drought*

LEAVES

NO HOLES PESTS VISIBLE	Barely visible, narrow yellow to brown insects under leaves, leaves scarred and silvered	*Western flower thrips*
	Green to pink pests clustered under leaves and on shoot tips	*aphids*
	Mealy insects at leaf bases	*mealy bug*
	Pale pests under leaves making short leaping flights when disturbed, bleached spots on leaves	*glasshouse leafhopper*
	Scab-like insects stuck under leaves close to veins, also found on stems	*scale insects*
	White, moth-like pests under leaves, fly off when disturbed, no bleached spots	*whitefly*
	Winding mines in leaves	*leaf miner*

NO HOLES NO PESTS VISIBLE	Pale stippling on top of leaves, barely visible greenish mites underneath	two-spotted mite
	Leaves of cyclamen and other plants crinkled	cyclamen mite
HOLES PESTS VISIBLE	Green or brown caterpillars present	caterpillars
HOLES NO PESTS VISIBLE	Ragged holes, slime trails present	slugs/snails
SCORCHED	Pale markings in ring patterns on saintpaulia	sun scorch
	Tips of leaves dried up, or patches on leaves	dry air, sun scorch, drought
FUNGAL GROWTHS OR SPOTS PRESENT	Black, sooty coating on upper surfaces of leaves	sooty mould
	Powdery yellow, orange, red or black spots under leaves	rust
	Various dry spots above or below leaves	leaf spot
	White, powdery fungus present	powdery mildew
CORKY PATCHES	Pale, corky areas under leaves	oedema, faulty growing conditions when on cacti
BROWN, ANGULAR PATCHES	Brown areas bounded by leaf veins	eelworm

BUDS AND FLOWERS

	Buds dropping off before opening	bud drop
	Chrysanthemum flowers covered in furry fungal growths	bloom damping
	Petals turning brown at the tips	petal blight

APHIDS (GREENFLY AND BLACK-FLY) (*SEE ALSO ROOT APHID, BELOW*) Aphids feed on plant sap and excrete sugary honeydew as they feed. This falls on to the leaves and stems as well as on to tables or other items of furniture where the plants may be standing. Honeydew feels sticky and is soon colonized by sooty moulds which turn it black. Aphids can spread virus diseases and generally weaken plants by their feeding. Build up of aphid infestation is rapid as greenfly produce living young.

Control: Inserting card 'pins' containing butoxycarboxim will prevent attacks building up and also control existing infestations. The chemical moves out of the card into the compost and is taken up by the roots to give a systemic control of the pests.

Biological control is also possible using the predatory midge-like fly, *Aphidoletes*, or the parasitic wasp, *Aphidius*. Alternatively, the plants can be sprayed with a suspension of spores of the fungus *Verticillium lecani,* which infects the greenfly and kills them. The dead pests then become covered with fungal spores to spread the control (*see Biological control, pp. xvi–xxi*).

Should insecticide sprays be preferred, use bioallethrin, bifenthrin, fatty acids, dimethoate, heptenophos, pirimicarb, pirimiphos-methyl or pyrethrins.

Main aphid species:

- Chrysanthemum aphid, *Macrosiphoniella sanborni*, is normally specific to chrysanthemum, feeding on leaves, buds and open flowers. Flowers are distorted and the aphid is also a carrier of chrysanthemum vein mottle virus and chrysanthemum virus B.
- Glasshouse and potato aphid, *Aulacorthum solani*, is a shiny yellow/green aphid with long antennae which feeds in unheated greenhouses and is commonly found on zonal and regal pelargoniums and winter cherry *(Solanum capsicastrum)*.
- Melon and cotton aphid, *Aphis frangulae gossypii*, is usually a dark blue-green and is often found feeding on begonia, chrysanthemum and cineraria. Damaged leaves often wilt, turn brown and die. It breeds continuously under heated greenhouse or indoor conditions.
- Mottled arum aphid, *Aulacorthum circumflexum*, is pale greenish-yellow often with a black horseshoe-shaped mark on its back. It feeds on a very wide range of flowering plants, weakening them, soiling them with honeydew and also spreading several virus diseases.
- Peach-potato aphid, *Myzus persicae*, is a major vector of virus diseases and can be found feeding on a wide tange of greenhouse and conservatory plants including begonia, carnation, chrysanthemum, fuchsia, primula, saintpaulia, and winter cherry.

BACTERIAL **WILT** Bacterial wilt is caused by the bacterium, *Xanthomonas begoniae*, and attack on winter-flowering begonias results in leaf spotting and wilting.

Control: There is no direct control. Badly affected plants should be destroyed, although it is possible to save lightly attacked ones by cutting out the affected parts or taking tip cuttings from any healthy shoots. Strict hygiene is necessary following an attack, disinfecting the knife used and cleaning down the greenhouse benches.

BLACKLEG Blackleg is the name used to describe a problem affecting the bases of zonal pelargonium ('geranium') cuttings and plants. It is generally thought to be caused by the Pythium fungus and can quickly spread though a pot or box of cuttings, especially if the compost is on the wet side.

Control: When taking cuttings, use clean pots and boxes and new compost and select shoots from the tops of healthy plants. Keep cuttings and plants on the dry side and pick over the plants regularly to remove dead or dying leaves and stems.

BLOOM **DAMPING** Bloom damping occurs on chrysanthemums following a severe attack by the grey mould fungus *Botrytis cinerea*. The blooms become covered with a grey, furry mould and rot away. Bloom damping is encouraged by an over-humid atmosphere in the greenhouse.

Control: Prevent by keeping humidity in check with plenty of ventilation and apply an occasional light treatment of sulphur dust. Should an attack occur, put a plastic bag over the infected bloom before cutting it off for disposal; this will prevent masses of spores being shaken into the air.

BUD **DROP** In greenhouses and indoors, bud-drop can often be a problem with gardenia, stephanotis, camellia and Christmas cactus. With gardenia and stephanotis it usually follows a period of compost dryness or low air humidity. Camellia drop their buds in spring particularly following insufficient watering in autumn, and Christmas cactus drops buds in reaction to overwatering or to too much movement of the plant once it is in bud.

Control: Avoiding the conditions mentioned will reduce the chances of bud drop occurring.

CATERPILLARS Several different types of caterpillar can be found from time to time feeding on greenhouse flowering plants, but are less common on house plants. Very severe bud and leaf loss can occur in a short time. Carnation tortrix moth caterpillars, for example, web the leaves together and feed under the protection, killing leaves and destroying developing flower buds.

Control: Hand-picking as soon as the caterpillars or the damage is seen is often sufficient. As an alternative, spray the plants with the bacterial biological agent *Bacillus thuringiensis*, or use bioallethrin, bifenthrin, fatty acids, permethrin or pyrethrins.

CROWN ROT Various rots of the lower parts of plants are grouped together as root, crown and stem rots, or simply as foot rots. They may be due to waterlogging, to disease attacking tissue damaged by other agents, or to a rotting disease such as black root rot. Stems turn brown or black and rot, and if the condition is not controlled the plants collapse and will probably die. Cineraria, calceolaria and *Primula obconica* are all prone to attack.

Control: Use clean pots and new compost at all times, and water with clean water. If using rain water, ensure the tank or butt is kept well covered and filter out old leaves and other debris, for example, by tying the foot of a nylon stocking over the end of the downspout. Cut out any diseased tissue as soon as seen, using a sterilized knife, and dust the cut tissue with sulphur dust. Regular addition of a copper fungicide to the water should reduce the risk of these rots to a minimum.

CYCLAMEN MITE Cyclamen mite, *Phytonemus pallidus*, is an important pest of many flowering and foliage plants grown in the greenhouse or the home. In addition to attacking cyclamen, the mite can be found causing damage to begonia, gerbera, ivy, pelargonium and many other plants. Feeding by the mite causes the foliage to become brittle, particularly around the leaf edges which frequently curl upwards. Growth is stunted and flowers are deformed. Badly infested plants can be killed by the mite. Build-up of mite populations is very rapid and it takes only two to three weeks from egg to adult at summer temperatures in the lower 20°Cs (68–75°F).

Control: Cyclamen mites move to the new foliage as soon as it starts to unfold and it is sometimes possible to gain the upper hand by regularly removing all the young foliage. Naturally, this does set the plants back a little, but not as much as an uncontrolled mite attack would do. Cyclamen mites are not usually controlled by sprays, even those that are effective against two-spotted mite. Where leaf removal has not proved effective, destruction of the whole plant is the only option.

DROUGHT Lack of water is one of the main causes of plant deaths. Temperatures in a greenhouse or in a conservatory can reach extremely high levels in summer, even where full ventilation is given. Under such conditions, watering two or even three times per day may not be too much.

Control: Apply shade or fix blinds to reduce the level of sunlight reaching the plants. Where hand watering is likely to be a problem during the daytime, grow plants in troughs fitted with capillary matting. It may also help to incorporate water-retentive granules in the compost as is often recommended for hanging baskets.

DRY AIR Dry air probably affects more house plants than waterlogging, drought, pest or disease put together. Leaves die round the edges, and then frequently turn yellow and fall, flower buds dry and drop and the plants generally look unhealthy.

Control: Spray the plants each day with water at room temperature to create some humidity round the foliage. It will also help to put plant pots on large saucers or other containers with a few centimetres of pebbles under the pots and then to water the pebbles each day, keeping the level of water below the base of the pot. Alternatively, put the pot inside a larger one and pack the space between with compost which can be kept moist, without the water entering the pot and causing waterlogging.

ELWORMS Leaf nematodes, particularly *Aphelenchoides ritzemabosi*, are the main eelworm pests of greenhouse flowering plants. They feed in and on leaves, buds and growing points resulting in a range of symptoms. Frequent among these is the angular leaf browning between the main veins as seen on affected chrysanthemum foliage. Each

such leaf may have as many as 15,000 individual nematodes, each approximately 1mm (½₄in) long, and affected foliage usually withers and dies but remains attached to the stem. Other symptoms include distortion and thickening of shoots, stunting of plants and small, badly formed flowers. This species of nematode also attacks saintpaulia, cineraria and crassula among others, and different species can be found on other ornamental plants. Eelworms can survive in dried-out leaves for several years but soon die in the soil. With chrysanthemums, the eelworms usually spend the winter in the shoots of the overwintering stools, and become active as growth starts in spring. The nematodes also live on a number of common weeds.

Control: Strict hygiene is essential with removal and burning of infected leaves and plants the first step. Care should be taken when purchasing new plants to ensure that only healthy-looking ones are bought. No effective chemicals are available for use by the gardener, but stools of valued chrysanthemum varieties can be cleaned up by hot water treatment. Clean off the old soil and wash thoroughly, pouring the water down the drain not on to the soil. Cut down the stems and then immerse the stools for five minutes in water held at 46°C (115°F). After the hot water, immediately plunge the stools into cold water and then plant up in clean compost and new boxes and grow on at 10°C (50°F) for cutting production.

FAULTY GROWING CONDITIONS This heading hides a multitude of sins, including growing shade-loving plants on hot, sunny windowsills and sun-loving plants in the shade, regular watering of plants that prefer a resting period after flowering, overwatering and underwatering, and generally not providing the conditions that any particular plant would prefer. Cyclamen, for example, prefer a cool but well lit position to grow well and *Epiphyllum* cacti develop corky patches if kept in too bright sunlight.

Control: Read the instructions (if any) on the plant label, consult gardening books and magazines, and above all watch the plant for signs of yellowing, poor growth, wilting or anything else that could suggest that something is not quite right. Experiment, but learn from any mistakes.

FOOT ROT (*SEE CROWN ROT, ABOVE*)

GLASSHOUSE LEAFHOPPER Glasshouse leafhopper, *Hauptidia maroccana*, breeds throughout the year at 'indoor' temperatures. The nymph stages and adults feed on the lower leaf surfaces, generally alongside a main vein, and the upper leaf surfaces develop a number of bleached spots. In severe cases, large patches of the leaves will turn yellow to white. The pale adult leafhopper, which is about 4mm (⅙in) long, pale yellow and with a couple of brown chevron marks on the back, takes short, leaping flights when disturbed. The nymphs, which are in various stages of wing development, remain on the leaves and evident there will also be the cast skins of the nymphs.

Control: Hang sticky, yellow traps over the plants and shake the stems and leaves regularly to increase the numbers caught on the sticky coating. For severe attacks, spray with bifenthrin, dimethoate, permethrin, pirimiphos-methyl or pyrethrins. Biological control agents for leafhoppers are being refined in commercial use and could be available to gardeners in the

near future. Keep weeds round the greenhouse under control as they can act as alternative hosts.

GREY MOULD The grey mould fungus *Botrytis cinerea* can attack any type of dead or dying plant and often then spreads to living tissue. It is encouraged by over-crowded, over-humid conditions.

Control: Keep plants well picked over to remove fading leaves and flowers. Maintain a balanced atmosphere with no excess moisture and spray with benomyl or carbendazim, alternatively spray or dust with sulphur.

LEAF MINER Various leaf miners can attack ornamental greenhouse and conservatory plants, but chrysanthemum leaf miner, *Phytomyza syngenesiae*, is among the more common. This species can also be found on cineraria and other plants as well as outside on sowthistle, groundsel and other related weeds. Attack results in winding mines as the larvae tunnel their way inside the leaves. The adult flies probe the leaf tissue to feed and to find egg-laying sites and these spots can be seen as small bleached dots.

Control: Commercial growers now use the parasitic wasps *Diglyphus* and *Dacnusa* to keep leaf miners under control, and at least one of these parasites is available for gardeners to use (*see Biological control, pp. xvi–xxi*). Good weed control also has a part to play, and infested leaves should be picked off or the larvae squashed within the mines. To protect from attack, sprays of permethrin could be applied.

LEAF SPOT Leaf spot fungi attack results in small spots on the leaves, which are often followed by a general yellowing and leaf fall. Aspidistra, cineraria, cyclamen, carnation, orchids, pelargonium,

Sansevieria (mother-in-law's tongue) and others each have their own species of leaf spot.

Control: Remove the worst affected leaves and then spray with a copper or mancozeb fungicide.

LEAFY GALL Twisted or bunched leafy outgrowths at soil level on chrysanthemum plants indicate infection by the bacterium, *Corynebacterium fasciens*. The infection is carried over in the soil.

Control: There is no chemical control. Remove infected plants and destroy, together with the compost from the pot. Disinfect any tools that have been used on the infected plants.

MEALY BUG (*SEE ALSO ROOT MEALY BUG, BELOW*) Various species of mealy bug infest greenhouse and conservatory flowering plants and house plants, sucking the sap, making the leaves sticky with honeydew and the plants unsightly with their presence. The mealy-covered pests become established particularly at the nodes where the leaves join the stems, but then spread out to the leaves and over the stems.

Control: Biological control agents are available for the control of mealy bugs (*see Biological control, pp. xvi–xxi*). Crypto-laemus montrouzieri* is a relative of the ladybird and both adults and larvae seek out and eat the pests. *Leptomastix*, *Anagyrus* and *Leptomastidea* are all tiny parasitic wasps that lay eggs in the citrus mealy bug. Alternatively, spray the plants thoroughly with dimethoate, fatty acids, permethrin or pirimiphos-methyl, wetting the mealy coatings well. At one time, gardeners used to dab the individual mealy bugs with methylated spirit using a fine paintbrush, but now, thankfully, there are quicker methods.

Main mealy bug species:
- Glasshouse mealy bug, *Pseudococcus affinis*, feeds on a very wide range of plants but seems to be particularly attracted to cacti and passion flower. Several generations occur per year and at suitable temperatures breeding continues throughout the year. Each female can produce up to 500 eggs and the life cycle takes around eight weeks at 20°C (68°F) or only four weeks at 30°C (86°C).
- Citrus mealy bug, *Planococcus citri*, has a similar life cycle and despite its name is found on a wide range of plants including cacti, ferns and orchids.
- Long-tailed mealy bug, *Pseudococcus longispinus*, is distinguished from the other two by having two or three long extensions at the 'tail' end. As with the previous two species, there is a wide host plant range.

OEDEMA Oedema, or dropsy, occurs when the roots are taking up more water than the leaves can loose by transpiration. It can result from too much water being applied or too humid an atmosphere reducing evaporation. Cells in the leaves rupture resulting in corky patches developing. Ivy-leaved pelargonium, camellia and peperomia are particularly susceptible to oedema.

Control: Reducing both watering and humidity will stop the problem but damaged leaves will remain on the plants.

PETAL BLIGHT Petal blight, caused by attack of the fungus, *Itersonilia perplexans*, is primarily a problem with greenhouse-grown chrysanthemum. Outer petals develop water-soaked spots which soon turn black as the infection spreads towards the centres of the flowers. In a short while, the whole flower is a dark, soggy mass and is often further attacked by grey mould (*see above*).

Control: Pick off damaged petals when first seen. If the infection is too advanced, enclose the bloom in a plastic bag and cut if off for safe disposal.

POWDERY MILDEW Chrysanthemum and begonia, especially the begonia 'Rex' types, are often attacked by powdery mildew fungi. Other plants are also subject to damage, including cineraria and greenhouse-grown roses and sweet peas. Leaves become coated with a white powdery deposit of mildew spores and then turn brown and die, growth slows down and plants may die.

Control: Remove the worst-affected leaves or shoots and then spray a few times at fortnightly intervals using benomyl, carbendazim, propiconazole or triforine or use a sulphur fungicide.

ROOT APHIDS The auricula root aphid, *Thecabius auriculae*, feeds on the roots of auricula and other primula species. (*See also Aphid, p.87.*) The aphids are small and pale and are covered with a mealy coating. Infested plants may wilt and die or leaves may become yellow or mottled. There is often a collar of mealy 'wool' around the neck of an infested plant.

Control: Insert a butoxycarboxim 'pin' into the compost or drench with diluted systemic insecticide such as dimethoate or heptenophos.

ROOT MEALY BUG Root mealy bug, *Rhizoecus falcifer*, can be found feeding on the roots of a number of ornamental plants under glass or in the home. Like roots aphid (*above*), the pests are covered with a white mealy coating but there is

also a mass of white waxy threads in the compost. Infested plants grow poorly and often wilt and die.

Control: Drench the compost with diluted dimethoate or heptenophos. For severe infestations it is better to remove the plant from its pot, remove the compost and dispose of it safely, spray the roots with insecticide and then pot up in new compost.

ROOT ROTS (*SEE CROWN ROT, ABOVE*)

RUST Various species of rust fungus can be found attacking a range of plants grown under glass or in the home, particularly *Uromyces dianthi* on carnation, *Puccinia chrysanthemi* on chrysanthemum, *Puccinia lagenophorae* on cineraria, *Pucciniastrum epilobii* on fuchsia and *Puccinia pelargonii-zonalis* on zonal pelargonium ('geraniums'). Masses of orange or brown spores are produced from pustules on the leaves, the pustules often erupting in outward-spreading concentric circles, although on carnation the pustules are more like long slits down the leaves.

Control: Keep plants well spaced to reduce local humidity around each pot and destroy badly-infected plants. Spray others with mancozeb or sulphur to protect from attack, or use the systemic propiconazole both to eradicate and protect.

SCALE INSECTS Most perennial plants of greenhouse, conservatory or house can be attacked by scale insects, the main species being the brown soft scale, *Coccus hesperidum*, and the hemispherical scale, *Saissetia coffeae*, both of which feed on a wide range of plants including camellia, citrus, ficus, oleander, poinsettia, stephanotis and ferns. The orchid scale, *Diaspis boisduvalii*, attacks most orchid types as well as palms while the oleander scale, *Aspidiotus nerii*, feeds on acacia, asparagus fern, cyclamen, *Dracaena* and palms as well as on oleander (*Nerium oleander*). Scale insects have a hard, rounded or oval shell and affix themselves to stems and leaves of their chosen host where they feed on the sap and produce honeydew (*see also Sooty moulds, below*). Each hemispherical scale (they are all female) produces around 2,000 eggs under the scale protection and then dies, while the brown soft scale (again all are female) gives birth to 1,000 or so nymphs. Eggs and young can be present at any time of the year given a suitable temperature and the young of both species wander over the plants, find a suitable site and settle down to feed.

Control: Biological control can be achieved by introducing *Metaphycus* into the greenhouse or conservatory (*see Biological control, pp. xvi–xxi*). Alternatively, scale insects are controlled by butoxycarboxim 'pins' inserted into the compost or by drenching sprays of fatty acids, permethrin, pirimiphos–methyl or pyrethrins.

SCIARID FLY The sciarid fly, *Bradysia* spp., is attracted in numbers to the organic content of composts where the eggs are laid. The sciarid larvae are small and colourless, apart from a small black head. They feed on organic matter, which can be peat or bark in the compost or plant roots, and in severe cases they burrow up into the plant stems. Young plants are killed by the root loss and other damage while the adult flies, like tiny gnats, are a nuisance as they constantly fly up off the compost during watering and other operations.

Control: Sticky, yellow plastic strips hung around the plants will trap quite a lot of adult sciarid flies. For more severe attacks, water the compost with the nematode *Heterorhabditis*, which also kill vine weevil (*see below*) or introduce the predatory mite *Hypoaspis* (*see Biological control, pp. xvi–xxi*).

SLUGS/SNAILS Slugs are normally minor pests in the greenhouse, conservatory and house, but occasionally greenhouse plants in particular may be severely damaged. Leaves are consumed, young stems are rasped away and even *Opuntia* cactus pads may be eaten.

Control: A late evening visit to the greenhouse with a torch will often reveal the culprits for easy removal. Alternatively, water the plants, greenhouse floor and staging with a metaldehyde solution or scatter metaldehyde or methiocarb pellets thinly around plants being attacked and close to possible hiding places.

SOOTY MOULD Sooty mould, species of *Cladosporium* and other fungi, grows on the sugary honeydew which is excreted by a number of sap-sucking pests as they feed. Aphids, scale insects, mealy bugs and whitefly are the main producers of honeydew. The mould does not attack plant tissue, but by reducing the amount of sunlight reaching the leaves it does interfere with food production in the plant.

Control: The honeydew and moulds can be gently sponged off plant leaves and stems, and off any furniture below them, with tepid soapy water. To prevent the sooty moulds, take appropriate action to control the honeydew-producing insects.

SUN SCORCH Sudden bursts of bright sun, especially in the morning on leaves still wet from overnight condensation, can result in leaf edges becoming burned and in a spotting of the leaf surface. Watering plants in direct sun can result in a burning of the leaves where any water falls, and with saintpaulia the damage takes the form of pale rings on the leaves. **Control:** Avoid hot, direct sun on the leaves by shading, by moving susceptible plants to a more shaded spot and by adequate ventilation as appropriate to allow any water applied in the evening to evaporate away.

TWO-SPOTTED SPIDER MITE

Two-spotted spider mite, or red spider mite, *Tetranychus urticae*, can be a major problem on all plants under protection. The tiny mites, barely visible to the naked eye, are pale green to slightly yellow and have two dark spots on their backs. They feed under the plant leaves and their sap-sucking activities result in a pale stippling on the upper leaf surface. With severe attacks, the mites produce a mass of fine webbing over the foliage and tops of the plants. Two-spotted spider mites are active from spring through to early autumn and at a minimum temperature of 21°C (70°F) the egg to adult life cycle is completed within 12 days. At a lower temperature of 10°C (50°F) the cycle takes 55 days to complete. At the higher rate, a population of 600 mites could increase to 50,000 in just one week. When the day length falls below 14 hours in autumn, the mites develop the orange-red winter female forms which mate and then hide away in the greenhouse structure and other suitable places over winter. **Control:** Two-spotted spider mites are encouraged in a dry atmosphere so regular damping-down of the greenhouse floor and benches, as well as misting over

the plants with water will help to prevent attack. When an attack is found, the predatory mite *Phytoseiulus* can be introduced and this will seek out and feed on the spider mites (*see Biological control, pp. xvi–xxi*). Alternatively, insert butoxycarboxim 'pins' into the compost or spray with bifenthrin or fatty acids. Two-spotted spider mite is likely to be resistant to most other pesticides.

VINE WEEVIL

The larvae of vine weevil, *Otiorhynchus sulcatus*, can be extremely damaging to plants in pots, feeding on roots, corms and tubers. Cyclamen, begonia and primula are all attacked, but very few plants escape when the adult weevil is laying her eggs. In heated greenhouses, conservatories and homes, overlapping stages of the life cycle from egg – through larva and pupa to adult – can be found, but in unheated conditions the overwintering stage is a larva. The adult weevils notch plant foliage, adding to the damage done to the roots by the larvae. **Control:** The best control is to water the compost with a suspension of one of the nematodes *Heterorhabditis megadis* or *Steinernema carpocapsae* to attack the vine weevil larvae (*see Biological control, pp. xvi–xxi*).

WATERLOGGING

Waterlogging is a source of many plant deaths as the water drives air out of the compost and the roots suffocate. Often the first sign of waterlogging is a wilting of the foliage, and often the first response of the plant owner is then to apply water, believing the wilting to be due to water shortage. Cinerarias are commonly damaged or killed in this way. **Control:** Test the weight of the pot before watering to check that it is light and therefore dry. When watering, give a good soak, but then allow to drain before replacing the pot on a saucer or in the pot holder. Alternatively, if the plants are standing in a tray, water well and leave for half an hour or so before pouring away any remaining water. Plants will always survive a short period without water better than a short period with an excess of water.

WESTERN FLOWER THRIPS Western flower thrips, *Frankliniella occidentalis*, is a relative newcomer to Europe, having arrived on chrysanthemum cuttings. It will attack a very wide range of greenhouse ornamentals, causing a scarring of the leaves and a bleaching and silvering of petals. Breeding continues throughout the year under suitable temperature conditions, and affected flowers can be distorted or may abort. Western flower thrips spreads tomato spotted wilt virus which attacks a number of different types of plants.

Control: This pest is difficult to control, having a resistance to most insecticides. It is also subject to statutory control in some countries so expert guidance should be sought where the pest is suspected or where normal control measures are failing.

WHITEFLY The glasshouse whitefly, *Trialeurodes vaporariorum*, is probably the most troublesome of the pests attacking greenhouse and conservatory plants. The pests suck the plant sap, excrete honeydew, and all attacks are likely to be severe ones; infested plants can be killed. Fuchsia, regal pelargonium, poinsettia and solanum are amongst the most favoured hosts of whitefly. The small white adults each lay up to 250 eggs over a three to six week lifespan, laying them on the leaves in a ring pattern. The young that hatch are known as scales and they feed for a period before pupating, with the adults then emerging to repeat the cycle. Egg to adult takes 27 days at 21°C (68°F), and successive generations through the spring to autumn build up very high population levels.

Control: From early summer onwards the temperatures will be high enough for the whitefly parasite *Encarsia* to be effective (*see Biological control, pp. xvi–xxi*). Trapping early-season whitefly on sticky, yellow plastic traps will help to keep levels down and also act as a monitoring system to give an indication as to when spraying is needed. For spraying, use fatty acids or pyrethrins if *Encarsia* is to be introduced later when temperatures are suitable. For chemical control without biological help, use bifenthrin, bioallethrin, fatty acids, permethrin or pyrethrins, repeating frequently as necessary.

WILT Chrysanthemum, carnation and a number of other plants can be attacked by either or both of the main wilt fungi, namely fusarium wilt, *Fusarium oxysporum* f. *dianthi*, and verticillium wilt, now named *Phialophora cinerescens*. Plants wilt and leaves turn yellow and death can follow quickly. Cutting the stem down its length will show a brown discolouration in the water-conducting vessels.

Control: Use clean pots and new compost when growing all plants. Following a wilt attack, dispose of plants and compost and wash the pots with an approved disinfectant and then rinse. Also use an approved disinfectant to wash down benches and/or the floor where the plants were growing.

WOODLICE Woodlice eat the bases of plant stems and also shred any leaves that are touching the soil. They hide by day in any debris available or under piles of pots or seed trays.

Control: Remove all debris and tidy away pots and trays. Dust around plants and under benches with a bendiocarb, gamma-HCH or pirimiphos-methyl powder. Methiocarb pellets for slug or snail control would also be effective against woodlice.

INDOORS 2

EDIBLE CROPS GROWN UNDER GLASS, INCLUDING TOMATO, PEPPER AND AUBERGINE, CUCUMBER AND MELON, LETTUCE, CLIMBING FRENCH BEANS, GRAPES, PEACH

ROOTS

DYING	Grey/black specks along roots, plants wilt and may die	*black root rot*
	Shrivelled and/or brown	*waterlogging*
	Soft rotting	*root rots*
EATEN	Small, black-headed colourless maggots feeding on roots	*sciarid fly*
	White creatures, 6mm (1/4in) long, feeding on roots	*symphilids*
GALLED	Numerous small galls along tomato roots	*potato cyst nematodes*
	Numerous large galls along tomato, lettuce, cucumber and French bean roots	*root-knot nematodes*

STEMS

EATEN	Eaten into or off at soil level, slime trails present	*slugs/snails*
	Seedlings and young plants damaged, jumping pests present	*springtails*
	Seedlings and young plants eaten, leaves shredded	*woodlice*
ROTTING	Covered in grey, furry fungal growths	*grey mould*
	Rotting at base	*crown, foot and root rots*
	Tomato stems with dark, sunken lesions at base or at leaf joints	*stem rot*
	White, fluffy fungal growth at stem base	*sclerotinia disease*
SPOTTED	Pink depressions on cucumber stems or fruit, later turning black	*anthracnose*
WILTING	No internal stem discolouration	*faulty root action*
	Plants wilting, brown discolouration visible running up inside cut stems	*wilt*

LEAVES

DISCOLOURED/ SPOTTED	Large dry patches on vine leaves	*scorch*
	Pale spots on top of lettuce leaves, downy mould below	*downy mildew*
	Pale spots on top of tomato leaves, grey/brown mould below	*tomato leaf mould*
	Pale stippling of leaves, minute pests just visible under leaves	*two-spotted spider mite*
	Pale spots becoming dry and brown	*anthracnose*
	Tomato leaves show bronze spots and curl down	*tomato spotted wilt*
	Various spots, mottles, distortions and paleness of veins	*virus*
	Yellow areas turning brown between veins of older leaves	*magnesium deficiency*
	Yellow areas on young leaves with veins green	*iron deficiency*
	Yellow areas on younger leaves and dark spotting	*manganese deficiency*
PESTS VISIBLE	Green insects clustered under leaves and shoot tips	*aphids*
	Pale insects with 'V'-shaped mark on back, fly off leaves when disturbed	*glasshouse leafhopper*
	White moth-like insects, flying off when disturbed	*whitefly*
VISIBLE FUNGAL GROWTHS	Powdery white mould, cucumber, melon, vine	*powdery mildew*
WATER DROPLETS	Water exuding from vein tips at vine leaf edges	*guttation*

FLOWERS

	Dropping without setting	*pollination, dry air*

FRUIT

Cucumbers oozing amber fluid	*gummosis*
Cucumbers with bitter taste	*pollination*
Cucumbers withering	*faulty root action*
Grapes shrivelling as fruit stalks die, other fruits bitter	*shanking*
Ripening tomatoes with green shoulders	*green back*
Ripening tomatoes with yellow/orange patches	*blotchy ripening*
Small raised spots on grapes	*oedema*
Tomatoes and grapes split	*faulty watering*
Tomatoes partially eaten, green or brown caterpillars present	*tomato moth*
Tomatoes with bronzed colouration	*virus*
Tomatoes with flat, dark area away from stalk	*blossom end rot*

ANTHRACNOSE Anthracnose is a condition caused by the fungus, *Colletotrichum lagenarium*, which affects cucumber stems, leaves and fruits. Pale spots occur on the leaves, then turn brown and the leaf dies, while on the stems sunken lesions develop, pinkish at first but then turning brown. The lesions expand and can girdle the stems, killing the plants. Infected cucumber fruits develop similar pink then brown lesions.
Control: Anthracnose is encouraged by over-high humidity so ventilate as much as conditions allow. Should an attack occur, remove the affected parts and spray a few times with a sulphur-based fungicide.

APHIDS (GREENFLY AND BLACKFLY) Various species of aphid are found on greenhouse-grown edible crops where they feed on the sap, excrete honeydew on which grow black sooty moulds, and spread virus diseases.
Control: Biological control is possible using the predatory *Aphidoletes*, the parasitic *Aphidius* or the fungus, *Verticillium lecani* (*see Biological control, pp. xvi–xxi*). Aphids can be controlled chemically with sprays of bioallethrin, bifenthrin, dimethoate, heptenophos, pirimicarb, pirimiphos-methyl and pyrethrins.

Main aphid species:
- Glasshouse and potato aphid, *Aulacorthum solani*, is mainly a pest in unheated greenhouses or conservatories where it feeds on a number of different crop types, including tomatoes. It is a shiny yellow-green and has long antennae.
- Melon and cotton aphid, *Aphis frangulae gossypii*, is normally a dark blue-green colour. It breeds

throughout the year under suitable temperature conditions and its feeding can result in leaves wilting, turning brown and dying.
- Peach-potato aphid, *Myzus persicae*, can be pink, grey, yellow or olive-green in colour and feeds on many different plants, outside as well as under glass. Peach trees are one of the main host trees for the winter eggs and from there the young aphids spread out in spring. They do not usually form dense colonies, but do spread a number of important virus diseases.

BLACK ROOT ROT Cucumber black root rot is caused by the fungus, *Phomopsis sclerotioides*, and can be very difficult to eradicate if it should become established in the greenhouse border soil. Attack results in grey to black specks along the roots and decay of the roots and stem base. Leaves wilt and plants are stunted; death follows a severe or early infection.
Control: Prevent attacks by removing all root fragments from the soil after growing the crop, or by growing cucumbers only in growing bags, isolated from the greenhouse border soil. Early infections may respond to sprays of benomyl or carbendazim, but plants seen to be dying should be removed and burned.

BLOSSOM END ROT Blossom end rot describes the physiological disorder which affects young tomato fruits at the end away from the stalk. A dark, flat area appears, and although the fruit continues to develop the dark area and tissue immediately underneath is inedible. The basic cause of the condition is a lack of calcium uptake into the fruits, but more often than not the deficiency is related to watering. Lack of water or fluctuating water supplies in the early stage of the fruit development leads to a lack of nutrients including calcium. Blossom end rot is often most prevalent on plants closest to the greenhouse door or under the vents, again related to more rapid drying of the plants in those positions, with the consequent lack of water and nutrient uptake. Once plants have set two or three trusses of tomatoes, blossom end rot usually ceases to be a problem.

Control: It is important to incorporate of plenty of organic matter into the soil prior to planting, and careful attention should be given to providing sufficient and regular volumes of water. This should prevent blossom end rot becoming troublesome but in case of attack, water the leaves and the soil with calcium nitrate using 30g per 5l (1oz/1gall) of water and apply 1 litre (2 pints) of the solution to each plant every week.

CROWN, FOOT AND ROOT ROTS (*SEE ALSO ROOT ROTS, BELOW*) Various fungi can be involved in these rots including *Thielaviopsis basicola*, *Pythium*, *Phytophthora* and *Rhizoctonia*. Plants wilt and collapse and examination will reveal a rotting of the roots or stem bases.

Control: Strict hygiene at the end of each cropping season to remove all crop residues plus good soil preparation should prevent these fungi being troublesome. Should an attack occur and be spotted early, it may be possible to control at least some of the diseases with some thorough drenches of a copper-based fungicide. Tomatoes and cucumbers root readily from their stems, and it is often possible to save the plants by earthing up around the stem bases with clean soil or with potting compost.

DOWNY MILDEW Lettuce downy mildew, *Bremia lactucae*, and brassica downy mildew, *Peronospora parasitica*, appear as pale blotches on the upper leaf surface and an off-white downy mould underneath the leaf. Seedlings can be killed or very badly checked, and cauliflower seedlings being grown for planting outside may fail to produce decent curds. Excess humidity and crowded pots or trays of seedlings or young plants encourage the diseases.

Control: Grow seedlings with plenty of ventilation. Resistant varieties of lettuce are available, but there are several different strains of the downy mildew fungus which makes it difficult to rely solely on the resistance factor. To control an attack, remove the worst-affected plants or leaves and spray those remaining with mancozeb fungicide.

DRY AIR Lack of adequate humidity in the greenhouse can result in flowers drying up and falling instead of setting fruit. Dry air also provides ideal conditions for the two-spotted spider mite in its attacks.

Control: Adequate watering of plants and soil plus frequent damping-down of paths and staging will help to maintain a good level of humidity. Take care, however, not to create excess humidity as this can encourage grey mould and cucumber anthracnose.

FAULTY ROOT ACTION Poor root activity affects plants in a number of different ways. Cucumber fruits wither when partly developed, plants suddenly appear unthrifty, and in extreme cases the whole plant may die.

Control: Thorough soil preparation before planting is the key to success. Break up any underlying hard pan of soil by deep digging and add plenty of well rotted manure or good quality garden compost. These measures will encourage the development of better root systems and help to even out water supplies.

GLASSHOUSE LEAFHOPPER Glasshouse leafhopper, *Hauptidia maroccana*, feeds on a number of greenhouse edible crops, causing bleached spots to develop on the leaves. The pale pest, with a darker 'V'-shaped marking, makes short, leaping flights off the leaves when disturbed, but never flies far. The young nymph stages remain on the leaves, feeding alongside the main veins, together with a scattering of cast skins, moulted as the nymphs develop through five instars (stages of development).
Control: Good weed control around the greenhouse will help by removing alternative resting and feeding sites. Hanging sticky yellow traps over the plants and shaking the stems each day will help catch quite a number of leafhoppers, and biological control agents will shortly be in use commercially. Where more complete control is needed for severe infestations, spray with bifenthrin, dimethoate, permethrin, pirimiphos-methyl or pyrethrins.

GREY MOULD Grey mould, caused by the fungus *Botrytis cinerea*, affects all types of plant, usually starting on dead or dying tissue but then frequently attacking adjacent living parts. Grey mould is particularly devastating on lettuces which rot off at soil level. Tissue affected by grey mould develops a soft rot and is soon covered with a furry grey growth of the fungus. Over-humid and crowded conditions encourage the disease.
Control: Remove any fading leaves and flowers, keep plants well spaced out and ventilate freely. Sprays of benomyl or

carbendazim, or sprays or dusts with sulphur are also effective.

GUMMOSIS Gummosis is a disease caused by the fungus, *Cladosporium cucumerinum*, that can damage cucumbers quite severely, affecting stems, leaves and fruit. Small, irregular spots appear on stems and leaves, but they are not always noticed until the fruit damage occurs. With the fruit attack, sunken areas appear and from these oozes an amber-coloured liquid.
Control: Remove affected fruit and leaves and reduce humidity. No chemical control exists.

GUTTATION Drops of clear or slightly green fluid exude from the tips of the veins of vine leaves. This exudation is termed guttation. Plants in humid conditions tend to be more prone, but guttation can simply indicate that the roots are taking up plenty of water and growing well and that excess water is being discarded by the plant.
Control: Rarely necessary, but humidity could be reduced if found to be on the high side.

IRON DEFICIENCY Lack of iron affects the youngest growths due to the fact that iron is not very mobile in the plant so, when in short supply, the available iron is used by the lowest leaves, where it stays (unlike magnesium deficiency, see below). The veins stay green except in conditions of severe deficiency. Shortage of iron results in poor growth and fruiting and may arise due to an actual shortage in the soil, or because alkaline conditions render any iron present insoluble.
Control: Water the leaves and soil with a sequestered or chelated iron preparation and repeat as necessary. These forms

of iron supply the element in a way that the plant foliage and roots can absorb without the soil locking it up in insoluble salts.

MAGNESIUM DEFICIENCY Shortage of magnesium affects the oldest growth first and causes the lower leaves to develop a yellowing between the veins. Unlike iron, magnesium is mobile within the plant so reserves are moved from the older leaves to the new growth. After a few weeks the yellow areas turn brown in colour, and with tomatoes there is generally a curling of the leaves. Magnesium deficiency is a particular problem with tomatoes, cucumbers, peach and vines, and the condition can be aggravated by excess applications of potassium fertilizers.

Control: Water the leaves and the soil with a solution of Epsom Salts (magnesium sulphate) using 100g per 5l (4oz/1gall) of water. With tomatoes, always use a tomato fertilizer, liquid or solid, that includes magnesium in the analysis. Repeat application a few times at two-week intervals.

MANGANESE DEFICIENCY Manganese deficiency is an occasional problem with tomatoes, especially those not grown in the border soil. An inter-veinal yellowing occurs, starting with the youngest growth but more general over the plant than with iron deficiency symptoms. All the veins stay green, not just the main ones as with magnesium shortage, so the yellowing is less intense than with a shortage of magnesium.

Control: Water leaves and soil with a solution of manganese sulphate using 5g per 5l (⅙oz/1gall) of water, plus wetting agent. Repeat a few times as necessary.

POLLINATION Lack of pollination of tomatoes, aubergines, peppers or melons will result in a lack of crop. On the other hand, greenhouse-grown cucumbers should not be pollinated otherwise they develop a bitter taste.

Control: Maintain a buoyant atmosphere in the house by damping-down and spraying plants as necessary. Tapping or shaking the strings supporting tomato plants will help and melons can be fertilized by hand using the male flowers (the ones without the small immature melons at the base of the petals). Cucumbers can be helped by removing all the male flowers as soon as they appear and before they open, or by growing modern, all-female varieties.

POTATO CYST NEMATODES (*SEE ALSO ROOT-KNOT NEMATODE, BELOW***)** Potato cyst nematodes, *Globodera rostochiensis* and *G. pallida*, attack tomato and aubergine as well as the potato, but are only a problem when tomatoes are grown year after year in the same greenhouse border soil. Affected plants grow poorly, are spindly with small fruit trusses and often wilt. If dug up, the roots will be seen to have numerous bead-like galls along their length. Often root rots and nematode attack occur together and the combined damage is then greater than the two separately.

Control: Guard against attack by regularly changing the soil if growing tomatoes or aubergines in the greenhouse border. Alternatively, grow using ring culture with the aggregate completely separated from the sub-soil by thick plastic, and replace the aggregate should a nematode attack occur, or else use growing bags. There is no control for an existing attack other than to remove and destroy the affected plants.

Tomatoes resistant to many common problems are available, but as yet none has been developed with resistance to potato cyst nematodes.

POWDERY MILDEW Various powdery mildew species can attack greenhouse edible crops but the ones normally causing most trouble are vine powdery mildew, *Uncinula necator*, and cucumber powdery mildew, *Sphaerotheca fuliginea*. Both are more likely in dry soil conditions, and both can be devastating to the crops. Vine leaves are rapidly covered with the powdery white spores while the grapes become coated then harden and crack, becoming quite inedible. Cucumber leaves are similarly coated and the resulting impairment of leaf function appears virtually to stop further cucumber production.
Control: Keep the soil well watered as necessary and when preparing the beds incorporate plenty of water-holding organic matter. To control attacks, spray with sulphur or with the systemic fungicides benomyl or carbendazim.

ROOT–KNOT NEMATODES Root-knot nematodes, *Meloidogyne* spp., can attack the roots of tomato, cucumber, lettuce and French beans resulting in galls up to 2cm (¾in) or more, often joining together. The resultant impairment of root function leaves plants short of water and nutrients, causing wilting and poor, pale growth. Severe attacks can kill the host plant and the nematodes pass into the soil where they will survive if the soil is moist. With climbing French beans under glass, remember that all beans produce bacterial nodules on their roots which are beneficial, as they fix nitrogen from the air. Such nodules are much smaller than the 2cm (¾in) size of a large root-knot nematode swelling.
Control: There is no chemical control available to gardeners. Plants suspected of harbouring nematodes should be dug up and burned and the soil kept dry for several weeks. Following an attack it would be safer to grow the next crop in growing bags rather than in the greenhouse border soil.

ROOT ROTS Root rots are generally due to attack by one or more of a number of soil-inhabiting diseases including *Thielaviopsis basicola*. Plants rot off at or just below soil level, or wilt and die as the roots rot away.
Control: Change the soil on a regular basis to prevent any build-up of soil diseases, or grow the crops in growing bags, isolated from the greenhouse border soil. At the first suspected sign of attack, or as a routine preventative, add a copper fungicide to the water once a week and spray the leaves with a complete foliar feed.

SCIARID FLY Sciarid fly, *Bradisia* spp., feeds on dead and decaying plant tissue so is attracted to the peat or bark in composts and to other forms of organic matter in the soil. The fly maggots, colourless creatures with small black heads, hatch in the soil from eggs laid by the adult flies, but soon turn their attention to living plant roots and root hairs. The maggots also bore up into plant stems, and can kill the host plant. The tiny midge-like flies are a nuisance as they fly up from the compost during watering.
Control: Sticky yellow traps will catch a number of the adult flies, but the best control now is achieved by using the predatory mite, *Hypoaspis,* or the beneficial nematode, *Heterorhabditis* (*see Biological control, pp. xvi–xxi*).

SCLEROTINIA DISEASE Sclerotinia disease of cucumber follows attack by the fungus, *Sclerotinia sclerotiorum*. Attack occurs at soil level and the stem becomes covered with a fluffy white fungal growth studded with black sclerotia that are the resting bodies by which the fungus persists in the soil through adverse conditions.

Control: Avoid by changing the greenhouse border soil on a regular basis or by using growing bags. Should an attack be found, remove and burn the plants with all the attached fungal growths together with a bucketful of soil from the planting site. Rest the soil from cucumbers for several years.

SCORCH Vine leaves are prone to scorch from hot sunshine falling on leaves still wet from condensation or watering.

Control: Shade the glass before the sun gets really hot, refrain from watering in the heat of the day, and ventilate well so any excess water dries up rather than settling as condensation on the leaves.

SHANKING Shanking occurs on grapes and is evident as a shrivelling of the individual stalks of the berries. The grapes then shrivel and become sour, with white varieties often appearing translucent and black varieties appearing red. Waterlogging, drought and poor soil conditions may be involved.

Control: Prepare the soil well and to a good depth, incorporating plenty of well rotted organic matter before planting to provide good drainage with adequate retention of water. Should shanking occur, remove affected grapes and try to improve conditions by applying more water in hot, drying weather and less in cool, slow-drying conditions. A few applications of a foliar feed may also help.

SLUGS AND SNAILS Slugs or snails can occasionally be troublesome in the greenhouse, feeding on stems and leaves. The ragged marks left by these pests are open to invasion by rotting fungi, particularly grey mould.

Control: Water plants and soil with a metaldehyde solution or scatter metaldehyde or methiocarb pellets thinly over the soil around the plants. Clear up any old pots or seed trays under benches to deny snails a hiding place.

SPRINGTAILS Springtails, *Onychiurus* spp., feed on young plants in the greenhouse soil, eating away the stems at ground level or skeletonising leaves touching, or close to, the soil. The ragged damage which results is then susceptible to grey mould attack.

Control: Avoid over-wet conditions which encourage springtails. For an existing attack, treat the soil with an insecticide in dust form.

STEM ROT Stem rot of tomato is caused by the fungus, *Didymella lycopersici*. With an early attack, a black lesion occurs at or around soil level and the plants wilt and die as the rot girdles the stem. On more mature plants, attacks often occur at waist or head height, and frequently on damaged tissue where a leaf has been cut off. Again, a dark lesion occurs and stem girdling may result. Fruit can also be attacked and infection shows as a round black mark spreading from the calyx end (away from the stalk) to cover most of the fruit. The disease persists from year to year in the structure of the greenhouse, on canes and strings, on old plant remains and in the soil.

Control: Remove and burn infected plants, placing them in plastic bags in order to carry them through and from the greenhouse to prevent the spores spreading to other plants. Take care subsequently with watering and apply carefully to the soil rather than over the plants. Thoroughly scrub down the greenhouse structure with an approved disinfectant at the end of the season and use new canes and string to train the next tomato crop. Following an attack in one year it would be worth applying fungicide treatments at the start of the next cropping year to guard against attack, and benomyl or carbendazim stem base sprays should be used within three days of planting. When any major de-leafing routine is carried out it would be worth spraying again with one of these fungicides to protect the scars from infection. This would also keep grey mould in check.

SYMPHILIDS Glasshouse symphilid, *Scutigerella immaculata*, can breed throughout the year and attacks seedling and young plants, feeding on the root hairs and fine roots. Affected plants wilt and examination will reveal the white creatures, up to 9mm (⅓in) long with 12 pairs of legs and long antennae. The pest is sometimes known as the white centipede, but this is unfair to the true centipede which is a beneficial creature, helpful to gardeners by eating various lesser soil creatures.
Control: Apply an insecticidal dust to the soil at planting time where damage has occurred previously.

TOMATO LEAF MOULD Tomato leaf mould is the result of attack by *Fulvia fulva*, (formerly *Cladosporium fulvum*). Pale yellow areas appear on the upper leaf surface while underneath a grey to pale brown mould develops. Infected leaves wither and die but stay attached to

the stem. The disease spreads to all the foliage, and crops are greatly reduced.
Control: The disease exists in a number of different variants but there are varieties that can be grown which are resistant to all the known forms of the disease (*see Resistant varieties, pp. x–xiii*), so consult seed catalogues and seed packets for details of tomatoes resistant to tomato leaf mould. For chemical control, sprays of benomyl, carbendazim or copper can be used on an existing attack, coupled with plenty of ventilation and careful watering to avoid splashing the disease spores around.

TOMATO MOTH Tomato moth, *Lacanobia oleracea*, can occasionally cause considerable damage to greenhouse tomatoes. Eggs are laid underneath the leaves, in batches of as many as 200 at a time, from the beginning of the year in heated greenhouses and from late spring to early summer in unheated conditions. The caterpillars feed on leaves and fruit and grow to around 4cm (1½in) long, so they can cause a great deal of damage. They feed on carnations and chrysanthemums as well as on tomatoes, and may be green or brown in colour and are not easy to see until the damage becomes quite severe. When fully fed the caterpillars pupate in the soil.
Control: At the first sign of eaten leaves or fruit, inspect the plants carefully and remove all caterpillars found. Repeat a few times at daily intervals until damage stops. Alternatively spray with the biological control bacterium, *Bacillus thuringiensis*, or use bifenthrin, fatty acids, permethrim or pyrethrins.

TOMATO SPOTTED WILT Spotted wilt is a virus disease that can attack quite a range of greenhouse plants. Of the edible crops under glass, lettuce and tomatoes are susceptible to damage, the virus being spread by thrips. On tomatoes the leaves tend to curl downwards and develop an irregular bronze spotting between the veins, often alongside the central vein. Plants are stunted, cropping is greatly reduced, and young plants are killed. Lettuce leaves become wilted, spotted or twisted to one side resulting in distorted plants that often die.

Control: Remove and burn all infected plants. Blue sticky traps attract thrips, so by hanging them up in the greenhouse when the crop is planted it is possible to monitor thrip numbers. Should considerable numbers of the narrow, black thrips be trapped it would be helpful to spray the plants with fatty acids, permethrin or pyrethrins.

TWO-SPOTTED SPIDER MITE Two-spotted spider mite, *Tetranychus urticae*, (formerly glasshouse red spider mite) can be a major pest of greenhouse crops and particularly so in the case of cucumbers. Damage takes the form of a pale stippling of the leaves as the mites feed underneath and in severe attacks a fine webbing covers the tops of infested plants. Breeding and feeding carry on from spring through the summer until the daylength drops to below 14 hours in autumn. At that point feeding ceases and orange-red winter forms are produced that hide away in the greenhouse structure until spring. Many generations are produced during the active season and the higher the temperature the shorter the life cycle from egg through nymph to adult; vast populations can build up in a short time. The rapid breeding rate helps the mite either to develop pesticide-resistant strains or for such resistant strains to

be selected out, so chemical control is not always easy.

Control: Two-spotted mite is encouraged by dry conditions, so regular damping-down of the plants and the greenhouse paths and benches will help to deter attacks. For an existing, light attack, introduce the predatory mite, *Phytoseiulus* (*see Biological control, pp. xvi–xxi*). For chemical control of dense populations, use bifenthrin when there is no intention to switch to biological control, or repeated applications of fatty acids or pyrethrins if biological control later is a possibility.

VIRUS (*SEE ALSO TOMATO SPOT-TED WILT, ABOVE*) Various viruses attack greenhouse edible crops resulting in a range of leaf spots, mottles, distortions, tomato fruit bronzing or vein clearing. Cucumber mosaic virus is perhaps the most far-reaching, affecting a vast range of different crops. Lettuce big vein virus, on the other hand, is specific to lettuce where it causes the veins to swell and become more prominent. Infected lettuces often fail to heart-up.

Viruses can be spread by aphids, thrips and other pests as they feed, on hands and tools, or by nematodes or fungi in the soil.

Control: There is no control for virus infection other than removal and burning or otherwise safely disposing of diseased plants. Care should, therefore, be taken in matters relating to pest control, to hygiene and to crop rotations to prevent virus infection as far as possible.

WATERLOGGING In waterlogging the air in the greenhouse soil is replaced with water so the plant roots suffocate through lack of oxygen. Plants wilt and leaves become pale and, if the waterlogged conditions persist for any length of time, the plants will die.

Control: Take care when watering not to saturate the compost or soil so much that the roots could suffer. Prepare soil well so that excess water is allowed to drain away and if standing pot-grown edible crops on trays, ensure that the pot is not allowed to sit in excess water that has drained through the compost.

WHITEFLY Glasshouse whitefly, *Trialeurodes vaporariorum*, is probably the most common and serious of the greenhouse pests. The whitefly population can increase 100-fold in six weeks in spring and in just three weeks at summer temperatures, so infestations build up very rapidly. Leaves are quickly blackened by sooty moulds growing on the honeydew excreted by the insects. Cucumbers, melons, tomatoes and many lesser crops can be seriously affected by a severe whitefly attack and produce little edible fruit.

Control: Once temperatures approach a minimum of 18°C (64°F), the parasitic wasp, *Encarsia formosa*, can be introduced and will keep pace with an existing light attack. To control whitefly before the temperatures are high enough for biological control, trap the pests with yellow, sticky plastic strips hung just over the crop and also by spraying with fatty acids or pyrethrins. Alternatively, if relying on chemical control, spray regularly with dimethoate, permethrin or pirimiphos-methyl or use a permethrin or pirimiphos-methyl smoke.

WILT Tomatoes and cucumbers and their relatives can be infected by both *Verticillium* and *Fusarium* wilt fungi. Infection is carried in the soil and as the disease develops the water-conducting vessels in the plants become blocked and turn brown. Plants wilt during the day but generally recover at night until the disease is advanced. Overall general health and cropping will be reduced and plants may be killed.

Control: Prevent attacks by growing only varieties listed in seed catalogues or on the seed packet as resistant to wilt diseases. Alternatively, replace the greenhouse soil regularly if growing direct in the border soil or grow the crops in growing bags. For an existing attack, as soon as wilt is suspected, earth up the stem with new compost and keep moist to encourage extra roots to develop from the stem. Drenches of benomyl or carbendazim are also effective controls.

WOODLICE Woodlice can attack seedlings and young plants, eating the stems at ground level and shredding the lower leaves where they touch the ground. The woodlice may be the pill bug type, *Armadillidium* spp., that roll into tight balls when threatened or the slater types, *Oniscus* and *Porcellio*, that remain flat.

Control: Keep all old pots and seed trays tidy and remove any plant debris or old wood so the woodlice have nowhere to feed or hide. Methiocarb-based pellets applied for slugs and snails will normally keep woodlice in check, otherwise dust the soil and any potential hiding places with gamma-HCH or pirimiphos-methyl powder.

VEGETABLES 1

VEGETABLE SEEDLINGS AND YOUNG PLANTS OF ALL VEGETABLE TYPES

SEEDS

EATEN	Holes in soil	*birds, mice*
	No holes in soil	*millipede, wireworm*
FAIL TO GERMINATE	Rot in soil	*seed rots*
	Do not rot	*old seed, dry soil*

SEEDLINGS

EATEN	Slime trails present	*slugs, snails*
	No slime trails	*birds, mice, rabbits*
ROT OFF	Dark area at soil level	*damping off, seedling rots*
GROW POORLY	Leaves scorched, plants may die, or die back	*frost or low temperatures*
	Leaves small but undamaged	*dry soil*

BIRDS Rooks, pigeons and a few other birds take pea, bean and sweet corn seeds from the soil, leaving holes where their beaks have penetrated.
Control: Firm the soil after sowing and cover over with netting.

DAMPING OFF Damping off, the term used to describe the death of young seedlings in patches, is normally a problem when seedlings are raised under glass, but overcrowded seed beds can still suffer, especially in wet weather. The problem is due to attack by species of *Pythium* and *Rhizoctonia* fungi. Typically, a constriction at the base of the stem is visible and the seedlings topple over and rot.
Control: Always sow thinly. At the first sign of damping off, remove the worst affected seedlings and then water those remaining with a copper-based fungicide.

DRY SOIL Seeds need a steady supply of moisture to enable them to germinate and grow. Under dry soil conditions the seeds will simply remain dormant, and may then be eaten by soil pests.
Control: To hold moisture close to the seeds, line seed drills with fine, composted bark or good, sieved garden compost and water well before sowing. Firm the soil over the seeds, and water as necessary in very dry weather.

FROST OR LOW NIGHT TEMPERATURES Seedlings of all kinds can be susceptible to frost or low night temperatures but these are particularly troublesome where the plants are not hardy, as with runner and dwarf (French) beans, for example. Seedlings and young plants may not be killed completely, but leaves will be scorched and shoots may die back, and it may be several weeks before replacement growth starts.

Control: When cold conditions prevail, putting cloches or ventilated plastic sheeting over the plants would be helpful. When frost threatens, protect vulnerable seedlings and young plants with a woven fleece covering, or with several thicknesses of newspaper held in place by netting or string. Should a frost occur without protective measures having been taken, put a water sprinkler on to the plants before the morning sun reaches them. This will slow down thawing and may save the plants. When sowing runner or dwarf (French) beans out of doors, grow a few extra plants in a greenhouse or cold frame to act as replacements in an emergency.

MICE Mice eat peas, beans and some other larger seeds, generally leaving holes in the ground, as with bird losses. Where the crop is netted and losses of seeds still occur, mice are the likely culprits.

Control: Firm the soil over the seeds and try laying sharp twigs, such as gorse or hawthorn, in the drills after sowing and before covering with soil. Alternatively, use mouse traps, suitably protected inside drains or under ridge tiles to avoid harming other animals. At one time gardeners dipped the seeds in paraffin before sowing, but this is no longer practised.

MILLIPEDES Millipedes find many seeds attractive as food sources and peas, beans and marrow seeds are most frequently attacked. If the attack occurs before germination, the seed may fail to produce any shoot. Where the attack is later, the shoot will be poor and will probably die after making a little growth. It is usually the spotted millipede, *Blaniulus guttulatus*, that attacks seeds. This species is up to 1.8cm (⅔in) long, pale in colour with small red spots along the back and two pairs of legs on each of the 50 or so body segments. Millipedes move slowly through the soil and, when disturbed, they curl up in spiral fashion.

Control: Treat the soil with chlorpyrifos/diazinon insecticide. Millipides are most active in soils with plenty of organic matter and in damp conditions. Attack often follows initial damage by wireworms or slugs, so control of those pests will reduce the likelihood of severe millipede attack.

OLD SEED Seed has a limited life in the packet, and this varies according to the type of vegetable. Generally, the larger seeds have a longer expected storage life but suppliers of seeds are obliged to supply vegetable seed that is of a guaranteed germination standard. It is possible to use home-saved seed, and acceptable germination can usually be obtained, provided that soil and temperature conditions are correct and pests or diseases are not involved. If the seed is more than a year or two old, however, it cannot be relied upon to germinate satisfactorily. Remember, also, that many of the best varieties are hybrids and do not come true to type from home-saved seed.

Control: Avoid disappointment and use fresh seed each year. If saving seed, however, store in moisture-proof jars rather than in paper bags or seed packets.

RABBITS Rabbits can cause much damage to seedlings and young plants in the vegetable garden. Whole rows can be grazed down to soil level overnight and, although a few types of vegetable may send out replacement shoots, most seedlings will die.

Control: Protecting seed beds and rows of young plants with wire netting is probably the only truly safe method. Where this is not possible, rags soaked in bone oil could be hung along or round the rows or beds. When large, local populations of rabbits are involved, some form of rabbit clearance operation would be the most successful control.

SEED AND SEEDLING ROTS Various fungi can attack seeds and seedlings in the ground resulting in rotting and death, with many of the fungal attacks following initial damage by soil pests or entering through damaged areas on the seed coat. *Pythium*, *Rhizoctonia*, *Fusarium*, *Phytophthora* and *Thielaviopsis* can each be involved, depending on the soil conditions and the plant involved.

Control: Grow seedlings in proprietary compost under cover and plant out when large enough and after hardening off the plants.

SLUGS Slugs are potentially serious pests of tender young seedlings, feeding on the stems at soil level and also on the foliage. Damage is most severe on heavy soils and in wet seasons.

Control: Control slugs before sowing by using the beneficial nematode *Phasmarhabditis hermaphrodita*, which seeks out slugs in the soil and penetrates via the mantle. There, bacteria carried by the nematode attack and kill the slug and the nematodes live on the breakdown

products and breed. The new nematodes then leave the host, complete with bacteria, to seek new hosts (*see Biological control, pp. xvi–xxi*). Alternatively, protect small areas of seedlings with paper barriers impregnated with metaldehyde and for larger areas, water soil and seedlings with metaldehyde solution or scatter pellets containing metaldehyde or methiocarb thinly over the soil.

SNAILS Snails are usually less of a problem than slugs, but can be troublesome in wet years.

Control: Protect with metaldehyde-impregnated strips, watering with metaldehyde solution or by scattering metaldehyde or methiocarb pellets thinly over the area to be protected. Soot, lime, crushed eggshells and grit have all been tried and tested, but with only a moderate success rate.

WIREWORM Wireworms are the larvae of click beetles, *Agriotes lineatus*. They take up to five years to complete their development and in that time can devour many seedling roots as well as killing many plants. Wireworms are most troublesome in new gardens or new beds made from old meadow or grassland. However, once soil is being regularly cultivated and disturbed, click beetles are less likely to use that area for egg-laying.

Control: Regular soil cultivations and hand removal of wireworms while preparing the seed bed should take care of the pest. For particularly heavy infestation levels, treat the soil with a chlorpyrifos/diazinon soil insecticide at sowing time.

VEGETABLES 2

BRASSICAS INCLUDING BROCCOLI, CALABRESE, CABBAGE,
CAULIFLOWER, CHINESE LEAVES, KALE, KOHL RABI, SPROUTS

ROOTS

EATEN	Small white maggots on roots	*cabbage root fly*
GALLED	Round galls at stem base, hollow or with grub feeding inside	*turnip gall weevil*
	Irregularly-shaped galling of roots	*club root*

STEMS

GALLED	Stems with warty galls	*hormone weedkiller contamination*
	Purple to brown cankers on stem followed by rotting	*canker*
WITHERING	Stems shrink around soil level with dark discolouration, plants may die	*wirestem*

LEAVES

PESTS VISIBLE HOLES	Green, brown or black and yellow caterpillars present	*caterpillars*
	Small holes in seed leaves and first few true leaves	*flea beetle*
PESTS VISIBLE NO HOLES	Mealy grey pests under leaves	*mealy cabbage aphid*
	White, moth-like pests under leaves	*whitefly*
NO PESTS VISIBLE HOLES	Leaves reduced to network of veins	*pigeons*
NO PESTS VISIBLE NO HOLES		
DISCOLOURED	Leaf edges turn blue-green then yellow	*potassium deficiency*
	Pale mottling between veins	*magnesium deficiency*
DISTORTED	Leaves crumpled	*turnip mosaic virus*
	Leaves narrowed to thin strips	*whiptail*
	Leaves stunted and deformed	*boron deficiency*
SPOTTED	Circular brown areas about 12mm (½in) across with black dots in concentric rings	*ring spot*
	Irregular dark or yellow blotches	*turnip mosaic virus*

SPOTTED cont.	Pale spots on upper surface, patches of downy fungus below	*downy mildew*
VISIBLE FUNGAL GROWTHS	Greyish mould on sprouts, leaf stalks and old cabbage hearts	*grey mould*
	Powdery white mould	*powdery mildew*
	Raised white pustules on leaves	*white blister*

CABBAGE HEARTS

	No hearts develop (and cauliflowers fail to produce a head)	*faulty growing conditions*
	Hearts split	*heavy rain*

STORED WHITE CABBAGES

	Brown, soft rotting	*grey mould*
	Dark burn-like marks	*cauliflower mosaic virus, turnip mosaic virus*

BORON DEFICIENCY A lack of boron shows up on cauliflowers as a stunting and distortion of the leaves surrounding the curds, while the curds themselves become brown with water-soaked areas and have a bitter taste. Brown discolouration can also be found in the curd stems and down into the main stem. Stem discolouration is also found on cabbages, kale and sprouts. Soft rot bacteria often invade the discoloured tissue.

Control: Apply borax (sodium tetraborate) to the soil at a rate of 1–3g per square metre ($\frac{1}{30}$–$\frac{1}{10}$oz per yd^2), depending upon the severity of the symptoms seen, ideally treating before sowing. Dissolve in a convenient volume of water to assist in the application.

CABBAGE ROOT FLY Cabbage root fly, *Delia radicum* (formerly known as *D. brassicae* and *Erioischia brassicae*), attacks all kinds of cultivated brassica plants as well as a range of flowers and weeds from the cabbage family. The most severe damage is done by the first generation of the pest which hatches from eggs laid in mid- to late spring. In the southern half of the UK, egg-laying coincides with flowering of cow parsley, *Anthriscus sylvestris*. The maggots feed on the root hairs and surface layers of the root and seedlings and young plants are killed. Older plants are stunted in growth and the leaves take on a dull purple discolouration. A second generation of adult flies appears in midsummer and sometimes a third generation in late summer. In the later attacks, some eggs are laid into developing sprout buttons. The maggots feed in the sprouts and remain largely undetected until harvest, when the sprouts are found to be brown and partially eaten.

Control: Cabbage root fly eggs, maggots and pupae are eaten by a number of natural enemies in the soil, and in trials it has been found that up to 90 per cent of the eggs are eaten by various predatory beetles, with further predation and parasitism of larval and pupal stages. Even then, the survivors were enough to cause economic damage, so further control measures are needed.

Probably the best method is to screen the crops with fine netting which keeps out the flying adults. To use this method satisfactorily, all the brassicas are best grouped together (*see Crop rotation, pp. viii–ix*) so they can all be protected. The netting should be in place by early spring, otherwise the first generation flies will have laid their eggs and the succeeding generations will be confined under the netting rather than being kept out.

A further method of excluding the egg-laying adults is to fit close-fitting rings or squares of roofing felt or carpet underlay around the stems of cabbages and other brassicas at planting time. Sowings or plantings made outside the main egg-laying times are less likely to be attacked, and good control of cabbage family weeds, such as shepherd's purse and hedge mustard, will also be of help.

Should insecticidal control be preferred, a chlorpyrifos/diazinon soil insecticide can be used, but keep the application close to the stems to avoid unnecessary damage to beneficial insects elsewhere in the vegetable garden.

CANKER Caused by the fungus, *Phoma lingam*, canker can attack most brassica types. Pale brown to purple cankers appear at the bases of the stems and on the roots, and the infection can also be found on leaves, flower stems, seed pods and on the seeds. Seed-borne infection used to be a common cause of spread. The attacked stem and root tissue decays and plants die, followed by the production of fungal bodies in the dead areas which spread the disease further.

Control: Use good quality seed to protect against spread of infection. Destroy any infected plants found and dispose of old brassica residues as soon as the crops have been harvested. Crop rotation will keep old plants and new plantings apart and help to prevent any cross-infection.

CATERPILLARS Several different types of caterpillar attack brassicas, feeding on the leaves, boring into hearts or curds and generally reducing the attractiveness and palatability of the crops. Details of the main pest species are given below.

Control: Netting over the crops during the period that the adults are in flight would prevent eggs being laid on the foliage, although in the average garden it may not be practical to guard against all the different species in this way. Regular hand-picking of the caterpillars could be carried out, or the crops can be sprayed with the antagonistic bacterium, *Bacillus thuringiensis*, which prevents caterpillars feeding within two hours of application, then kills them. Alternatively, spray with bifenthrin, fatty acids, permethrin or pyrethrins. Apply at the first sign of egg-laying or caterpillar feeding and before the boring types have had chance to bury themselves down away from the spray. Repeat the bacterium or insecticides as necessary to maintain the level of control.

Main caterpillar species:
- Cabbage white butterflies. The large white, *Pieris brassicae*, has white wings with black markings and lays eggs in batches of up to 100, mainly underneath the leaves. The butterfly is on the wing in late spring with a second generation in mid- to late summer. The caterpillars feed on the leaves of cabbages and rarely

penetrate into the hearts. They grow up to 4cm (1½in) long and are basically pale green with yellow and black spots and bands.

- The small white, *Pieris rapae*, lays eggs singly and so can attack a much greater number of individual plants. The green caterpillars have a thin yellow line along their bodies, grow to a length of 2.5cm (1in) and cause more serious damage than those of the large white as they bore into the hearts of cabbages and deep into the curds of cauliflowers. Plants are fouled by the caterpillar droppings.

- The cabbage moth, *Mamestra brassicae*, flies at night during late spring and early summer and lays eggs in small batches underneath leaves. The caterpillars are light green at first but can be quite variable as they become older, ranging from green through brown to black-backed. The skin is smooth and not hairy, unlike the cabbage white butterfly caterpillars. The fully-grown caterpillars are around 3cm (1¼) long and leave the plants in order to pupate in the soil.

- The diamond-back moth, *Plutella xylostella*, is a much smaller species, the adult moths being only 6mm (¼in) when fully grown. The caterpillars feed only on the underside tissue of the leaves, leaving 'windows' of the upper surface behind them. They also construct a flimsy sort of web or hammock. The name 'diamond-back' comes from the diamond-shaped patterns that are made as the wings are folded together.

CLUB ROOT Club root, caused by the fungus *Plasmodiophora brassicae*, is probably the most serious of all the diseases affecting brassica plants, as well as attacking other plants in the cabbage family including weeds. Attack through the soil causes the root tissue to swell up into large galls in which the fungus multiplies. The plants become unthrifty and may die, and the fungus remains in the soil in the diseased roots. Resting spores develop which can persist in the soil for 20 years or more, and when brassicas are again planted in the same site, motile spores are produced which swim in the soil moisture to infect the roots.

Club root is encouraged by acid and wet soil conditions, and can be spread in soil on boots and tools, in manure from animals fed on contaminated plants, and in flood water where the spores are washed out of the soil to come to rest in a new site.

Control: Following a crop rotation plan (*see Crop rotation, pp. viii–ix*) and liming the soil where the brassicas are to be grown will help. Aim for a soil pH (acid/alkaline reading) of 7.3 to 7.5. If the soil is on the wet and heavy side, try to improve drainage to a soakaway. Where club root has already occurred, raise seedlings in pots of proprietary compost and not in outdoor seed beds to ensure a good, healthy root system is established by planting-out time.

Seedling roots can be dipped in a solution of thiophanate-methyl, benomyl or carbendazim, which will reduce the severity of attack and enable a crop to be grown in infected soil, but will not reduce the level of infection in the soil. As soon as any crops are found to be dying from club root, or at the end of cropping where disease has not proved fatal, dig out all the roots and burn them before they start to rot. Keep cabbage family weeds – such as shepherd's purse and charlock – under control, as well as other weeds on which the disease has at times been found. If buying in, or if given, young brassica plants, examine the roots very carefully to ensure there is no disease present. See also the description of turnip gall weevil (below), which can be confused with club root disease.

DOWNY MILDEW Downy mildew, *Peronospora parasitica*, is most damaging when it attacks seedling brassicas, and can often be troublesome on cauliflower seedlings being raised in the greenhouse. Pale yellow patches appear on the upper leaf surfaces with a downy white mould below. Water drips or ;ack of ventilation can encourage the disease in the greenhouse, while overcrowded seedlings or plants are vulnerable in the open garden.
Control: Avoid drips in the greenhouse and keep plants well spaced out at all stages in their lives. Prevent or control attacks with sprays of a copper or mancozeb fungicide.

FAULTY GROWING CONDITIONS Faulty growing conditions can result in plants running to seed early, in cabbages not hearting up, in cauliflowers failing to produce a head and in sprouts being 'blown' (open and loose instead of being firm). Brassicas grow best in slightly alkaline, well-firmed soil. If not firmed in well at planting time, or after any lifting due to frost, cabbages may fail to heart up, sprout buttons become blown and cauliflowers may become blind. Regular availability of water is necessary for good cropping of cabbages, but excess water may cause cabbage hearts to split open so good drainage is also of benefit. Where cauliflowers are starved of nutrients in the early stages of

growth blindness usually follows, even if feeding is adequate later on.
Control: Prepare the soil well before planting, adding lime as necessary and ensuring there are adequate reserves of organic matter from previous crops to help even out water reserves. Feed during the early stages of growth to ensure a sound start.

FLEA BEETLE The turnip flea beetle, *Phyllotreta cruciferae*, attacks all brassica seedlings and young plants, attacks being particularly serious on the seed leaves. The larvae eat the plant roots while the adults attack the leaves, leaving small round pits where they have fed. Most damage occurs in spring, and severe attacks can greatly reduce plant vigour.
Control: Treat the seedlings and the soil with rotenone dust, repeating as necessary at weekly intervals.

GREY MOULD The grey mould fungus, *Botrytis cinerea*, attacks damaged tissue and therefore it can be a problem where the leaves or stems have been injured by frost, or on sprouts where cabbage root fly has fed on the buttons. Old, fading leaves may be the source of the initial attack, especially in wet weather.
Control: Remove all old leaves and damaged parts of plants. Avoid excess nitrogen, which could make the plants soft and more prone to attack. A dusting with sulphur dust could be helpful as a first-aid measure.

HEAVY RAIN Heavy rains after a long, dry period result in rapid uptake of water and a sudden spurt of growth. This may be too much for cabbage hearts that are almost ready for harvest, and splitting across the heart is a common result. Heavy rains will also wash soluble nutrients, such as nitrogen and magnesium, out of the surface soil layers.

Control: Incorporating organic matter into the soil will help to even out water supplies. When dry weather prevails, water sufficiently to prevent the soil drying out too much.

HORMONE WEEDKILLER CONTAMINATION Contamination of brassicas by hormone weedkillers, as used for lawn weed control, has a much greater effect than would be expected. Stems develop warty swellings along their length and cropping is greatly reduced. Cabbage and sprouts appear to be more susceptible to this kind of damage than other brassicas. Spray-drift while treating a nearby lawn and residues of weedkiller in the watering-can are the most common sources of the contamination.

Control: Treat lawns only in still, windless weather and keep a watering can solely for weedkiller application. It is virtually impossible to wash out every trace of some weedkillers, and only a few parts per million are needed for damage to occur. Affected plants are best removed and burned although lightly affected plants may still produce a usable crop.

MAGNESIUM DEFICIENCY A shortage of magnesium results in the older leaves turning yellow between the veins, while the veins themselves remain green. This symptom can be quite common at the end of a rainy summer as magnesium is most likely to be in short supply in light, acid soils and in wet years when the rain washes it through the soil. Too much potassium in the soil, or applied in fertilizers, makes magnesium less available.

Control: When applying lime during preparation of the brassica plot, use magnesium limestone or calcified seaweed instead of ordinary garden lime. For an early-season deficiency, water plants and soil with Epsom Salts (magnesium sulphate) using 100g per 5l (4oz per gall) of water plus wetting agent.

MEALY CABBAGE APHID Mealy cabbage aphid, *Brevicoryne brassicae*, is one of the most disgusting of the greenfly species, covering the crop with a sticky, mealy coating, distorting the growth and causing yellow patches on the leaves where it feeds. The pest also penetrates into the centres of cabbage hearts and sprout buttons and gets into the curds of cauliflowers, rendering the crops inedible. The aphid spends the winter in the egg stage on old brassica stems, so it is close at hand to start new attacks in the following spring.

Control: Remove all old plant remains at the end of cropping and spray infested plants with a systemic insecticide such as dimethoate or heptenophos at the first sign of attack. Attacks can sometimes be prevented by covering brassica crops with a fine netting, but the success of this operation depends on the completeness of the cover, which should reach right down to soil level.

PIGEONS Pigeons will feed actively on newly-planted brassicas and also on older specimens, often reducing the leaves to a network of the larger veins. In winter they often perch on top of sprout plants to feed.

Control: Cover smaller plants with netting or criss-cross black cotton over the plants. Alternatively, protect the plants by stretching 'humming' strips of plastic overhead to vibrate in the wind and frighten the birds. In areas where wood pigeons are particularly plentiful, growing winter brassicas inside a fruit cage is probably the only certain answer.

POTASSIUM DEFICIENCY A shortage of potassium (potash) leads to the leaves turning a blue-green colour and a scorching of the leaf edges, starting with the older leaves. Potassium shortage is often a problem on light sandy soils and on soils with a high peat or chalk content. **Control:** Normal dressings of a balanced fertilizer should provide adequate potassium for the season. In cases of shortage, apply potassium sulphate (often sold as sulphate of potash) or a proprietary tomato fertilizer. An excess of potassium can make magnesium deficient, so do not overdo the potassium treatment.

POWDERY MILDEW Crucifer powdery mildew, *Erisiphe cruciferarum*, is becoming more common on brassicas, although a frequent problem already with turnip and swede (*see also Powdery mildew, p.144*). Kale and sprouts are attacked, the fungus coating the leaves with a dry, powdery deposit of spores. The same species attacks poppy, as well as cabbage family weeds, so infection can come from a variety of sources. **Control:** As with other powdery mildew species, the crucifer type is encouraged by dryness at the roots, so it is wise to pay attention to building up the water-holding capacity of the soil with compost and watering in dry weather. For an existing infestation, spray with a sulphur fungicide or use benomyl or carbendazim. Weed control is also important.

RING SPOT Brassica ring spot fungus, *Mycosphaerella brassicicola*, is chiefly a wet-winter fungus, attacking broccoli, savoy and other winter cabbage and sprouts. It is more common where no crop rotation plan is followed and on soil that has received a lot of manure, leading to over-lush growth. Circular brown spots around 2cm (¾in) across appear on the leaves and stems, each one dotted with black spore bodies. Infected leaves soon turn yellow and then wither. **Control:** Follow a regular system of crop rotation and do not apply an excess amount of manure or nitrogenous fertilizer. Should growth be over-lush, balance it by applying a potassium fertilizer. Remove affected leaves and spray once or twice using a copper fungicide. Other leaf spot fungi also attack brassicas but the same control measures would apply to them.

TURNIP GALL WEEVIL The turnip gall weevil, *Ceutorhynchus pleurostigma*, attacks the stem bases and roots of brassicas, resulting in a series of rounded galls developing. These may be confused with club root although the galls are a regular, rounded shape and not knobbly or elongated as with club root. If the galls are cut open a legless larva will be found feeding if the gall is still an active one, or a hollow if the pest has finished its development and left. Late-sown brassicas are most at risk from attack as the majority of eggs are laid in late summer to early autumn. **Control:** Remove and burn all old stems and roots as the brassica crops are harvested and practise crop rotation. Treat the soil with chlorpyrifos/diazinon as recommended for control of cabbage root fly.

TURNIP MOSAIC VIRUS Early signs of the virus include a vein clearing, where the veins lose their normal green colour, and a yellow mottling of the leaves together with some distortion and crinkling. Probably the most serious effect is on hard, white cabbage where, together with cauliflower mosaic virus, the virus causes sunken brown spots to appear in the leaves, a condition known as 'cigar burn'. Hard cabbages infected with turnip mosaic virus are more susceptible to later rots due to grey mould attack than healthy cabbages.

Control: No effective control measures exist. Breeding for resistance offers the best hope for control.

WHIPTAIL Whiptail is the name given to the symptom of molybdenum deficiency seen on cauliflower and broccoli leaves. The leaves are reduced to little more than the main vein and usually the plant will be blind. Molybdenum shortage occurs on acid soils and most commonly in dry weather.

Control: Normal liming of the soil, carried out as part of the crop rotation scheme, will ensure that molybdenum remains available to the plant roots. Where the whiptail symptoms have appeared, protect later plantings with a few applications of a complete foliar feed that lists molybdenum (Mo) among its contents. To supply molybdenum to a deficient soil, water as the seedlings emerge using a solution of ammonium molybdate of 30g per 5l (1oz/1gall) of water to 10 square metres (10yd^2) of soil.

WHITE BLISTER The white blister fungus, *Albugo candida*, causes shiny white raised spots to appear on the leaves. Later, the spots appear less shiny due to the production of spores on their surfaces. Sprouts are more severely attacked than other brassica types, but the same fungus also attacks cabbage family weeds

and flowering plants such as honesty, although these may be different forms of the fungus which do not attack brassicas. Severe attacks can weaken plants as infected leaves usually turn yellow and then fall, and cabbage hearts and cauliflower heads can also be distorted.

Control: Remove and burn infected leaves or severely infected plants as soon as seen. Sow or plant new brassicas away from the previous year's old crops in a crop rotation system and try a few protective sprays with a copper fungicide.

WHITEFLY Brassica whitefly, *Aleyrodes proletella*, is a more vigorous-looking relative of the glasshouse whitefly and can survive even the hardest winters outside. The larval stages, known as scales, and the adults feed on plant sap and excrete honey dew as they feed. This makes the leaves sticky and likely to be colonized by black sooty moulds. Even though whitefly feed underneath the leaves, they are quite conspicuous as they fly off in swarms when disturbed.

Control: Little real damage is caused, but if control is required a few weekly applications of bifenthrin, dimethoate, permethrin or pirimiphos-methyl should prove effective.

WIRESTEM Wirestem is a problem suffered by brassica seedlings and young plants due to infection by the fungus, *Thanatephorus cucumeris*. The base of the stem becomes narrow, brown and hardened and plants often collapse and die. Older plants may survive but will not thrive.

Control: Keep any greenhouse-grown seedlings and young plants away from drips and do not overwater. Out of doors, sow or plant into a good tilth and again do not overwater.

VEGETABLES 3

PEAS AND BEANS INCLUDING RUNNER, DWARF AND BROAD BEANS

ROOTS

Brown, irregular swelling on roots of all legumes	*nitrogen fixing nodules*
Roots and bases of stems rot	*root and foot rots*
Small brown bodies on roots of peas and broad bean	*pea cyst eelworm*
White, legless grubs feeding on nodules on roots	*pea and bean weevil larvae*

STEMS

Bases of broad bean stems blackened, followed by white fungal growth	*sclerotinia disease*
Leading shoots twisted and deformed, white grubs present	*pea midge*
Stems and leaves wilt, brown discolouration evident when stem cut lengthways	*wilt*
Stems bored into by maggots	*bean seed fly*
Stems with elongated dark brown cankers	*anthracnose*

LEAVES

PESTS VISIBLE	Green or black insects clustered over leaves and stems	*aphids*
	Tiny green or reddish pests under leaves of beans	*two-spotted spider mite*
PESTS NOT VISIBLE	Leaf edges notched	*pea and bean weevil*
SPOTTED	Chocolate-brown spots	*chocolate spot*
	Brown patches or yellow mottling	*virus*
	Small pale spots or larger, darker ones	*leaf spots*
	Small pale spots surrounded by yellow ring	*halo blight*

FLOWERS AND/OR PODS

PODS SPOTTED	Chocolate-coloured spots	*chocolate spot*
	Round, dark, sunken spots	*anthracnose*
	Small purple spots	*leaf and pod spots*
	Grey, mouldy areas and rot	*grey mould*

PESTS PRESENT	Pods with white, jumping insects	pea midge
	Small black or yellow pests causing silvery streaks on pods	thrips
	White caterpillars feeding on peas	pea moth

FLOWERS

	Lack of pods	lack of flower set

SEEDS

EATEN	Holes bored into peas and beans in store	pea and bean beetles
	Legless maggots feeding in runner beans in the soil	bean seed fly
	Round, brown spot in centre of peas	marsh spot

A NTHRACNOSE Anthracnose, caused by the fungus *Colletotrichum lindemuthianum*, attacks dwarf (French) beans and results in elongated brown cankers on the stems, yellowing and withering of the leaves and a dark, sunken spotting of the pods. The disease spreads from the pods on to the beans inside which are also spotted. Anthracnose is most troublesome in cool, wet weather.

Control: Destroy infected crops and never save seed, even from lightly infected beans. Follow a normal crop rotation so the new crop will not be in contact with any of the old plant debris (*see Crop rotation, pp. viii–ix*). No chemical control is available.

APHIDS (GREENFLY AND BLACKFLY)
Black bean aphid, *Aphis fabae*, and pea aphid, *Acyrthosiphon pisum*, are the species involved. Dense colonies of the black bean aphid build up in summer and feed on leaves, flowers and pods of broad and other beans and on peas. They are capable of spreading at least five different viruses to peas and/or beans. Feeding can greatly reduce crop yields especially in dry, warm conditions which favour rapid

reproduction by the pests. The aphids fly off in autumn to spindle tree (*Euonymus europaeus*) or guelder rose (*Viburnum opulus*) where the winter eggs are laid.

As well as feeding on beans, the black fly also attacks a wide range of vegetable and flowering garden plants. Pea aphid, on the other hand, only feeds on plants in the pea family and a severe attack may be damaging enough to prevent any peas being formed.

Control: Aphids do have a number of natural enemies in the form of ladybird larvae and adults, hoverfly and lacewing larvae, plus parasitic and predatory midges and wasps. Often these beneficial insects are not numerous enough or timely enough in their action to control the pests completely, so some help is needed. Spray with pirimicarb which is virtually aphid-specific. Alternatively, where no beneficial insects are present, spray with bifenthrin, fatty acids, dimethoate, heptenophos or pyrethrins.

B EAN SEED FLY There are two species of bean seed fly, *Delia platura* and *D. florilega*, that attack seeds of runner and dwarf beans as well as attacking pea and bean plants and a range of other crops. When runner bean seeds are damaged, the appearing seedlings will be weak and inspection will show considerable mining within the seed, often enlarged by subsequent millipede feeding. With dwarf beans where the damaged seed leaves appear above the ground, they will shrivel and die. Stems are often twisted into a 'snake-head' position.

Control: Where bean seed flies are a problem, grow beans in pots or trays of compost to get the seedlings off to a strong start. Alternatively, spend time creating a good seed bed so the seeds germinate quickly.

CHOCOLATE SPOT The chocolate spot fungus, *Botrytis fabae*, occurs on broad beans where it causes pale brown spots on the leaves and long brown streaks on the stems. Pods and seed coats also show a brown spotting. Defoliation and even plant death can follow an early attack in the winter on late-sown broad beans, since the fungus thrives in moist weather.

Control: Chocolate spot persists on plant remains so removal and careful disposal of infected plants is essential. Sow in well drained, fertile soil. Where there are thought to be high nitrogen levels in the soil, balance them by applying potassium and phosphates. Good air circulation will also help so a slightly exposed site would be preferable to a hidden away, cosy one. Should a severe attack develop, a few sprays with copper fungicide should help to prevent further spread of the disease.

GREY MOULD Grey mould, *Botrytis cinerea*, can be found in wet and humid weather attacking the pods of

peas and beans. Often attack starts following very wet weather when the flowers become rotted and the rot then spreads to nearby pods. Diseased pods become soft and are soon covered with the typical grey, furry coating of fungus.

Control: Remove affected pods when seen. If damage is severe, follow with a few sprays of benomyl, carbendazim or sulphur.

HALO BLIGHT The aptly-named halo blight is seen as a fine spotting on the leaves of dwarf beans, each spot surrounded by a pale halo. The spots may join together, resulting in the whole leaf turning brown and withering. Caused by the bacterium *Pseudomonas phaseolicola*, halo blight is carried in the seed coat and attack via the seed usually results in seedlings that die soon after emergence. Any that do survive will carry stem lesions and pods will show circular, water-soaked spots.

Control: Do not save home-grown seed if there has been any halo blight around, and purchase new seed from a reliable source. When saving seed from healthy plants, examine it carefully and reject any with raised blisters. Grow in a new site each year, preferably following a set three or four year rotation (*see Crop rotation, pp. viii–ix*).

LACK OF FLOWER SET Failure of flowers to set a crop is a problem besetting runner beans and can be due to a number of factors, some controllable, others not. Dryness of the soil is a major cause which is easily preventable, lack of pollinator activity due to bad weather, however, is not.

Control: Ideally, grow runner beans in a sheltered spot to encourage bees and other pollinators (and also to prevent high winds blowing the crop over). Add plenty of compost to the planting site to act as a reservoir for water and water well, if necessary, in dry weather. Sometimes 'robber' bees attack the flowers, nibbling out holes at the base of the flowers to get at the nectar without the bother of entering the flower. Such flowers are unlikely to set a crop as other pollinators will probably follow the same, easy route. If this type of damage is seen, pick off the damaged flowers. Picking on a regular basis, and picking before the beans have grown to a large size, will also help to prolong the cropping season.

LEAF AND POD SPOTS Leaf and pod spots of peas can be caused by a number of different fungi but the most important is *Ascochyta pisi*. Pale brown, sunken spots with darker margins appear on leaves and pods and the disease also infects the peas, which develop sunken brown or purple spots. Wet weather favours the disease.

Control: Pull out and burn infected plants and follow a long rotation of crops (*see Crop rotation, pp. viii–ix*). Do not save peas for sowing from infected plants or from neighbouring ones and carefully collect up and dispose of all plant remains. Some seed companies will supply fungicide-treated pea seeds.

MARSH SPOT When peas are grown in soils that lack manganese, typically in wet or marshy ground, the crop appears normal but when cut open the peas are found to have a rounded dark mark at the centre. If these are then dried for use as seed in the following year, they will fail to germinate or will produce poor yellow shoots that soon die.

Control: Where peas have to be grown on wet ground, supply the necessary manganese by treating the soil before sowing with a fritted or chelated manganese product.

NITROGEN–FIXING NODULES The roots of peas and beans, in common with those of other legumes, are home for special bacteria that are able to fix nitrates from the soil. In this symbiotic relationship, the bacteria supply nitrogen to assist plant growth and the roots produce the nodules in which the bacteria live. The nodules are often slightly pink in colour and of irregular sizes, not to be confused with the tiny cysts of pea cyst eelworm, below. At the end of cropping the roots die and the nodules rot to release the nitrogen into the soil.

PEA AND BEAN WEEVIL Pea and bean weevil, *Sitona lineatus,* is probably the most common and frequent pest of peas and beans. The adults feed on the leaves, resulting in characteristic notched edges, while the larvae feed on the nitrogen-fixing nodules on the roots. The weevils transmit two viruses as they feed. Damage done to the leaves is rarely of any significance as far as crop yields are concerned, but the nodule damage by the larvae can be serious in dry years when nitrogen uptake from the soil is reduced.

Control: Where leaf damage is severe, on young seedlings for example, prevent further attacks by dusting with gamma-HCH or spraying with permethrin.

PEA CYST EELWORM Pea cyst eelworm, *Heterodera goettingiana*, also known as pea cyst nematode, is becoming a locally serious pest of gardens and allotments.

Peas and broad beans can be attacked, but not dwarf or runner beans. Infested plants grow poorly, often turn bright yellow, then wither and die prematurely. When lifted, the roots will be seen to have numerous small white cysts, each about half the size of a pin-head and an absence of nitrogen-fixing nodules will also be evident. Each cyst contains up to 300 eggs and the cysts pass into the soil as the crop dies. The eggs can remain viable for several years.

Control: A normal three or four year rotation should prevent pea cyst eelworm becoming a problem although if an attack is confirmed a much longer rest between pea or broad bean crops would be required (see Crop rotation, pp. viii–ix). No other control measures exist.

PEA MIDGE Larvae of pea midge, Contarinia pisi, are dirty white in colour and their feeding in the growing points of pea plants results in curling and distortion of the growth. Beans, particularly broad beans, can also be attacked. The flowers fail to open fully and crops can be ruined by a severe attack. The grubs also get into the pods and as many as 300 have been counted in a single pod.

The larvae are quite active jumpers and, when fully fed, will propel themselves down into the soil where they pupate.

Control: Crop rotations are of benefit as the adults are not very strong fliers, but try to grow the current year's peas and beans as far as possible from the site of the previous year's crops. No certain chemical control exists but spraying with dimethoate or permethrin as soon as the flower buds appear may help.

PEA MOTH Pea moth, Cydia nigricans, is the cause of maggoty peas. Eggs are laid on the leaves from early to late summer and the caterpillars enter the young pods to feed on the seeds. When fully fed they leave the pods, drop to the ground and spin cocoons in which they spend the winter before pupating in spring. A severe attack is very damaging and most unpleasant to find, as infested pods look quite normal from the outside.

Control: Early-sown and late-sown crops will escape most, if not all, of the attack by being in the 'wrong' stage of growth during the main flight time of the moths. Insecticides are effective if timed correctly and it is possible to obtain a pheromone trap for pea moths (see Pheromones, pp. xv–xvi).

The pheromone traps attract and catch the male moths as they seek their female counterparts and so provide an indicator as to the best time to spray. Although pheromone traps for codling moths of apples can help control the resident codling population, pea moth traps cannot be used in this way, as mated female pea moths travel quite long distances to find the crops. Permethrin and pirimiphos-methyl would be suitable insecticides to use, provided the timing is correct.

ROOT AND FOOT ROTS Various root and foot-rotting fungi can attack peas and beans and, being soil-borne, they are present when the crops are sown. In severe cases roots are killed, stem bases turn black or dark brown and plants collapse and die. With a lighter attack the plants will survive but cropping will be reduced.

Control: Crop rotations will be of help by preventing build up of the diseases from year to year in the same site (see Crop rotation, pp. viii–ix). If the symptoms are spotted sufficiently early, watering the stem bases and soil with a copper-based fungicide may reduce the disease sufficiently for a crop to be taken.

SCLEROTINIA DISEASE Sclerotinia disease, caused by the fungus *Sclerotinia sclerotiorum*, is an occasional problem with runner beans. The base of the main stem, or sometimes further up the plants, becomes coated with a dense white fungus in which develop large black fungal resting bodies. Upper parts of the affected plants wilt and cropping is likely to stop. The same disease affects a number of other vegetable crops.
Control: Remove and burn affected plants before the resting bodies get into the ground. Do not dig any plant remains into the soil at the end of cropping.

THRIPS Pea thrips, *Kakothrips robustus*, feed on both the leaves and the pods, but it is the pods that show most damage as they develop a dull, silvery or brown discolouration. The adult thrips are narrow and black, while the young are yellow, but both stages puncture the cells to feed.
Control: Spray at the first sign of damage with fatty acids, dimethoate, permethrin or pyrethrins.

TWO-SPOTTED SPIDER MITE The two-spotted spider mite, *Tetranychus urticae*, can be a major pest on runner and dwarf beans in hot years. It often first infests plants being raised in the greenhouse and then continues to breed when the plants are set out in the garden. Attack results in a fine stippling of bleached spots on the leaves, and in severe cases the plants may fail to set pods. At the end of the season the mites will seek suitable hibernation quarters indoors, perhaps on the bean poles in a potting shed.
Control: Spray as necessary using fatty acids, dimethoate or pyrethrins. It may be possible to use the predatory mite *Phytoseiulus* successfully in warm summers but advice should be sought from the suppliers of biological control for their latest recommendations (*see Biological control, pp. xvi–xxi*).

VIRUS Various virus diseases of peas and beans exist, causing mottling, spotting and brown streaks and patches on leaves and stems but they are rarely found in gardens. Many are spread by pests, including aphids and pea and bean weevil.
Control: Good pest control is important to prevent a virus gaining a hold.

WILT *Fusarium solani* f. *pisi* attacks peas while *F. s.* f. *phaseoli* attacks dwarf and runner beans. Both fungi result in a wilting of the crops and the whole of the above ground parts of the plants wither, turn yellow and die. Attacks often start just as the crops are coming into flower, which may be just too late in the season to sow another crop. If the stems are cut lengthways, a pale orange to deep red discolouration will be seen in the central water conducting vessels.
Control: The disease is generally more severe on poorly drained soils so any action that can be taken to improve drainage would help. Wilt persists in the soil and on infected plant remains, so gather up and safely dispose of all diseased material and use a new site for the succeeding pea or bean crops.

VEGETABLES 4

STEM AND LEAF CROPS INCLUDING ASPARAGUS, CELERY,
CELERIAC, CHICORY, LETTUCE, LOVAGE, MINT, PARSLEY, RHUBARB,
SEA KALE, SPINACH, SPINACH BEET, SWISS CHARD

ROOTS AND CROWNS

PESTS VISIBLE	Mealy white pests on lettuce roots	*aphid (lettuce root)*
	Parsley roots mined by white maggots	*carrot fly*
	Tunnels in celeriac made by white, translucent caterpillars	*swift moth*
NO PESTS VISIBLE	Rhubarb crowns rot, leaves yellow and die	*crown rot*
	Roots covered with violet fungal threads	*violet root rot*

PLANTS

PESTS VISIBLE	Eaten off at ground level by large, off-white caterpillars	*cutworm*
NO PESTS VISIBLE	Lettuce rot off at soil level	*grey mould*
	Plants run up to seed	*bolting*
	White fungal growth over base of celery plants	*sclerotinia disease*

LEAVES AND LEAF STALKS

PESTS VISIBLE	Greenfly feeding on parsley	*aphid*
	Grey grubs/black and yellow beetles eating asparagus leaves	*asparagus beetle*
NO PESTS VISIBLE	Blister-type mines, celery, lovage, Swiss chard	*leaf miner*
	Brown marks on celery stalks	*boron deficiency*
	Brown or yellow spots on most plant types	*leaf spot*
	Cracked celery stalks	*faulty growing conditions*
	Irregular holes in leaves and leaf stalks, slime trails present	*slugs*
	Leaf stalks of rhubarb mined, jelly exuding	*rosy rustic moth*
	Leaves of parsley turning yellow or red, plants small	*motley dwarf disease*
	Rusty orange pustules on mint leaves	*rust*
	Various leaf mosaic patterns, distortions, discolourations	*virus*
	Yellow patches above, pale mould below on lettuce and spinach leaves.	*downy mildew*

NO PESTS VISIBLE	Yellow patches and upward rolling on spinach and spinach beet leaves	*manganese deficiency*
	Yellow patches turning brown on spinach beet and Swiss chard leaves	*magnesium deficiency*

APHID (GREENFLY AND BLACK-FLY) Various aphid species can be found on the vegetables in the groups above, but the two most important are lettuce root aphid and willow-carrot aphid. The willow-carrot aphid, *Cavaviella aegopodii*, is green in colour, feeds on parsley (as well as on carrot) and transmits motley dwarf disease (*see below*). Lettuce root aphid, *Pemphigus bursarius* (*see also Lettuce root aphid, p.72*), spends the winter in the egg stage on Lombardy poplars and then multiplies in spring inside galls on the poplar leaf stalks. Winged forms develop in mid- to late spring and fly to lettuce and related weed plants such as sowthistle where they attack the roots. Feeding results in weak, wilting plants and death may follow a severe attack. Most of the aphid population will fly back to poplars in autumn, but where lettuce are grown throughout the year and on light soils some may spend the winter on the lettuce roots. The pests are white and powdery and are usually present in large numbers.
Control: Control willow-carrot aphids by spraying as soon as seen with fatty acids, dimethoate, heptenophos, pirimicarb or pyrethrins, but it is doubtful if spraying would prevent the transmission of motley dwarf disease. Prevent damage by lettuce root aphids by growing resistant varieties (*see Resistant varieties, pp. x–xiii*). Where an attack has occurred, a drenching application of malathion may give control. Use a new site each year, and pull up and destroy any overwintering lettuce identified as having a root aphid infestation, easily distinguished because the plants wilt by day and recover over night. Good weed control, especially of sowthistles, is also important.

ASPARAGUS BEETLE Asparagus beetle, *Crioceris asparagi*, can be a very damaging pest of asparagus, since the insect lives on no other host plant, and both larvae and adults feed on the foliage. The grey, humped larvae hatch from eggs laid on the leaves in mid-summer, become fully fed after only two weeks, pupate in the soil and emerge as new adults shortly afterwards. There are, therefore, two or three generations per year. The adults have a black double cross on their backs with yellow between the bars.
Control: Spray with fatty acids, permethrin or pyrethrins whenever larvae or adults are seen.

BOLTING Bolting describes the way certain vegetables produce premature flowering stems which shoot upwards very rapidly. Lettuce, parsley, rhubarb and spinach are probably the worst offenders. The usual causes are poor soil and hot dry weather.
Control: Prepare the soil well before planting and water when needed in prolonged dry spells.

BORON DEFICIENCY Celery can suffer from a shortage of boron and reacts by producing stalks that are cracked and marked with a brown corky mottling. Leaf yellowing and poor growth are also symptoms.

Control: Apply borax (sodium tetraborate) to the soil before planting using 10g per 10 square metres (⅓oz per 10yd²), dissolved in a convenient volume of water to ensure accurate application. Should the problem arise during growth, apply twice the above rate.

CARROT FLY Carrot fly, *Psila rosae*, also attacks parsley. The roots are mined by the larvae and small plants may be killed.
Control: Grow the crop under a cover of fine netting or apply chlorpyrifos/diazinon or pirimiphos methyl before sowing.

CROWN ROT Crown rot can be found on rhubarb in wet soils and is seen as a decay of the central buds followed by a brownish rot down into the roots. The bacterium *Erwinia rhapontici* is normally thought to be involved in crown rot, but other diseases can be found attacking the dying parts.
Control: Remove and burn affected crowns, including as much of the root system as possible. Grow future plants in a different location on well prepared ground.

CUTWORM Cutworms are the soil-dwelling larvae of certain species of moths. The larvae are usually off-white to green or pale brown and feed at soil level, eating seedlings and mature plants. Lettuce are particularly at risk. Attacks are more severe in dry summers as, in wet years, the caterpillars are usually attacked and killed by a number of diseases.
Control: Regular hoeing will often expose the cutworms for removal by hand. Where high populations are present it would be worth treating the soil with the beneficial nematode, *Steinernema carpocapsae*, as recommended for vine weevil control (*see Biological control, pp. xvi–xxi*). Alternatively, apply a chlorpyrifos/diazinon insecticide at planting time or pirimiphos-methyl when the damage is first seen.

DOWNY MILDEW Downy mildew of spinach, *Peronospora effusa*, is evident as a pale yellow spotting on the upper leaf surface with a greyish-purple mould below. Affected plants may die, particularly when they are growing in crowded conditions and in wet seasons. Lettuce downy mildew, *Bremia lactucae*, is more troublesome under glass than on outdoor crops but attacks can be severe during wet springs and dewy autumns. Yellow patches appear on the upper leaf surfaces with a fine grey fungal coating under the leaves.
Control: Sow thinly and thin out in good time to leave spinach plants 15cm (6in) apart and lettuce 25cm (10in). On heavier soils and in wet areas use resistant varieties (*see Resistant varieties, pp. x–xiii*).

GREY MOULD The grey mould fungus, *Botrytis cinerea*, will attack any dead or dying tissue but is particularly aggressive on lettuce. Winter lettuce are frequently attacked, the mould starting at stem bases or on lower leaves and resulting in a complete rot through the base of the plants.
Control: Plant in well drained soil and keep the lettuce seedlings and young plants well above soil level when planting. Dusting the lower leaves and the soil under and around the plants with sulphur will help to delay or prevent attacks.

LEAF MINER Blotch-type leaf mines occur on celery following attack by celery fly, *Euleia heraclei*, and on spinach beet and Swiss chard following attack by beet leaf miner, *Pegomya hyoscyami*. There are two or even three generations of each pest per year and crops can be reduced by severe attacks, particularly on spinach beet and chard.

Control: Squash the pests within the mines when seen, or remove leaves where damage is extensive. Dimethoate sprays may control existing attacks.

LEAF SPOT Several different vegetables in this group are attacked by leaf spot fungi, including celery by *Septoria apiicola*, parsley by *Septoria petroselini*, spinach by *Heterosporium variabile* and rhubarb by *Ramularia rhei*. The spinach and rhubarb spots are quite large and pale with a darker border while the parsley and celery spots are small and dark. Leaf yellowing and death may follow a serious attack when the spots merge together.

Control: Remove the most seriously-affected leaves and, if necessary, spray with a copper or mancozeb fungicide.

MANGANESE DEFICIENCY Manganese deficiency can be a problem with spinach beet, resulting in leaf rolling and a yellow spotting between the veins. Typically manganese can be in short supply in thin, peaty soils overlying chalk and in wet seasons.

Control: Water or spray the leaves and the soil with manganese sulphate using 15g per 5l (½oz/1gall) of water plus a wetting agent. Where the problem occurs regularly, add manganese in chelated or fritted form when preparing the site prior to sowing.

MOTLEY DWARF DISEASE Mainly a problem with carrots, this trouble can also affect parsley. The problem follows feeding by aphids carrying the carrot mottle virus and carrot red leaf virus.

Leaves of infected parsley turn yellow and red and plants are stunted.

Control: There is no control available, but spraying with fatty acids, dimethoate, heptenophos, pirimicarb or pyrethrins may help prevent infection by reducing aphid numbers.

ROSY RUSTIC MOTH Rosy rustic moth, *Hydraecia micacea*, is an occasional, but damaging, pest of rhubarb. The dull pinkish caterpillars, up to 4.5cm (1¾in) long, burrow through the leaf stalks leaving behind a series of jelly-filled tunnels. Attacks start early in the growth of the rhubarb leaves so the presence of the pest is difficult to detect until the damage has been done.

Control: Remove and burn infested leaf stalks when seen. An application of a permethrin insecticide at the start of growth in spring may prevent attack.

RUST Rust disease, *Puccinia menthae*, can attack mint leaves and stems causing an orange blistering and a distortion of the shoots.

Control: Dig up and burn infected plants and grow new stock on a new site. It is possible to raise healthy plants from infected stock by taking tip cuttings from underground runners but it is better to start with new, clean plants.

SCLEROTINIA DISEASE Celery plants can be attacked by *Sclerotinia sclerotiorum*, resulting in a fluffy, white fungal coating and rapid rotting of the plants. Black resting bodies develop in the mould, contaminating the soil for future crops.

Control: Remove and burn the diseased plants quickly, ideally before the black resting bodies reach the soil. Follow a rotation system (*see Crop rotation pp.viii–ix*).

SLUGS Slugs can be very troublesome, especially in wet years, eating ragged holes out of leaves and feeding between celery stalks. Lettuce can also suffer considerable damage.

Control: By day, most slug species burrow into the ground to avoid the desiccating effect of the sun and there they are susceptible to control by the beneficial nematode, *Phasmarhabditis hermaphrodita*. The nematodes are supplied in a form ready to be dispersed in water and applied to a given area of soil, which should then be kept moist (*see Biological control, pp. xvi–xxi*). Alternatively, control slugs by watering plants and soil with a metaldehyde solution or by using metaldehyde or methiocarb pellets.

SWIFT MOTH The white, translucent caterpillars of ghost swift moth, *Hepialus humuli*, and the garden swift moth, *H. lupulinus*, can be sometimes found tunnelling into the swollen stem bases of celeriac. In severe cases all the tissue is eaten away.

Control: The caterpillars take two or three years to complete their development, so thorough soil preparation before sowing or planting would expose any resident pests. When planting, treating the soil with chlorpyrifos/diazinon or pirimiphos-methyl would protect from attack through the early weeks of establishment. For later attacks, use of the beneficial nematode, *Steinernema carpoc apsae* or *Heterorhabditis megadis* should give control (*see Biological control, pp. xvi–xxi*).

VIOLET ROOT ROT Violet root rot is caused by the fungus *Helicobasidium purpureum*, which attacks asparagus, sea kale and other plants, covering the roots with red-violet fungal strands. Affected plants turn yellow and die. In an asparagus bed the fungus gradually spreads throughout all the plants and any substantial weeds present in the area.

Control: Dig up and burn affected plants and keep the areas free from asparagus, sea kale or root crops for as long as possible. Elsewhere in the vegetable garden, practise a four year rotation of crops (*see Crop rotation, pp. viii–ix*), to reduce the chances of violet root rot or other soil-borne diseases gaining a hold.

VIRUSES In addition to motley dwarf disease, several other virus diseases may attack stem and leaf crops. Arabis mosaic virus, spread by *Xiphinema diversicaudatum* nematodes in the soil and cucumber mosaic virus, spread by *Myzus persicae* aphids are probably the two most common and serious. Cucumber mosaic virus infection of spinach gives rise to spinach blight, in which leaves turn yellow and die, eventually just leaving a few narrow and puckered ones at the centre. Lettuce may suffer from four or more virus diseases with big vein being amongst the most severe. Lettuces with big vein virus develop a pale banding of the veins, the leaves become puckered and the plants fail to heart. Rhubarb is also subject to virus attack which causes various ring spots and mottles, with the nematode-transmitted arabis mosaic virus and aphid-transmitted turnip mosaic viruses being among the more usual ones.

Control: There is no control available other than safely to incinerate affected plants and limit spread by aphids.

VEGETABLES 5

ONIONS (BULB AND SPRING), LEEKS, SHALLOTS, GARLIC, CHIVES

ROOTS, BULBS AND STEM BASES

EATEN	Small maggots present	onion fly
DISTORTED OR SPLIT	Bloated and distorted base	eelworm
	Bulbs splitting	faulty growing conditions
ROTTING	Going soft at top of bulb	neck rot
	Leeks rotting at soil level, pink discolouration present	foot rot
	Soft rot at side with blue–green fungus	blue mould
	Soft, smelly rot, mainly at side	bacterial rot
	White mould present at base	white rot

LEAVES

DISCOLOURED	Bright orange spots present	rust
	Brown spotting with grey mould coating on spring onions	grey mould
	Dark strips under scales bursting to reveal black mass of spores	smut
	Dying from tips with fine downy fungal covering	downy mildew
	Silvery streaking down the leaves	thrips
	Tips of leek leaves becoming water-soaked then white and withering	white tip
	Yellow streaks on leaves of shallots and onions	shallot virus yellows
EATEN	Onion and leek leaves holed and eaten	leek moth
TWISTED	Bloated and crumpled	eelworm

PLANTS

	Onions with thick necks	faulty growing conditions
	Running to seed	bolting

BACTERIAL ROT A soft rotting of onions occurs in storage due to attack by the bacterium, *Erwinia carotovora* var. *carotovora*, and other bacteria, resulting in the tissue becoming soft and foul-smelling. Bacterial attack often follows damage by other agencies, and particularly injury during harvesting.
Control: Dry the onions off thoroughly after harvest and handle carefully. If

making into ropes for hanging, ensure the old leaves are thoroughly dry before tying them in. Store in a cool, frost-free place, examine at regular intervals and remove any showing signs of rot.

BLUE MOULD Blue mould is a fungal disease caused by *Penicillium* spp. Like bacterial rots, blue mould is more common on onions damaged by other agencies, and diseased bulbs develop round tufts of blue-green fungus.
Control: Treat as for bacterial rot, *above*.

BOLTING Bolting is used to describe the production of a flowering stem which will then often prevent formation of an onion bulb or a decent leek stem. Bolting can be due to shortage of water, planting too early, or onion sets being stored at incorrect temperature prior to planting.
Control: Prepare the soil well by incorporating plenty of manure or compost to help conserve moisture. Cut off flowering stems as soon as they are seen (but not in the case of chives, where flowering is normal) and, should a harvestable crop be produced, use as soon as possible without attempting any long storage.

DOWNY **MILDEW** Onion downy mildew, *Peronospora destructor*, attacks onions and shallots and has also been found on Egyptian 'tree' onions. Attacks are worst in wet years, but downy mildew can also be a problem in dry years in the more humid areas. Pale spots appear on the foliage and this becomes covered with a fine, felted fungal coating. Spores from there spread the disease further and the infection enters the soil where it can persist for four or more years. Infected bulbs will rot in store.
Control: Wherever possible, grow onions on well-drained soil where there

is good circulation of air, and follow a three or four year rotation to keep one year's crop away from where the previous crop was grown (*see Crop rotation, pp. viii–ix*). Dig up and burn any diseased plants found, then spray the remaining, unaffected plants with a mancozeb or copper fungicide to protect against attack. Where the disease has been troublesome in previous years, spray new crops as a routine before any disease is seen.

EELWORM Onion eelworm, *Ditylenchus dipsaci*, is a member of a very widespread type of pest, recorded as affecting over 400 different plant species. On onions, it causes the leaves to become puckered and bloated. The bulbs may crack or split and little further growth is made once the attack is established. If the attack comes late in the season a bulb may be produced but it is likely to be split and will be infective in store so the eelworms will continue to breed and spread.
Control: Bulbs suspected of being infested with eelworms should not be stored. Onion eelworm can attack many other vegetables and so infested onions are best dug up and burned. Brassicas are not attacked by onion eelworms, however, so could be grown in soil suspected of carrying such infection in the course of a three or four year rotation (*see Crop rotation, pp. xvi–xxi*). No chemical controls exist.

FAULTY **GROWING CONDITIONS** Planting too early, as mentioned above, can result in the plants bolting, or running up to flower in the first year rather than in the second, as can very dry growing conditions. Heavy rains following a dry period can cause the bulbs to split at the base, while over-wet and lush conditions may result in bull neck, in which onions grow with very thick necks and an attendant poor storage ability.

Control: All these growing problems can be overcome or reduced by thorough soil preparation before planting, incorporating sufficient well-rotted manure or compost to act as a reservoir of moisture in dry spells and as a sponge in wet weather. To prevent bull neck, avoid an excess of rich manure or over-fertilizing.

FOOT ROT Foot rot of leeks is due to attack by *Fusarium culmorum*, a fungus that causes the outer leaves to rot at soil level. There is a pink or red coloration of the affected tissue and the rot may spread gradually into the centre of the leeks. Plants wilt and may die. Foot rot is worst in hot, warm weather.

Control: Foot rot is usually only a problem when leeks are grown on the same site year after year so a normal rotation should prevent attacks (*see Crop rotation, pp. xvi–xxi*). If an attack does occur, remove and burn all infected plants.

GREY MOULD Grey mould, *Botrytis cinerea*, can attack spring onions during wet winter weather, resulting in oval white spots, often with a water-soaked margin, towards the leaf tips. Other diseases can be involved including *Sclerotinia* (*Botrytis*) *squamosa* and *Sclerotinia* (*Botrytis*) *porri*. In milder, damp weather the typical, grey, mouldy fungal growth appears on the spots. Growth can be checked and plants are made rather unappetising by the damage.

Control: Sprays of sulphur, benomyl or carbendazim should be effective in controlling grey mould.

LEEK MOTH Leek moth, *Acrolepiopsis assectella*, feeds mainly on leeks, but onions, shallots and garlic can also be attacked. The caterpillars mine in the growing points and then eat through the young, folded leaves resulting in a shothole effect when the leaves unfold. In the case of onions and shallots the caterpillars feed within the hollow leaves. There are three generations per year and plants may be killed by attacks in late summer.

Control: Remove and burn old and dead leaves on which the pest may be pupating. Deep digging and regular cultivations will also be helpful by disturbing or killing the pupating stage. Treatment of the plot with a soil insecticide should also prove effective.

NECK ROT Neck rot is caused by *Botrytis allii*, a fungus that attacks large bulb onions as well as pickling varieties, sometimes causing considerable losses in store. Losses of 50 per cent were reported in the early 1970s in Britain. There is often no sign of the damage to come when onions are lifted in autumn for storage, but a softening of the tissue in the neck of the bulb is evident two to three months later. Under the bulb scales will be found masses of hard, black resting bodies of the fungus, known as sclerotia. The fungus moves vertically through the bulb until the rot is complete, when the bulbs will become dry. Leeks are largely immune from attack but shallots and garlic can suffer the same damage.

Control: Infection may be present on the seed coat, so buy new seed each year from a reputable source, requesting fungicide-treated seeds if the disease has been a problem previously. Alternatively, dust seed and sets with benomyl before planting. As harvest time approaches, do not cut off or forcibly bend over the tops of onions but let them die down naturally. When lifting, discard any bulbs with a softening of the neck and dry thoroughly before storing in a frost-free place (the infection cannot spread through the dry tissue at the neck of a properly dried bulb). Follow a crop rotation to avoid spread from old crop residues in the soil (*see Crop rotation, pp. viii–ix*).

ONION FLY Onion fly, *Delia antiqua*, attacks onions, leeks and shallots, with early summer being the worst time for damage. The adult, which looks rather like the common housefly, lays eggs in late spring on the leaves and necks of the young plants or on the soil near to the plants. The maggots hatch a few days later and burrow into the plants to feed. When fully fed after three weeks feeding, the maggots will be around 8mm (⅓in) long and they leave the plants to pupate in the soil. There will then be a second generation and, in some years, a third one.

The maggots bore through the scales causing a wilting of the leaves and as many as 30 maggots can be found in a single bulb. Heavy infestation levels result in the bulb rotting in the soil before harvest, but lightly infested ones may appear sound until they are cut or until rots take over, having gained entry as a result of the damage caused by the maggots. The related bean seed fly, *Delia platura*, causes similar damage although attacks by this insect start slightly earlier so seedlings are more likely to be attacked and killed.
Control: Protect plants from attack by these pests by treating the soil with chlorpyrifos/diazinon, or pirimiphos-methyl insecticide.

RUST Leek rust, *Puccinia allii*, is mainly found on leeks although onions, chives and garlic are also susceptible. Infected plants develop oval pustules on the foliage on which the orange spores appear. Rust attack looks quite serious although there is actually very little effect on cropping. Wet weather is a predisposing factor to attack.
Control: Crop rotation will help by isolating older, possibly infected plants from the new seedlings (*see Crop rotation, pp. viii–ix*). Balancing any tendency to lush, excess growth by an application of sulphate of potash may reduce the chances of attack, and a few protective sprays with copper or mancozeb fungicide would be worthwhile where the disease has been a problem previously.

SHALLOT VIRUS YELLOWS This virus disease causes a yellow streaking in the first leaves to appear from infected shallot bulbs and similar damage can also occasionally be seen on onions. Later leaves are more yellow, crinkled and sometimes flattened and the plants may collapse. The disease is spread by aphids as they feed, so healthy seed-raised plants can be infected by aphids previously feeding on infected material.
Control: Remove and burn infected plants. Where an attack has occurred, purchase healthy sets the following year from a reliable supplier rather than saving any of your own shallots for planting.

SMUT Onion smut fungus, *Urocystis cepulae*, is a seed and soil-borne disease that can be very serious in its effect. It can attack both bulb and spring onions as well as leeks, shallots, chives and garlic. Infection spreads throughout the plant causing dark grey stripes to appear. The striped areas then burst open to reveal masses of black powdery spores. These contaminate the soil for some years. Legislation prevents the sale of infected plant material in Britain.

Control: Grow seedlings in a seed bed where no infection has been detected in previous years. Collect up and burn all infected and suspect plant material and follow a three or four year rotation to avoid most of the threat of soil-borne infection (*see Crop rotation, pp. viii–ix*). No chemical control for garden use exists although seed suppliers can be relied upon to supply clean seed.

THRIPS The onion thrips, *Thrips tabaci*, can be found on onions and leeks in large numbers during heavy, humid weather. The small, thin black insects, orange in the larval stages, puncture plant cells as they feed, leaving silvery streaks and stripes. Distortion and stunting of growth can follow a severe attack. The onion thrips is also a major pest of greenhouse plants and spreads the spotted wilt virus.

Control: Spray at the first sign of silvering with fatty acids, permethrin or pyrethrins and repeat as necessary.

WHITE ROT White rot is caused by the fungus, *Sclerotium cepivorum*, which attacks all kinds of onions as well as leeks, garlic and shallots. Attack results in a fluffy white mould developing over the base of the plant and the death of roots and leaves. Black resting bodies, known as sclerotia, appear in the white mould and these fall into the soil where they survive to infect subsequent crops, and losses of 90 per cent of crop have been experienced. Attacked plants often rot due to bacterial infection of the damaged tissue, giving the whole plant a foul smell.

Control: Remove and burn infected plants together with some of the surrounding soil and follow a three or four year crop rotation system. Raise plants in trays of proprietary seed compost to ensure a clean start.

WHITE TIP White tip, caused by the fungus *Phytophthora porri*, is a local problem with leeks. The leaf tips become waterlogged and then die back becoming pale and papery. Affected leaves usually rot down to soil level, and growth and cropping are reduced. Damage is evident by late summer and in autumn.

Control: Collect and burn all diseased plants residues; do not dig in or compost. Follow a regular crop rotation (*see Crop rotation, pp. viii–ix*). Applications of copper fungicide may protect plants from attack.

VEGETABLES 6

POTATOES

ROOTS	Small white, then brown, half-pinhead sized cysts	*potato cyst eelworm*

STEM	Blackening and rotting	blackleg
	White crusting on stem, dark canker below soil level	stem canker
LEAVES	Green pests clustered on leaves and growing points	aphids
	Leaf rolling, spots and mosaic patterns	virus
	Pale brown markings on leaves from early summer, plants dying back	blight
	Pale brown scorching of leaf edges early in growing season	frost
	Pale green or yellow discoloration with small dark spots along veins	manganese deficiency
	Red and black larvae or orange and black beetles feeding	Colorado beetle
	Small dark spots and tattered holes	capsid bug
	Yellowing, and later browning, between veins	magnesium deficiency
TUBERS EXTERNAL SIGNS	Clusters of small raised spots	skin spot
	Dark spots with star-like outline	common scab
	Round dark spots with raised edge, may also be outgrowths of distorted flesh	powdery scab
	Warty outgrowths	wart disease
TUBERS INTERNAL SIGNS	Brown arcs seen in cut tuber	spraing
	Centre hollow, often small potatoes budding out from main tuber	secondary growth
	Irregular, large cavities	slug
	Rings of dark spots just under skin, seen when cut across tuber	net necrosis
	Rusty brown spots throughout flesh	internal rust spot
	Small entry hole, larger cavities inside	millipede
	Small, round holes and cavities	wireworm
	Various rots, soft or firm, pale or coloured, during storage	storage rots

APHIDS (GREENFLY AND BLACKFLY)

At least six different species of aphid can attack potatoes, with the peach–potato aphid, *Myzus persicae*, being the most common. Severe aphid infestations can have a serious effect on crop yields, particularly when attack coincides with the start of tuber development. Aphids can also spread a number of viruses and some of these affect cropping, although viruses are not normally a problem unless the tubers from infected plants are used as seed potatoes. Aphid attacks on the sprouts of potatoes set up to chit before planting can result in virus infection in the seed. Where leaf roll or potato virus Y are involved, growth and cropping will be poor in the year of infection.

Control: Spray with fatty acids, dimethoate, heptenophos, pirimicarb or pyrethrins and repeat as necessary. Where ladybirds, hoverflies or lacewings are present and feeding on the aphids but are failing to keep up with the spread of the pests, use pirimicarb which is virtually aphid-specific. Do not save home-grown potatoes to use as seed for the next year, particularly when aphids have attacked the crop.

BLACKLEG Blackleg is a bacterial disease caused by *Erwinia carotovora* var. *atroseptica*. Attack occurs in late spring and causes the foliage to turn yellow prior to the plants dying. A blackening of the stems will be seen at soil level and, if the stems are cut across, a black discolouration of the water-conducting tissue will be visible, in line with the 'wings' on the stem edges. The blackening of the stems may continue into any potato tubers that are produced. Blackleg disease is spread on infected seed potatoes and the problem is at its worst in wet soil. Potatoes from infected plants do not store satisfactorily.

Control: Dig out and burn affected plants and then harvest and store in dry conditions any potatoes that are produced by neighbouring plants. Do not used any home-produced potatoes as seed for the following year. When planting, do not cut the seed potatoes.

BLIGHT Potato blight, *Phytophthora infestans*, is a very damaging fungal disease that can wipe out the crop in a very short time. It is a matter of historical record that in the mid 1840s the Irish potato crop was devastated for several years in succession by potato blight and this resulted in the death, or emigration to avoid starvation, of millions of people. The introduction in 1885 of the copper fungicide, Bordeaux Mixture, altered the situation dramatically.

Potato blight first shows as a browning of the leaflets followed in rapid succession by the whole leaf and then the entire plants turning brown and dying.

The disease is encouraged by warm, damp weather and attacks can be expected following a period of two days with a temperature not less than 10°C (50°F) and a relative humidity of not less than 90 per cent for at least 11 hours each day. Infection from the leaves passes into the tubers where there is a superficial browning but no soft rotting. Infected tubers produce blighted shoots which spread the disease to the next year's crop. There are considerable varietal differences in susceptibility to blight on the leaves and on the tubers (*see Resistant varieties, pp. x–xiii*).

Control: Growing less susceptible varieties will help to keep blight in check. In the UK the usual times for attack to occur are known for each region of the country and protective applications of copper or mancozeb from that time will prevent infection. It will also help to keep potatoes well earthed up to stop any blight spores reaching the tubers, and the tops should be cut off and composted or burned before the tubers are lifted. This is again to keep the blight spores and the tubers apart.

When lifting the crop, remove every potato including the very tiny ones and dispose of unwanted ones safely, not by composting; any 'groundkeepers' left in the soil will sprout in the next year and could be carrying the blight fungus.

CAPSID BUG Potato capsid, *Calocoris norvegicus*, and other capsids bugs feed on the leaves, producing small dead spots. As the leaves expand, the dead spots open out to give a tattered look to the foliage. Severe damage may result in shoots withering and dying.

Control: Where necessary, spray with fatty acids, dimethoate, permethrin or pyrethrins, treating the soil as well as the foliage to catch the pests as they drop off the leaves.

COLORADO BEETLE Colorado beetles, *Leptinotarsa decemlineata*, are not yet established in Britain or Ireland but have spread through much of Europe. Both the yellow and black-striped adult beetles and the red and black larvae feed actively on potato foliage and extreme vigilance is necessary to keep the beetle out of the UK. Any suspect beetles found in Britain should be put in a secure container and sent, with details of where they were found, to the Ministry of Agriculture, Fisheries and Food, Harpenden Laboratory, Hatching Green, Harpenden, Herts, AL5 2DB, for official examination and action if confirmed.

COMMON SCAB Common scab, caused by *Streptomyces scabies* and other Streptomyces species, is a very common ailment of garden potatoes. Smallish dark spots with spiked edges develop on the skins, the spots being composed of brown corky tissue. The damage is superficial but unsightly. Common scab is worst on potatoes grown in light, sandy soils, in dry seasons and in soils lacking in organic matter. Liming increases common scab attack but there are some varieties with a degree of resistance to the problem (*see Resistant varieties, pp. x–xiii*).
Control: Grow resistant varieties and add plenty of organic matter when preparing the soil for potatoes. Fresh lawn mowings can be used if there is not enough compost available and one average barrow load to 4 square metres ($4yd^2$) would be around the correct rate. Alternatively, or additionally on soils very short of organic matter, add fresh lawn mowings to the trench or to the planting holes, but take care not to use too much

or the grass may overheat and damage the potato seed. Do not use mowings from a lawn that has been treated with a lawn weedkiller.

FROST Potatoes are very susceptible to frost damage and even a mild frost can cause the leaflet edges to turn brown. Later, the tissue dies and the damaged leaves turn yellow and often die. In the case of a severe frost, the plants may be killed down to soil level, although replacement shoots soon appear.
Control: Keep early potatoes well earthed-up and when frost is forecast earth them up again to protect the shoots with a covering of soil. For later frost forecasts, when the haulm is too tall to earth up, protect the crop with a covering of woven fleece.

INTERNAL RUST SPOT Internal rust spots are visible when the potato tuber is cut across, the spots being 5mm (⅕in) or so across, rusty-brown in colour and randomly distributed.
Control: No specific causes have yet been determined, but the condition appears to be less of a problem where the potatoes are growing well and there is plenty of organic matter in the soil. The 'King Edward' potato seems less prone to internal rust spot damage than most other varieties.

MAGNESIUM DEFICIENCY Potatoes appear to have quite a large demand for magnesium and when insufficient is available the leaves develop the characteristic yellow areas between the veins. Magnesium is easily washed out of the soil in rainy weather, particularly from light soils deficient in organic matter, and it is also in short supply where excess potassium has been applied.

Control: Water the plants and the soil with a solution of Epsom Salts using 100g per 5l (4oz/1gall) of water plus a wetting agent.

MANGANESE DEFICIENCY A deficiency of manganese results in the leaves showing an interveinal yellowing with numerous dark spots alongside the veins. Manganese is often in short supply in poorly drained, alkaline and highly organic soils.
Control: Water plants and soil with a solution of manganese sulphate using 15g per 5l (½oz/1gall) of water plus a wetting agent.

MILLIPEDES The spotted millipede, *Blaniulus guttulatus*, is rarely a primary pest of the potato tuber but causes a great deal of damage by extending the injury started by wireworms or slugs. The pest is mainly white in colour with a double row of pink dots down its body. Each of the 50 or so body segments has two pairs of legs and the creature will curl up in spiral fashion when disturbed.
Control: Application of a soil insecticide for wireworm control should also take care of millipedes. Lift the crop as it matures rather than leaving the tubers in the soil where continuing damage can be done.

NET NECROSIS Net necrosis can be seen, when the potato tuber is cut across, as a double ring of black dots just under the skin. This pattern indicates that leaf roll virus was present in the parent plant.
Control: Do not use such potatoes as seed. Leaf roll is one of the aphid-spread viruses for which no control exists.

POTATO CYST EELWORM Two types of potato cyst eelworms,

Globodera rostochiensis and G. *pallida*, attack the roots and cause stunted, weak plants. Lower leaves wilt and die, followed by the rest of the plant. On the roots will be found the small cysts, each about 0.5mm (⅟₅₀in) in size, creamy-white or golden in colour, and which pass into the soil. The infestation can be spread in soil on boots and equipment or even in wind-blown soil.
Control: Follow a long crop rotation and should an attack be experienced, dig out the plants plus the soil surrounding the roots and burn (*see Crop rotation, pp. viii–ix*). The best control method is to concentrate on growing early varieties which often escape attack.

POWDERY SCAB Powdery scab is due to the fungus, *Spongospora subterranea*, and can be distinguished from common scab by the raised edges and the rounded shape of the lesions. Spores from the lesions pass into the soil where they can persist for many years and damage is more severe in heavy wet soils and cool weather. Outgrowths of canker-like tumours may occur with some varieties, notably 'Pentland Crown'. 'Cara', 'Maris Bard' and 'Estima' are all susceptible to powdery scab.
Control: Follow a long rotation and avoid susceptible varieties.

SECONDARY GROWTH Secondary growth arises typically when rainy weather occurs after the tubers have virtually finished their development. Potatoes develop hollow centres lined with dark, discoloured cells and numerous small potatoes may grow out from the sides of larger tubers.
Control: Lift the crop as soon as it is ready and store it in an airy, frost-free place.

SKIN SPOT Skin spot, due to *Polyscytalum pustulans*, is seen as a number of pimples over the surface of the tuber, each pimple generally being surrounded by a dark, sunken area. The condition gradually develops during storage. If planted, such potatoes may produce no shoots as the buds are often killed by the disease.
Control: Follow a four year (or longer) rotation, do not plant seed with any sign of skin spot (*see Crop rotation, pp. viii–ix*). Sprout tubers before planting to ensure the 'eyes' produce shoots.

SLUGS Various slug species can attack the potato crop but the most serious by far are the keeled slugs, *Milax* spp., and particularly *M. budapestensis*. Keeled slugs are grey or black in colour with a ridge (keel) along the back and *M. budapestensis* has an orange sole. Keeled slugs rarely come to the surface of the soil. They are able to eat their way into the potatoes in the ground and then hollow out the inside, sometimes assisted by millipedes.
Control: Considerable variation exists between potato varieties regarding their susceptibility to slug attack (*see Resistant varieties, pp. x–xiii*). Where slug attack is expected, typically on heavy soil and in wet regions, grow only resistant varieties. Dig up the crop as soon as it is ready for harvest; it has been found that slug damage can increase 10 fold in one month in autumn. Existing slug populations can be controlled by using the beneficial nematode *Phasmarhabditis hermaphrodita*, keeping the soil moist after watering on the nematode suspended in water (*see Biological control, pp. xvi–xxi*). Ideally carry out this treatment before planting.

SPRAING The name 'spraing' is a dialect word meaning a stripe or streak and is used to describe the arcs of brown discolouration seen in the cut potato. 'Pentland Dell' potato is particularly prone to this condition. The markings occur when the potato is carrying tobacco rattle virus infection or, in the case of a small number of varieties, mop top virus infection. Tobacco rattle virus is spread in the soil by eelworms and mop top virus by the powdery scab fungus. Infected plants may produce stunted shoots and lower yields.
Control: Rotations and regular cultivations, plus measures to control powdery scab (*see above*), will help to keep spraing at a low level.

STEM CANKER Stem canker is caused by the fungus *Rhizoctonia solani*, and shows up as a cankering of the stem bases, generally covered with a white mould. When the canker girdles the stems the plants die. The fungus also causes a brown to black superficial marking on the tubers, referred to as black scurf, and badly affected potatoes may not produce sprouts. Stem canker is most common on light soils and in cold, dry weather.
Control: Chit the seed potatoes before planting to eliminate any that do not produce sprouts. Add organic matter to the soil and water well in dry weather. Practise crop rotation as the infection is both soil and seed borne (*see Crop rotation, pp. viii–ix*).

STORAGE ROTS Various rots can attack potatoes in store, each producing its own characteristic type of damage. Dry rot, caused by *Fusarium* spp., causes the tubers to shrink, starting at one end, and in time pink, white or blue pustules develop on the surface, while inside the cavities are filled with a fluffy mould in the same range of colours. Pink rot,

Phytophthora erythroseptica, spreads from the heel end (the end that was attached to the plant) and gradually spreads throughout the flesh turning it pink when exposed to the air. The colour changes through purple to brown and there is typically a vinegar-like smell. Watery wound rot, caused by *Pythium ultimum* attacks where the tuber has been damaged during lifting or by careless handling. The skin stays intact but inside the flesh becomes soft and wet and is soon invaded by bacteria, resulting in a smelly rot. Gangrene is due to *Phoma solanicola* f. *foveata* and first appears as irregular, dark sunken areas on the surface of the potato. Internal cavities develop, coated with a yellow or grey mould and black fungal bodies, about the size of a pin-head, are produced both internally and externally.

Control: Many of the rots start in areas of the tubers damaged during lifting and then develop later during storage. Most of the fungi are present in the soil, so a combination of careful handling and crop rotation will help to keep rots to a minimum.

VIRUS There is a very wide range of different viruses that can affect potato plants, most of them transmitted by aphids as they feed on the leaves. Symptoms and damage are usually most severe if infected potatoes tubers are planted and grown on, and such plants will then act as carriers from which aphids can pick up and spread the infection.

Control: No direct control exists although control of aphids may help a little. When harvesting the crop, try to ensure that every single potato is removed from the soil, no matter how small. This will help to prevent any virus-infected 'groundkeepers' from carrying the infection over to the following year. Follow a four year rotation and dig up any potatoes that come up in the wrong plot (*see Crop rotation, pp. viii–ix*).

WART DISEASE Wart disease, caused by the fungus *Synchytrium endobioticum*, is virtually a thing of the past now as a result of legislation and the development of immune varieties. Land may still be infective, however, from previous outbreaks of the disease and cases of a persistence of 30 years are known. Infected tubers develop cauliflower-like warty outgrowths and from these the infection passes into the soil.

Control: Grow only varieties stated to be immune to wart disease. In the UK, any outbreaks must be reported to the Ministry of Agriculture.

WIREWORM Wireworms, *Agriotes* spp., can cause severe damage to potatoes by boring into the tubers and the damage is then often extended by millipedes (*see above*). The orange or yellow larvae feed for up to five years before being fully fed and pupating to emerge as click beetles. Wireworms are typically pests of established grassland so they can be expected to attack potatoes when the crop is grown on land previously put down to grass.

Control: Treat the soil before planting with chlorpyrifos/diazinon or pirimiphos-methyl. Lift the tubers as soon as they are ready to harvest. Where large numbers of wireworms are seen during soil preparation, it is best to grow only early potatoes in the first year; these are less subject to severe attack than main-crop varieties.

VEGETABLES 7

OTHER ROOT CROPS INCLUDING BEETROOT, CARROT, JERUSALEM ARTICHOKE, PARSNIP, RADISH, SWEDE, TURNIP

ROOTS	Cankers on shoulders of parsnips	*canker*
	Dark or violet coating over any type of root crop	*violet root rot*
	Discolouration in centre of beetroot	*heart rot*
	Discolouration in centre of swede	*brown heart*
	Eaten on outside, any crop	*slugs*
	Galls on turnip, swede, radish	*club root*
	Mining of carrot and parsnip	*carrot fly*
	Mining of radish, swede, turnip	*cabbage root fly*
	Soft rotting, especially of swede and turnip	*soft rot*
	Splitting of roots, any crop	*faulty growing conditions*
	Tunnelled into by caterpillars	*cutworm, swift moth*
LEAVES	Blister-like mines, beetroot, parsnip	*leaf miner*
	Discolouration of carrot foliage	*motley dwarf disease*
	Green or grey pests present	*aphids*
	Pits in leaves of radish, swede, turnip	*flea beetle*
	Spots on beetroot leaves	*leaf spot*
	White powdery coating on swede and turnip	*powdery mildew*
GENERAL GROWTH	Running to seed	*faulty growing conditions*
	Stunted, especially carrots	*virus*

APHIDS (GREENFLY AND BLACKFLY)
Aphids are a common and widespread problem. Various aphids attack the different root crops, probably the most damaging being the mealy cabbage aphid on swede and turnip and the willow-carrot aphid, which is responsible for spreading virus infection to carrot and parsnip (*see Motley dwarf disease, below*). Attacks on the leaves and at the growing points will distort growth and a severe attack on young plants can be lethal.

Control: Spray at the first sign of attack with fatty acids, dimethoate, heptenophos, pirimicarb or pyrethrins and repeat if necessary.

Main aphid species:
- Mealy cabbage aphid, *Brevicoryne brassicae*, is a grey, mealy-covered insect which is very unsightly as well as damaging. It attacks swede and turnip, covering the leaves and growing points with a sticky, mealy coating. Populations nearly always build up rapidly, requiring prompt action.
- Willow-carrot aphid, *Caraviella aegopodii*, feeds on carrot and parsnip and infects the plants with two viruses, namely carrot motley dwarf and carrot red leaf. Together, the two viruses cause carrot motley dwarf disease (*see below*).

BROWN HEART Brown heart is a condition found in swedes after harvest, although in severe cases the leaves may be curled and easily snapped. The centres of the roots show a clear brown or grey area, seen as concentric rings in cross section and as an elongated area when the root is cut lengthways. Brown heart is caused by a deficiency of boron in the soil, and affected roots have a bitter taste and are rather woody when cooked.

Control: Treat the soil with borax (sodium tetraborate) before sowing using 1–3g per square metre (⅓₀–⅒₀oz per yd²), depending on the degree of severity. Boron shortage is more likely on soils with a high lime content (either naturally or following lime application) so use the higher rate where this occurs. Dissolve the borax in a convenient volume of water to ensure even application. Dry weather also increases the chances of boron shortage, so water well in dry weather.

CABBAGE ROOT FLY Cabbage root fly, *Delia radicum*, can be quite a serious pest on radish, swede and turnip, the small white maggots eating the smaller roots and root hairs as well as boring into the flesh. There are two and sometimes three generations of the pest each year.

Control: Protect the plants by growing them under a fine net covering to exclude the egg-laying adult flies. The flies are on the wing first in mid- to late spring, in the UK around the time that the cow parsley is in flower in local field edges or roadsides. Alternatively, treat the soil with chlorpyrifos/diazinon or pirimiphos-methyl.

CANKER Canker occurs on the shoulders of parsnip roots as a brown discolouration and cracking. The fungus *Intersonilia perplexans* is generally found to be involved, but other factors often combine to make the problem more troublesome. Such factors include wet weather following dry, attack by carrot fly, high levels of nitrogen and low levels of lime.

Control: Grow canker resistant varieties (*see Resistant varieties, pp. x–xiii*), prepare the soil well avoiding excess application of nitrogen-based fertlizer, and apply lime if necessary to bring the soil to around the neutral point of pH 7.

CARROT FLY Maggots of carrot fly, *Psila rosae*, feed on the surface of carrot and parsnip roots and then bore more deeply into the flesh of these vegetables. Typically the mines develop a rusty appearance, and early and severe attacks can ruin the crop. The first batches of eggs are laid in late spring and early summer with the second generation of adult flies appearing in late summer to lay more batches of eggs.

Control: Sowing the seed later than normal, around the time the first eggs are being laid in late spring, will avoid most of the damage from the first generation of carrot fly, as the maggots will hatch before the carrot seedlings are large enough to be attacked. Covering the crop with fine netting in mid-spring will exclude the egg-laying adults, and maincrop carrots should be lifted and stored as soon as they are ready to avoid losses from second generation maggots. The varieties of carrot 'Ingot' and 'Sytan' have a reduced susceptibility to attack and these should be grown as an additional safety measure. For chemical control, treat the soil with chlorpyrifos/diazinon or pirimiphos-methyl before sowing.

CLUB ROOT Club root disease, caused by the fungus *Plasmodiophora brassicae*, attacks swede and turnip resulting in tumour-like outgrowths from the roots and an internal mottling of the flesh. Infected roots generally rot away into a smelly mess. Club root fungus is encouraged by wet, acid soils and can be spread in soil on tools or boots and on the roots of seedlings from infected soil.

Control: Check the pH (acidity/alkalinity) of the soil using a meter or reliable soil-testing kit and add lime if necessary to bring the soil to the alkaline side of neutral before sowing the crop. Follow a three or four year rotation and include brassicas and other cabbage family plants, which are also affected by club root, in a similar rotation (*see Crop rotation, pp. xiii–ix*). Grow the swede variety 'Marian' which is resistant to club root.

CUTWORM Various moths in the Noctuid family lay eggs in or on the soil and these hatch into soil-living caterpillars known as cutworms. Typical of the Noctuid family is the turnip moth, *Agrotis segetum*, which bores into the edible roots of turnip and swede. The caterpillar is 3.5cm (1½in) long when fully fed, grey to brown in colour with darkish line patterns. Smaller plants will be eaten off at soil level and larger roots tunnelled. Attacks are worst in dry years and on light soils.

Control: Treat the soil with the beneficial nematode *Steinernema carpocapsae* (*see Biological control, pp. xvi–xxi*), or use chlorpyrifos/diazinon when planting or sowing or pirimiphos-methyl when the damage is seen.

FAULTY GROWING CONDITIONS Bolting of beetroot is one of the common signs of a hot, dry soil and one which could be improved by adding compost and applying more water in dry weather. Other root crops respond to poor, dry growing conditions by becoming hardened on the outside and then splitting, either when heavy rain falls or when water is given in quantity by the gardener.

Control: Work in plenty of organic matter to the soil when preparing the site but do not use fresh manure as this would cause the roots to fork. During dry spells apply water generously to reach down into the soil.

FLEA BEETLE Various flea beetles, *Phyllotreta* spp., attack radish, swede and turnip and the mangold flea beetle, *Chaetocnema concinna*, attacks beetroot. Small, rounded depressions are formed in the leaves where the pests have fed and these areas become larger and may fall out as holes as the leaves expand. The adult flea beetles are mainly dark with two yellow stripes along the wing cases on the back. Seedlings and young plants are particularly prone to damage from this pest and serious harm can set the plants back considerably.

Control: After emergence of the seedlings, dust soil and plants with a rotenone dust, repeating as necessary at weekly intervals.

HEART ROT Heart rot of beetroot is due to a deficiency of boron and shows up as dark rings inside the root as well as cankers on the outside.

Control: Treat the soil with boron as for brown heart (*see above*).

LEAF MINER Beetroot leaves are attacked by the beet leaf miner, *Pegomya hyoscyami*, better known to some gardeners as mangold fly. Several of the larvae live together in blister mines and the affected areas shrivel and die. Attacks early in the season can be quite damaging, although attacks later in summer are of little consequence.

Control: Pick off infested leaves or squash larvae within the leaves. For severe, early infestations, spray with dimethoate.

LEAF SPOT Beetroot leaves develop a brown spotting due to attack by the fungus, *Cercospora beticola* and sometimes by *Ramularia beticola*. In time, the centres of the spots dry and fall out. High temperatures and high humidity encourage the diseases.

Control: Space the seeds well when sowing and thin out seedlings to allow air to circulate, thus reducing local humidity. Pick off badly affected leaves and collect up and burn crop residues at the end of cropping. Follow a crop rotation to avoid new seedlings picking up any disease from infected crop residues (*see Crop rotation, pp. viii–ix*).

MOTLEY DWARF DISEASE Two viruses, carrot mottle virus and carrot red leaf virus, combine to produce the carrot motley dwarf disease. The viruses are spread by the willow–carrot aphid (*see above*) and cause stunting and twisting of the leaves, followed by a change of colour from green to yellow and red. Very poor crops of carrots are produced from infected plants.

Control: There is no control, so destroy infected plants. Spraying with dimethoate or heptenophos to kill the aphids may help, although not much feeding is needed to transmit the infection.

POWDERY MILDEW Powdery mildew of crucifers, *Erisiphe cruciferarum* (*see*

Powdery mildew, p.117), is particularly damaging on swede and turnip. Badly affected plants have leaves completely covered in the white mildew deposit and soon turn yellow, wither and die. Roots can also crack under mildew attack, and this leaf and root damage may let in soft rot bacteria (*see below*). Crops growing in dry weather and on light soils are most prone to attack.

Control: Good soil preparation to incorporate sufficient water-retaining organic matter, together with watering in dry weather will help to delay or even prevent powdery mildew attack. For existing attacks, spray with a sulphur-based fungicide.

SLUGS All root crops can be invaded by keeled slugs, *Milax* spp., which bore into the flesh. *M. budapestensis* is one of the most damaging species and can be recognised by the black body with a ridge or keel on the back and an orange sole. Keeled slugs rarely come to the surface of the soil, and so are not controlled by normal slug pellets.

Control: Dig up the crops as soon as they are ready; the longer they stay in the ground after that time, the greater the damage that will occur. To control keeled (and other) slugs, treat the soil with the beneficial nematode *Phasmarhabditis hermaphrodita* (*see Biological control, pp. xvi–xxi*), and keep the soil moist after application. The nematodes carry a bacterium into the slugs where it attacks the body tissue. Bacteria and nematodes build up within the slugs and the next generation of the nematode leaves to penetrate further slugs, carrying the bacteria within their bodies.

SOFT ROT Most root crops can suffer from a soft rotting of the tissue but swede and turnips are more commonly attacked by the bacterium *Erwinia carotovora* var. *carotovora*. Attack can occur while the crop is growing or later, during storage. The outer flesh remains firm while the inner flesh becomes a greyish-white, putrid mass. Many of the attacks start at points of injury caused by soil or foliar pests or by hoeing, and damage can also spread down from the crown to the root. Leaves wilting after severe powdery mildew attack may also allow the bacterium into the crown.

Control: Take measures to prevent damage from soil or foliar pests and diseases. As soft rot is also more troublesome in over-manured, wet soil, prepare the soil with these factors in mind, and follow a set crop rotation to reduce the risk of further attack (*see Crop rotation, pp. viii–ix*).

SWIFT MOTH Caterpillars of the ghost swift moth, *Hepialus humuli*, and the garden swift moth, *H. lupulinus*, bore into underground storage organs, creating tunnels in which they live. Jerusalem artichokes can be very severely damaged in this way. The translucent larvae have brown heads and wriggle backwards quite violently when disturbed. Ghost swift larvae may feed for three years before pupating, while the garden swift larvae usually feed for two years.

Control: Regular hoeing often disturbs or exposes the caterpillars. Otherwise, an application of chlorpyrifos/diazinon insecticide at planting time will clear up any resident swift moth caterpillar populations.

VIOLET ROOT ROT Violet root rot, *Helicobasidium purpureum*, is a soil-borne disease that can attack all underground plant parts. Roots become covered with red-violet strands of the fungus and rot, while the above-ground parts of the plants turn yellow and die prematurely. Infection persists in the soil and the disease can also attack a wide range of weeds.

Control: Dig out and burn all infected plants and where a severe attack has occurred, avoid growing any root crops for a few years. Elsewhere, follow a set crop rotation to avoid the disease building up (*see Crop rotation, pp. xvi–ix*).

VIRUS In addition to carrot motley dwarf virus on carrot, turnip mosaic and cauliflower mosaic viruses affect swede and turnip and yellows virus can infect beet. The virus responsible for yellows is common on sugar beet so gardens in rural areas where sugar beet is grown are at risk. Leaf yellowing and spotting, leaf distortion, paleness of veins and poor cropping are the end results of infection.

Control: There is no control for virus, but applications of dimethoate or heptenophos systemic insecticides to control aphids may help to prevent infection. Virus-infected plants should be removed and safely disposed of, preferably burned.

VEGETABLES 8

VEGETABLE FRUITS INCLUDING COURGETTE, GHERKIN, GLOBE
ARTICHOKE, MARROW, MELON, PUMPKIN, RIDGE CUCUMBER,
SWEET CORN, OUTDOOR TOMATO

SEEDS AND ROOTS	Lack of germination	*faulty growing conditions*
	Roots and stem bases rotting	*root and foot rot*
	Sweet corn seeds taken from soil	*mice*
	Seeds rotting in soil	*seed rots*
STEMS	Eaten, slime trails present	*slugs and snails*
	Green pests clustered on stems	*aphids*
	Grey fungal growths, mainly at leaf joints	*grey mould*
	Sweet corn shoots dying, side shoots growing out	*frit fly*
	Tomato stems blackening and dying from midsummer	*tomato blight*
	White fungal coating on cucumber and relatives	*Sclerotinia disease*
LEAVES	Courgette and relatives distorted with small holes	*capsid bug*
	Courgette and relatives distorted with yellow mottling	*virus*
	Courgette and relatives, white powdery deposit over foliage	*mildew*
	Distorted leaves with frilly edging	*hormone weedkiller contamination*
	Green pests clustered under leaves	*aphids*
	Tomato leaves blackening and dying	*tomato blight*
	Tomato leaves with mottling and spotting	*virus*
	Yellow patches between veins	*magnesium deficiency*
	White insects flying off when disturbed	*whitefly*
FRUITS	Black spots on tomatoes	*blossom end rot*
	Cucumbers shrivelling	*faulty growing conditions*
	Fruits rotting, covered with furry fungal growths	*grey mould*
	Lack of fruits	*poor pollination, faulty growing conditions*
	Swellings on sweet corn cobs, bursting to release black spores	*smut*
	Tomatoes splitting	*faulty growing conditions*

APHIDS (GREENFLY AND BLACK-FLY) Various species of aphid attack cucumbers and other cucurbits (courgette, gherkin, marrow and melon) and also attack tomatoes, feeding on the sap and having the potential to transmit virus diseases.

Control: Where natural predators such as ladybirds, hoverflies and lacewings are not present or adequate, spray with bifenthrin, dimethoate, fatty acids, heptenophos, pirimicarb or pyrethrins.

BLOSSOM END ROT Blossom end rot is evident on tomatoes as a blackening of the fruit at the end furthest away from the stalk. It is more of a problem with tomatoes grown in the greenhouse but can occur outside when water supply is variable. The actual reason for blossom end rot is a deficiency of calcium but it is more commonly a lack of uptake rather than an actual deficiency in the soil.

Control: Ensure adequate water is available at all times. Should the condition develop, water leaves and soil with calcium nitrate solution, using 30g per 5l (1oz/1gall) of water. Repeat at weekly intervals in association with regular watering until the condition is cured.

CAPSID BUG The capsid bug *Lygocoris pabulinus* can be a major problem pest for courgettes and marrows. The pests puncture the leaf tissue to feed and each puncture point becomes a small, brown dead spot. As the leaves expand the dead areas open into holes, resulting in a tattered appearance. Capsids drop off the plants at the first hint of danger or disturbance, so are not often seen at work.

Control: Spray the soil under and around the plants and then up over the plants themselves to catch the capsids as they drop off the leaves as well as any remaining on the plants. Use bifenthrin, fatty acids, permethrin or pyrethrins and repeat as necessary.

FAULTY GROWING CONDITIONS A number of different disorders can be related to faulty growing conditions, particularly a lack of adequate or regular water. Seeds fail to germinate and flowers fail to set fruit following dry conditions, and fruits split following heavy rain after drought.

Control: Thorough soil preparation and incorporation of plenty of organic matter to even out water supplies will do much to prevent problems. If dry weather does prevail, applications of regular and adequate volumes of water will ensure steady growth.

FRIT FLY Frit fly, *Oscinella frit*, attacks sweet corn plants in the early stages of their growth and the larvae burrow in the stems. Often the main stem dies and weak side shoots may then be produced. Crops of cobs may fail to develop.

Control: Grow seedlings in pots of compost under cover and do not plant out until at least six leaves appear. At this stage, the plants are too advanced for frit fly to attack. Alternatively, dust the seedlings growing from seed sown outside with gamma-HCH dust.

GREY MOULD Any damaged tissue is likely to be attacked by the grey mould fungus, *Botrytis cinerea*. Particularly at risk are tomato or cucurbit stems damaged by leaf removal, tomato fruits split by rain and marrows and melons attacked by slugs.

Control: Avoid physical damage to the plants. If leaf removal is necessary, to increase air circulation through tomato plants for example, cut off cleanly with a very sharp knife. Should the disease occur, cut off all damaged tissue and apply a sulphur dust. Control slugs, snails and other damaging pests.

HORMONE WEEDKILLER CONTAMINATION
Contamination by lawn weedkillers of the hormone type, such as 2,4-D, dichlorprop, mecoprop and MCPA, can be extremely damaging to crops and particularly to tomatoes. Leaves are reduced to fern-like fronds, stems are twisted, fruits become malformed and elongated, and full of liquid instead of seeds and flesh.
Control: Only apply lawn weedkillers during windless days. It is virtually impossible to wash out every trace of weedkiller from cans or sprayers and just a few parts per million will result in severe symptoms on tomatoes. Keep separate equipment for weedkiller application and do not store such equipment, or bottles of weedkiller, in the greenhouse.

MAGNESIUM DEFICIENCY
Magnesium deficiency shows up as a yellowing of the leaves between the main veins and can be a problem with several different cucurbits and with tomatoes. If the deficiency is not corrected, the yellow areas turn brown and may die, and cropping is reduced. The symptoms start with the oldest leaves as magnesium is a mobile element, and the plants take it from the older leaves to supply the new.
Control: Water the leaves and soil with Epsom Salts (magnesium sulphate) using 100g per 5l (4oz/1gall) of water and repeat as necessary. When growing tomatoes always feed using a proprietary fertilizer with magnesium (Mg) listed in the analysis.

MICE
Mice are attracted to sweet corn seeds and they will sometimes also dig up and eat marrow and courgette seeds as well.
Control: The best way to prevent mice taking the seeds is to grow the plants in pots of compost indoors or in a greenhouse or cold frame. If using a greenhouse or cold frame, cover the pots with plastic or netting to keep mice out. Plant out when the seedlings are well grown. If sowing direct into the ground, firm the soil well and cover with prickly gorse or hawthorn twigs. Where mice are known to be a problem use mouse killer bait, suitably protected from non-target species under ridge tiles or in drain pipes.

POWDERY MILDEW
Powdery mildew, *Sphaerotheca fuligenea*, can attack all the cucumber family plants, covering the leaves with a dense white powder of spores. Badly infected plants dry up and stop producing fruit. The disease is usually more serious in dry years and on light soils.
Control: To try to avoid the disease in the first place, prepare the soil well before planting, incorporating plenty of water-absorbing organic matter, and then water as necessary in any prolonged dry spells. Should an attack occur, spray with sulphur or with the systemic fungicides benomyl or carbendazim.

ROOT AND FOOT ROTS
Numerous different diseases attack the fruiting vegetables included in this section, particularly if they are grown on the same sites each year. Fluctuating water supply, ranging from dry soil to near waterlogged conditions, is another factor which encourages these diseases. The fungi associated with root and stem base

rots include *Fusarium, Phytophthora, Pythium, Thanatephorus (Corticium)* and *Thielaviopsis*. Affected plants wilt and then the whole plant will topple.

Control: Follow a normal three or four year crop rotation or grow the crops in growing bags. Good soil preparation is also important, with organic matter incorporated into the soil to help even-out water availability. There is no really effective control as, once attacked, plants are likely to die quite rapidly. Watering the stem bases and soil around a few times after planting out using a copper fungicide should help to protect from attack.

SCLEROTINIA DISEASE Tomatoes, cucumbers and other plants can suffer attacks from the *Sclerotinia sclerotiorum* fungus. Infected plants develop a thick, white, felted covering over the stem bases and the plants soon shrivel and die. In the white coating will be found hard black fungal bodies; these are the sclerotia or resting stage of the disease and can remain dormant in the soil for several years.

Control: Dig up and burn affected plants, endeavouring to ensure that no sclerotia reach the ground. Follow a rotation to reduce chances of any build up of the disease (*see Crop rotation, pp. viii–ix*). There is no specific control, but watering the plants and the soil after planting out using a copper fungicide may be of help.

SEED ROTS When soil temperatures are low and seeds stay a long time in the soil before germination they may be attacked by pests or diseases causing them to rot.

Control: Quite a high proportion of the sweet corn seed supplied by seedsmen is treated with fungicide to prevent

such rotting. For other crops, grow seedlings under cover and plant out when large enough and after the plants are hardened off.

SLUGS AND SNAILS Slugs and snails will attack virtually every type of garden plant and fruiting vegetables are no exception. Seedlings and young plants can be eaten off at ground level, leaves and petals can become full of holes and the pests also eat into developing fruits. Most damage occurs at night and can involve the garden snail (*Helix aspersa*) and the strawberry snail (*Trichia striolata*), or the garden slug (*Arion hortensis*), the field slug (*Drocerus reticulatus*), or various keeled slugs (*Milax* spp.).

Control: Keeled slugs can be cleared from the soil by watering on a suspension of the beneficial nematode *Phasmarhabditis hermaphrodita* (*see Biological control, pp. xvi–xxi*). As snails stay above ground, other treatments will be needed, and surrounding plants with sharp grit or soot may assist a little, coupled with nightly inspections by torchlight to collect and kill the intruders. Alternatively, water plants and soil with a solution of metaldehyde, surround the plants with a collar of metaldehyde-impregnated tape or scatter metaldehyde or methiocarb pellets lightly over the plot.

SMUT Smut, *Ustilago maydis*, can be a devastating disease of sweet corn in hot summers. Large pale swellings appear on the cobs and stems and, when fully grown, they break open to liberate masses of powdery black spores which contaminate the soil and nearby sweet corn plants.

Control: Inspect crops regularly and destroy any plants showing the pale swellings. Burn old plant residues after cropping and incorporate sweet corn into a four-year rotation to avoid re-using the same site for a few years (*see Crop rotation, pp. viii–ix*).

TOMATO **BLIGHT** Tomato blight, *Phytophthora infestans*, is the same fungus that causes potato blight. Attacks occur mainly during wet weather in late summer and early autumn and cause the leaves to turn black and die while the fruits develop dark brown areas on the skins. A whitish fungal growth develops on the leaves to spread the infection further and the fruits rot as secondary fungi take over. Tomato stems also turn dark and the whole plant will then collapse.
Control: Spray the tomatoes whenever a nearby potato crop is being sprayed for potato blight control. Copper or mancozeb fungicides would be suitable. The disease spreads most readily in periods of warm, humid weather so spray in advance of any attack during such conditions in order to protect the plants.

VIRUS Various viruses can attack tomato and cucumber family plants causing mottling, spotting and distortion of leaves and stunting and poor cropping of the plants. Tobacco mosaic virus is one of the most common on tomato plants, resulting in yellow mottling and distortion. Cucumber mosaic virus is another serious problem, affects many crops and is spread to cucumber and related plants by aphids as they feed.

Infected cucumber, marrow, melon, pumpkin and courgette plants show a mottling and distortion of the leaves and plants become stunted. Leaves become wrinkled and the few fruits that do set develop a yellow-green mottling starting at the stem end. The same virus attacks tomatoes causing a fern-leaf effect, with very narrow leaves and some mottling.
Control: No control for virus exists and affected plants should be removed and burned. Control of aphids may help although a virus-infected aphid does not have to feed for long to transmit the disease to the host plant.

WHITEFLY Mainly troublesome on greenhouse-grown cucumbers, melons and tomatoes, glasshouse white-fly, *Trialeurodes vaporariorum*, can be damaging on outdoor crops in warm summers, often being present on seedlings as they are planted out from the greenhouse. The pests feed on the sap and excrete sugary honeydew which makes the leaves sticky and is soon colonized by black sooty mould fungi.
Control: Spray with bifenthrin, fatty acids, dimethoate, permethrin or pyrethrins at the first sign of pest attack, paying particular attention to the under-sides of the leaves. The larval 'scale' stage of whitefly is little affected by most insecticides so applications need to be repeated frequently at weekly intervals, but, as always, follow carefully the instructions on the product label.

FRUIT 1

TOP FRUIT: APPLE, ALMOND, APRICOT, CHERRY, GAGE, HAZEL,
FIG, NECTARINE, PEACH, PEAR, PLUM, QUINCE, WALNUT

TRUNKS AND BRANCHES

PESTS VISIBLE	Bands of eggs around young shoots on most fruit types	*lackey moth*
	Irregular galleries eaten in bark of older fruit trees. Damage can be deep and branches may die	*cherry bark tortrix*
	Patches of white growths on apple, purple insects underneath, young shoots distorted and swollen	*woolly aphid*
	Round or elongated scaly insects on bark	*scale insects*
NO PESTS VISIBLE	Apple bark peeling off in thin, pale sheets	*papery bark*
	Bark eaten from base of stems	*vole, rabbit, deer*
	Branches dying back, wood hollowed out by large caterpillar, bore hole or 'sawdust' may be present	*goat moth, leopard moth*
	Dead areas on cherry and other stone-fruit stems or branches with exudation of gum	*bacterial canker*
	Death of shoots and branches after showing silvering of leaves	*silver leaf*
	Death of shoots and branches; no prior leaf silvering	*fireblight*
	Death of tree, loose basal bark with white fungal growths beneath and eventually clusters of pale toadstools	*honey fungus*
	Fig branches develop oval cankers, branches may die	*fig canker*
	Longitudinal cracks down trunks	*frost*
	Plum or cherry with clusters of tightly-growing twigs	*witches' brooms*
	Rough cankered areas on apple and pear	*apple canker*
	Shoots dying back, pinkish pustules present	*coral spot*
	Small dark pustules on young shoots of apple and pear	*scab*
	Young twigs dying back following wilting of blossoms	*bacterial blossom blight, blossom wilt*

LEAVES AND YOUNG SHOOTS

NO HOLES IN LEAVES PESTS VISIBLE	Blackish, slug-like grubs eating on surface of leaves of cherry and pear	*pear slug sawfly*
	Infestations of small, stationary insects, green or red to purple or black, foliage sometimes curled. All fruit crops	*aphids*
	Leaves, all fruit crops, becoming bronzed in summer, many small reddish mites under leaves	*spider mites*
	Leaves of most types of fruit trees become webbed together, caterpillars feeding inside	*tortrix*

NO HOLES IN LEAVES PESTS VISIBLE cont.	Leaves of most fruit tree types show pale stippling, active pests with leaping flights, cast skins present under leaves	*leafhoppers*
	Pale, flat insects under leaves of apple and pear, exuding drops of liquid, young foliage often distorted and sticky	*suckers*
NO HOLES IN LEAVES NO PESTS VISIBLE	Brown to black, irregular spots on apple and pear leaves and fruit	*scab*
	Elongated, raised spots on walnut, undersides with pale cream hairs	*walnut blister mite*
	Foliage and growth poor and pale, premature autumn tints	*nitrogen deficiency*
	Irregular, dark spotting on quince	*quince leaf blight*
	Large, yellow patches on cherry leaves. Patches turn brown and leaves fail to fall in autumn	*cherry leaf scorch*
	Leaves of peaches and nectarines become bloated and discoloured	*peach leaf curl*
	Leaves of all fruits, but especially plums, develop a silvery sheen	*silver leaf*
	Marginal browning and leaf spotting	*potassium deficiency*
	Powdery, white deposit on leaves of apple, peach, pear, quince	*powdery mildew*
	Purplish tints	*phosphorus deficiency*
	Rounded, orange spots on apple leaves	*Cox spot*
	Small, dark spots changing to yellow on walnut leaves, grey to black underneath. Fruits also affected by sunken spots	*walnut leaf blotch*
	Small, raised spots on pear leaves, green, yellow, red to black in sequence	*pear leaf blister mite*
	Small, rusty spots under leaves of peach and plum	*rust fungi*
	Winding mines present on most fruit types	*apple leaf miner*
	Yellow then brown zones between veins of older leaves	*magnesium deficiency or manganese deficiency*
	Yellow zones between veins of youngest leaves	*iron deficiency*
HOLES IN LEAVES PESTS VISIBLE	Black and yellow caterpillars feeding in large groups on apple, pear, cherry and plum	*buff-tip moth*
	Caterpillars feeding in colonies in or around silken tents on apple, pear, cherry, plum	*lackey moth, brown-tail moth*

HOLES IN LEAVES PESTS VISIBLE cont.	Generally green or brown caterpillars, walking with looping action on most types of fruit tree	*winter moth, March moth, mottled umber moth*
	Leaves of all fruit types with small holes and later a tattered look, active pests sometimes seen	*capsid bug*
HOLES IN LEAVES NO PESTS VISIBLE	Rounded, brown spots which fall out to leave holes in leaves of cherry, gage, nectarine, peach and plum	*shothole*

BUDS AND FLOWERS

	Apple flower buds fail to pass pink stage	*apple blossom weevil*
	Blossom and shoot buds wilt, stems die back	*bacterial blossom blight, brown rot blossom wilt*
	Buds of apples and pears become distorted, brown and fail to open	*sucker*
	Flowers turn brown overnight	*frost*
	Hazel buds become swollen but remain unopened in spring	*filbert bud mite*
	Looper-type caterpillars feeding on buds and blossom trusses	*winter moth and related types*

FRUITS

STILL ON TREE PESTS VISIBLE	Looper-type caterpillars feeding on fruitlets of apple, cherry, pear and plum	*winter moth and related species*
	Maggots feeding within developing plums which then fall	*plum sawfly*
	Maggots in tiny apple fruitlets which then fall. Older fruits show ribbon-like scars	*apple sawfly*
	Older apple, and less often pear, fruits eaten inside by creamy-pink caterpillar	*codling moth*
	Older plums eaten inside by reddish grubs	*plum fruit moth*
STILL ON TREE PESTS VISIBLE	Ripening fruits hollowed out, black and yellow striped insects found inside	*wasps*
	Small caterpillars feeding on surface of apple, cherry, pear and plum fruits, often under a webbed-on on leaf	*various species of tortrix moth*
	Young pear fruitlets swell then turn black and fall. White grubs inside	*pear midge*
STILL ON TREE NO PESTS VISIBLE	Apple and pear fruits with dark patches and cracks	*scab*
	Apple and pear fruits with vertical or horizontal corky cracks	*frost*
	Apples drop in early to midsummer	*June drop*

STILL ON TREE	Developing fruits split and soft rots may follow	*water fluctuations*
NO PESTS VISIBLE	Flesh pecked from neck and sides of ripening fruits	*birds*
cont.	Fruits of many kinds with roughness of the skin	*russetting*
	Hazel nuts are found to be hollow, with round exit hole in side	*nut weevil*
	Peach and nectarine fruits spit open from the stem; earwigs may be found inside	*split stone*
	Pears develop in distorted manner and contain hard gritty particles	*stony pit*
	Pears are distorted with brown spotting of flesh	*boron deficiency*
	Raised, corky patches on apple fruits	*apple capsid*
	Small plums become boat shaped, shrivel and drop	*pocket plum*
	Small spots on many fruits developing into corky patches	*capsid bugs*
	Soft, brown rotting following pest damage	*brown rot*
	White coating on peach and nectarine	*powdery mildew*
	Young apples deformed with lumpy appearance	*rosy apple aphid*

AFTER HARVEST

	Apple and pear flesh becomes brown and soft, blue-green tufts of fungus on skin	*blue mould*
	Apple flesh becomes glassy or waterlogged	*water core*
	Apples turn brown and develop concentric rings of buff-coloured spores	*brown rot*
	Eye rot of apples and pears	*apple canker*
	Light green caterpillars feeding on surface of apples and pears in store	*fruit tree tortrix moth*
	Spots of dark cells just under apple skin	*bitter pit*
	Sunken brown patches on apple, quince and rarely on pear, gradually spreading	*bitter rot*

APHIDS (*SEE ALSO WOOLLY APHID, BELOW*) Aphids are very common insect pests, with virtually all crops being subject to attack (*see also Aphid, p.177*). Some species of aphid are host-specific in that they spend their entire lives on one type of plant, others alternate between two or more hosts. In general, winter eggs are laid on woody plants and the newly hatched aphids are wingless. They insert feeding tubes into the host plant and feed on the sap, excreting large quantities of sugary honeydew as they do so. This often attracts ants which consume the sugary fluid and the ants also move the aphids around the tree and have been known to defend them from predators. Foliage can become blackened as sooty moulds colonize the honeydew. This is not directly harmful, but could reduce the ability of the leaves to function normally. The wingless aphids, which are all female and reproduce parthenogenitically (that is, without recourse to a mate), produce large numbers of living young and dense colonies build up. It is often stated that the daughter of the morning is the grandmother of the evening, and indeed aphids can be born with up to 36 embryos already developed in their bodies. As colony densities build up, winged forms are produced which fly of to other host plants, either of the same type or of a different type, depending on the aphid species involved. Aphid infestations build up on the young growths and leaves, producing various amounts of discolouration, distortion and leaf curl. In autumn a winged generation will return to the winter host tree to mate, and eggs are laid to survive the winter.

Control: A winter spray with a tar oil preparation will kill the overwintering eggs of most species and so prevent early damage the next spring. During spring and summer the aphids are preyed upon by ladybird adults and larvae, by lacewing and hoverfly larvae, and by other beneficial insects. Should control be necessary in spring or summer, spray with an insecticide based on bifenthrin, dimethoate, fatty acids, heptenophos, pirimiphos-methyl, pirimicarb or pyrethrins. Where beneficial insects are present, pirimicarb is preferable as it is virtually aphid-specific, but fatty acids would not be harmful once the spray had dried. Weed control is also helpful as many aphid species spend the summer on non-crop plants.

Main aphid species:

- Cherry blackfly, *Myzus cerasi*, causes severe leaf curling and stunting of growth of cherry before flying off to bedstraw and speedwells for the summer. It returns to the cherry to lay winter eggs.
- Green apple aphid, *Aphis pomi*, attacks apple, pear and quince and has no alternate host.
- Leaf-curling plum aphid, *Brachycaudus helichrysi*, feeds on plum and damson where it causes damage by severe leaf curling and rolling. This species can also spread plum pox virus. The summer host plants are asters and chrysanthemums.
- Mealy plum aphid, *Hyalopterus pruni*, is a very waxy aphid feeding in large colonies under leaves of plum, damson and sometimes peach. Honeydew can ruin the crop and affect growth. The summer host plants are reeds and waterside grasses.
- Peach aphid, *Brachycaudus schwartzi*, is confined to peaches where attacks cause severe leaf curling.
- Pear-bedstraw aphid, *Dysaphis pyri*, is an important and damaging species on pear, the mealy pink aphids sometimes present in vast numbers, swarming over trunks and stems. Breeding continues in summer on bedstraw plants (*Galium* spp.) with a return to pear trees in autumn for egg-laying.
- Rosy apple aphid, *Dysaphis plantaginea*, is pink to grey with a mealy, wax coating and attacks on apple result in shoot twisting, leaf curling, and a pimpling and malformation of the fruits. Apples ripen prematurely. The rosy apple aphid spends the summer feeding on plantains.
- Rosy leaf-curling aphid, *Dysaphis devecta*, attacks apples and causes a downwards curling of the leaves. The main identifying feature is the bright red discolouration of the foliage. Attacks have normally finished by mid- to late summer and eggs are laid deep in fissures in the bark, there being no alternate host. Winter washes with tar oil have little controlling effect, so spring and summer sprays are needed.

APPLE BLOSSOM WEEVIL Apple blossom weevil, *Anthonomus pomorum*, lays single eggs in blossom buds in early spring and each female can lay up to 50 eggs. The larvae feed on the essential floral parts and infested flowers fail to open, resulting in the characteristically capped blossoms. The larvae pupate inside the blossoms and then emerge a few weeks later when they feed on the leaves before seeking their winter quarters in midsummer. Apples are the main host plant but pears and quince can also suffer damage. This pest was much more of a problem in old, unsprayed orchards, before the advent of effective insecticides. A light attack may have a useful thinning effect by reducing surplus flowers in years of plentiful blossom. There is a natural parasite of the apple blossom weevil, namely the ichneumon *Scambus pomorum*. The grubs of this helpful insect feed on larvae and pupae of the weevil.

Control: For expected severe attacks permethrin applied at green cluster stage would prevent damage.

APPLE CANKER Apple canker, *Nectria galligena,* is a fungal disease that attacks apples and pears, mainly through wounds in the bark, and a common entry point is the scars left as leaves fall in autumn. Woolly aphid feeding sites are also frequently invaded by the canker fungus. Small, dead areas develop on the wood and the infection spreads, generally in concentric, cracked rings, gradually encircling the shoot or branch. Death of the branch is the final stage. Infection of the wood can occur at any time of year and the fungus also attacks in the 'eye' end of the apple (away from the stalk) which results in an eye rot during storage. Apple canker is more severe on trees suffering from poor growth due to waterlogging or lack of nutrients, and 'Cox's Orange Pippin', 'James Grieve', 'Fiesta' and 'Gala' apples and 'Fertility' pear are particularly susceptible to attack. Feeding and drainage, or selection of less susceptible varieties of apples, for example 'Bramley's Seedling' and 'Lane's Prince Albert', will help to reduce canker attacks.

Control: Cut out and burn larger cankers when seen and use a wire brush on the surrounding tissue to remove any peripheral infection. Paint exposed wood with a proprietary wound paint. Smaller cankered shoots should be pruned out completely and burned. Chemical treatment is aimed at protecting the leaf scars from the canker spores, and is achieved by two applications of a copper fungicide, the first at the start of leaf fall and the second half way through the leaf fall period. Control of woolly aphid is also of value.

APPLE CAPSID Apple capsid, *Plesiocoris rugicollis*, can be a serious pest of apple and also attacks currants and gooseberry. The adult capsid is around 6mm (¼in) long and fast moving. Normally a fairly minor pest, apple capsid can, nevertheless, cause considerable damage when present in numbers and not controlled. Leaves are punctured by the capsid to feed on the plant sap and small brown spots develop around the feeding points. As the leaves expand, the holes become larger and result in a tattered appearance. Punctures on the fruits start as similar small, brown spots but enlarge to give unsightly, raised, corky patches. When small apples are attacked they may fall prematurely.

Control: Control apple capsid with a spray at green cluster stage of permethrin, pirimiphos-methyl or fatty acids.

APPLE LEAF MINER Apple leaf miner, *Lyonetia clerkella*, is responsible for unsightly, winding mines in the leaves of apples, cherry and other fruit crops. Where the mines form a complete loop, the area enclosed turns brown and dies. There are usually three generations per year so the damage can be evident right through the growing season.

Control: Some reduction will be obtained by the pre-blossom application of permethrin or other insecticide for control of more important pests. For severe attacks in summer, a few repeats of the same insecticide may be needed. On small trees, removal and destruction of infested leaves may be worthwhile; alternatively the caterpillars can be squashed by hand inside the infested leaves.

APPLE SAWFLY Apple sawfly, *Hoplocampa testudinea*, can be a very damaging pest of apples. Eggs are laid singly in the flowers during blossoming and hatch within a couple of weeks. Each female sawfly can lay up to 30 eggs. The larvae bore into the young fruitlets and feed on the pips, resulting in the failure of the apple to develop further. The larvae then move out to attack other apple fruitlets and this process may be repeated until they are fully fed. Where the sawfly larvae feed on the surface of the apple, a ribbon-like scar develops. When fully fed, the larvae enter the soil to spin a cocoon in which they overwinter, pupating in spring. Most new adults emerge in the following spring but some may take two or even three years. Where there has been a severe attack it is necessary, therefore, to take preventative action for three years running to make certain of good results.

Control: Attacks can be prevented by spraying a week after 80 per cent petal fall to catch the larvae as they hatch but before they penetrate too deeply into the flesh. Dimethoate, permethrin or pirimiphos-methyl would all be suitable insecticides to use. In gardens where the soil is cultivated under the apple trees, soil movement during winter may expose or kill the overwintering sawflies. It will also be helpful to pick up all apple fruitlets that fall in early summer, as soon as possible after they fall, to catch any sawfly larvae before they can enter the soil.

APPLE SCAB Apple scab, *Venturia inaequalis*, is one of the most widespread diseases of apple trees. Infection is related to temperature and humidity and, after a certain time under the correct conditions, the spores of apple scab fungus will germinate and start up an attack. Most of the spring infection will come from fallen leaves, or from scab pustules on the wood of 'Cox' and some other varieties. Later infections in summer or autumn are generally the result of taking inadequate measures in spring. The first sign of scab attack on apples is the appearance of olive-green patches on the foliage and small dark spots on the fruits. Gradually, the leaf infections turn darker and expand while the fruit damage becomes more extensive. As the fruits mature, the scabby areas tend to crack, and this can let in brown rot and other diseases that result in the fruit rotting, either on the tree or later in store. Trees grown in crowded conditions, or subjected to excess nitrogen applications resulting in soft, sappy growth, will be more susceptible to scab attack. Attention to these details will help to reduce attacks. If planning new plantings, consult your supplier to find out any scab-resistant varieties on offer. Apples vary considerably in their susceptibility to the disease.

'Bramley's Seedling', 'Cox's Orange Pippin', 'Gala' and 'James Grieve' are all susceptible to scab, while 'Charles Ross', 'Discovery', 'Sunset' and 'Winston' exhibit some degree of resistance. Where scab has occurred, gathering up fallen leaves in autumn will reduce local infective sources, as will pruning out any scabby wood.

Control: On the chemical front, fungicide applications before and after flowering will do much to prevent damage. Continue the spray programme longer into the summer in a wet season. Suitable fungicides include benomyl, carbendazim and mancozeb. A sulphur fungicide could be used, but many varieties are sulphur shy and are damaged by this chemical, and most varieties tend to develop a hardening of the foliage and possibly a russetted skin when treated with sulphur.

APPLE SUCKER Apple sucker, *Psylla mali*, feeds by sucking the sap from blossom and leaf clusters in spring causing symptoms that look superficially rather like frost damage, namely a brown discolouration of petals. A severe attack can kill the entire blossom truss in a few days. Drops of honeydew are very noticeable where apple suckers are active. Feeding continues through to late summer, when eggs are laid to survive the winter and to hatch out in spring.

Control: A winter tar oil spray will normally take care of the overwintering eggs and so prevent the damaging, early spring attacks. Where a winter wash has not been applied, apple sucker would be controlled by the insecticides recommended for aphid control (*above*).

BACTERIAL BLOSSOM BLIGHT Bacterial blossom blight, *Pseudomonas syringae*, attacks pear blossoms particularly in cold, wet weather. Attack results in a withering of the blossoms and a dying back of the spurs.

Control: There is no direct chemical control although tar oil, applied for aphid control, does have a useful effect by killing weak buds and trusses in winter. Should flower trusses be seen to be turning brown and dying in spring, prune them out, cutting back to clean wood.

BACTERIAL CANKER Bacterial canker, *Pseudomonas mors-prunorum*, is particularly severe on cherry and plum but can attack any *Prunus* species, both culinary and ornamental varieties. Attacks can occur on the stems and branches as well as on leaves, smaller shoots and fruits. There is a winter, canker stage and a summer, leaf spot stage, but the end result can be cankers developing in the crotch region and in the angles between smaller branches. As with apple canker infection, much of the attack comes through the leaf scars left at leaf fall, but the bacterium also gains entry through physical or frost injury to the bark; areas damaged by chafing of tree ties are frequently attacked by bacterial canker. A common symptom, though not exclusive to bacterial canker, is the presence of amber coloured gum on the bark, especially with infection of cherry trees. If a canker girdles a branch then the branch will die. The summer, leaf spot stage results in small, rounded areas turning brown on the leaves. These areas then fall out to give a shothole effect. This is virtually identical to shothole caused by the fungus *Stigmina carpophila* (*see below*). The bacterium is encouraged by wet weather, particularly towards the end of the blossoming period. The newer rootstocks, 'Colt' and 'Pixie', which are replacing the older types, are resistant to bacterial canker infection.

Control: Cut out and burn dead branches and cankered tissue, painting exposed wood with a wound paint. Leaf scar infection can be greatly reduced by sprays of copper fungicide in late summer, early autumn and mid-autumn. These applications encourage early leaf fall and then protect the scars from infection by the bacteria.

BIRDS Birds can be important fruit pests, with bullfinches and other species eating fruit buds in winter, sparrows and finches pecking off flowers in spring, and starlings, blackbirds and thrushes attacking ripening fruits in autumn. When holes are pecked in the fruits, wasps and earwigs frequently enlarge the damage and can eat out the entire contents around the core. Damage by birds also lets in the spores of a number of fruit-rotting fungi.

Control: A reliable fruit cage is the only complete answer, but would only be suitable for cordon or other dwarf forms of fruit tree. Black cotton (not nylon) threads passed over a tree several times will help a little to protect fruit buds, and various bird-scaring devices are available in the form of cut-out cats, glittering strips and the like. Bird deterrent sprays are also available but need to be renewed after every fall of rain.

BITTER PIT Bitter pit is a physiological disorder, that is one caused by a growth malfunction and not by pest or disease. Slightly sunken spots can be found on the skin of apples and, after peeling, there remain spots of dark flesh. The spots are mainly near the surface, but some can be found more deeply in the apple and give the fruit a bitter taste. The damage can sometimes be seen while the apples are still on the tree, but more usually it develops after harvest. 'Cox's Orange Pippin', 'Bramley's Seedling', 'Lord Lambourne', 'Crispin', 'Gala', 'Jonagold' and 'Merton Worcester' appear to be particularly susceptible to the disorder. Bitter pit is most serious in dry years, and on fruit from trees bearing a light crop of large apples. It is related to excess of potassium or magnesium or to a deficiency of calcium in the fruit. Prevent by watering in dry weather, by mulching to conserve moisture in the soil, and by avoiding heavy pruning and excessive nitrogen applications, both of which can encourage smaller crops but larger apples. Liming acid soils helps, but mostly it is a reduced uptake of calcium rather than a shortage in the soil that is to blame.

Control: Spray the trees with a solution of calcium nitrate several times in summer and early autumn.

BITTER ROT Bitter rot can arise from attack by *Glomerella cingulata*, *Pezicula alba* or *P. malicorticis*. Attacks occur on apple, cherry, quince and less frequently pear. Sometimes on the tree but mainly in store, round depressed areas develop and gradually spread out until the whole fruit is affected. The fungi also cause a cankering of the fruit spurs. Fruit infection can start with cracks in the skin due to apple scab, and wood infection can follow damage by woolly aphid. Cankered wood should be cut away and general pruning carried out in late winter, as spore production from infected wood is less prevalent then. Fruit for storing should be gathered as soon as it is ready, as the longer the fruit stays on the tree, the greater the chances of infection occurring. Check stored fruit at frequent intervals and remove any found to be suffering from rots.

Control: Regular fungicide applications for scab control should also give a measure of control of these rots.

BLACKFLY (*SEE APHIDS, ABOVE*)

BLOSSOM WILT Blossom wilt, *Monilinia* spp., infects the flowers and the fungus grows down into the spur. Infected blossom trusses and leaves fail to develop and are often still present at leaf fall. Greyish spore masses appear in wet weather to spread the infection further. 'Cox's Orange Pippin', 'Lord Lambourne' and 'James Grieve' appear to be more susceptible to attack than most other apples, but the variety 'Bramley's Seedling' is little affected.

Control: It has been found that a tar oil spray, applied to control dormant pest eggs, will also reduce the sources of blossom wilt. A thorough scab fungicide programme will also be of value.

BLUE MOULD Blue mould is the name given to the fruit rot caused by *Penicillium expansum*. Apples and pears are affected and the disease results in a soft rot followed by the production of bluish pustules. Attack normally starts in points of damage, even though they may be too small to be clearly evident at picking time. Reduce the chances of spread in store by keeping each apple away from the next and by frequent examination to remove any found to be rotting.

Control: Adequate pest and disease control to prevent skin damage will help to keep blue mould infection away.

BORON DEFICIENCY Boron deficiency occurs mainly in apples and pears and results in the bark becoming pimpled, shoots dying back and in leaf distortion. Fruits develop cracks and numerous brown, corky spots appear in the flesh.

Control: Apply borax (sodium tetraborate) to the soil at the low rate of 3g per square metre (⅒oz per yd^2) or spray at petal fall with a solution of 16g per 5l (½oz/1gall) of water.

BROWN ROT Brown rot, *Monilinia fructigena* and *Monilinia laxa*, causes a rotting of all types of fruit. It is primarily a wound parasite, gaining entry through damage caused by codling moth and tortrix caterpillars, birds, wasps, scab or general russetting of the skin. Infected fruits soon turn brown and soft. Concentric rings of buff-coloured spores then break through the skin in cushion-like outgrowths and the whole fruit can be rotted within a couple of weeks. The infection passes by contact from fruit to fruit, both on the tree and in store. Brown rot can pass back from the apple to the spur in a similar way to the infection of blossom wilt, resulting in small cankers. If left on the tree, infected fruit will hang in mummified form all winter to infect the following season's fruit.

Control: Remove all infected fruits from the trees and from store and bury rather than just throwing them on to the compost heap. Cut out all dead spurs and small cankers seen, and also scrub down the storeroom shelves. The apple scab fungicide sprays will also reduce brown rot incidence, but take appropriate measures to prevent fruit damage by other agencies.

BROWN TAIL MOTH Brown tail moth, *Euproctis chrysorrhoea*, tends to be limited to coastal areas, but there it can cause severe damage to apple, pear and plum. The eggs hatch in autumn and the caterpillars make a communal silken tent in which to shelter. They feed actively on the tree foliage until winter and then rest until spring. Feeding starts again in late spring and whole trees may be stripped of leaves. There is additional concern regarding the silken tents as many people are sensitive to the larval hairs present.

Control: Cut out and burn the tents in winter, taking care to wear rubber gloves to avoid contact with the hairs. When new tents are seen, or the caterpillars are feeding away from the tent, spray with a contact insecticide like bifenthrin, permethrin, pyrethrins or fatty acids.

BUFF TIP MOTH Buff tip moth, *Phalera bucephala*, is a sporadic but sometimes very damaging pest of apple, cherry, pear, plum and some soft fruit bushes. The caterpillars are yellow with black lines and orange cross markings, and they feed together in large numbers.

Control: Complete defoliation is possible with a normal to severe infestation. If spotted sufficiently early, the pests can be removed by hand. Once damage has started, more complete control is usually required, and a spray of bifenthrin, permethrin, pyrethrins or fatty acids is recommended.

CALCIUM DEFICIENCY (*SEE BITTER PIT, ABOVE*)

CAPSID BUG (*SEE ALSO APPLE CAPSID, ABOVE*) Common green capsid, *Lygocoris pabulinus*, causes the same type of damage to leaves and fruit as apple capsid, above, but damage starts slightly later. There are two generations of common green capsid each year, compared to only one with apple capsid, and the insects feed on a wide range of weeds, particularly nettles, thistles and docks as well as on fruit trees. (*See also Capsid bug, p.179*.)

Control: In addition to controlling weeds in the garden, spray fruit trees immediately after petal fall with a contact insecticide as recommended for apple capsid.

CHERRY–BARK TORTRIX Cherry-bark tortrix, *Enarmonia formosana*, is widely distributed on older apple, cherry, pear, plum and other trees. Eggs are laid on rough or damaged areas of bark on the trunk and the caterpillars that emerge eat out extensive and deep mines under the bark. On plum and cherry there may be copious exudations of gum. In subsequent years, eggs tend to be laid in the previously mined areas so that even more damage is done and in severe cases branches or whole trees may be killed by this pest.

Control: Scrape away the loose bark from tree trunks to expose the caterpillars to birds, or remove them by hand. At one time painting the exposed areas with creosote or undiluted tar oil in winter was recommended; a contact insecticide drench over the area may be worthwhile.

CHERRY LEAF SCORCH Cherry leaf scorch, *Gnomonia erythrostoma*, is identifiable by the dead, brown cherry leaves hanging on the tree over winter. In spring, spores are produced on these leaves to infect the new growth. Hard spots may also be found in the cherry fruits. The disease is not usually too severe, but when a serious attack does develop it can be very weakening if allowed to go unchecked. 'Napoleon' and 'Turk' varieties of cherry are stated to be resistant to the disease, whilst 'Frogmore Bigarreau' and 'Waterloo' are susceptible.

Control: Remove all dead leaves left hanging after normal leaf fall.

CODLING MOTH Codling moth, *Cydia pomonella*, is probably the most widely distributed pest of apples and can also attack pears. The caterpillars enter the side or the eye of the apple and eat their way down to the core region. More than one apple per larva may be attacked, but they have usually (though not always) left the fruit by harvest time. When small apples are attacked they usually fall from the tree. Winter is spent in a cocoon under rough bark or in tree ties and similar hiding places. Sometimes there can be a second generation in the same year.
Control: Prevention of damage can be achieved by a number of different actions at different times of the year. Tying corrugated cardboard or sacking bands about 10cm (4in) wide around the tree trunks in summer will provide hiding places for the larvae seeking winter quarters, and these are then removed and burned in winter. Scraping any rough bark off the trunks will help to ensure that the larvae use the bands. By the end of petal fall, pheromone traps (*see Biological control, pp. xvi–xxi*) should be in place to lure and trap the male codling moths and one trap will protect the apple trees within a 30m (27 yard) radius. In larger gardens, more traps could be used, or one trap could be used as a monitoring system to determine when the codling moths were on the wing in numbers. A suitable insecticide such as bifenthrin or permethrin could then be applied.

CORAL SPOT Coral spot, *Nectria cinnabarina*, is normally confined to attacking dead or dying shoots, but it does seem that more active strains sometimes exist. The fungus enters through wounds, pruning cuts and similar areas and causes a die back of the shoot. Numerous coral-pink pustules appear on the shoots, and spores from these will spread the infection further.
Control: Cut out all dead wood, removing back to 5cm (2in) or more below any obviously dead area. Burn the dead wood, and check other old wood in the garden, such as pea sticks and any piles of old prunings for signs of infection.

COX SPOT Cox spot is a physiological disorder that shows up as variably-sized orange spots on the leaves of 'Cox's Orange Pippin' and some other varieties of apple. The exact cause of Cox spot is not known, but loss of nutrients from the leaves shortly after petal fall, faulty root action and magnesium deficiency have all been suspected of being involved from time to time.
Control: Improving drainage, and supplying trace elements to the leaves by means of foliar feeding may help.

DEER Deer can be very damaging to the bark and shoots of trees in certain rural areas of the country. Leaves and shoots are grazed extensively in spring and bark may be torn off the trunks in winter.
Control: The only complete answer would be 2m (6ft 6in) high fencing around the garden, or those parts of it subject to attack. Rags dipped in bone oil, creosote or tar oil may have some deterrent effect, whilst human hair hung in bags in strategic places is stated by some old gardeners to be effective.

FIG CANKER Fig canker, *Phomopsis cinerescens*, can be seen as an oval cankering on the bark, often located around an old pruning cut. Small black fruiting bodies arise on the cankered area and these exude masses of white spores in wet weather. The spores are spread by rain, insects, birds, and by hand and tools to infect new shoots.

Control: Cut out all dead wood and, when pruning, cut back flush with the main shoot to avoid snags being left. Paint any large cuts with a wound sealant.

FILBERT BUD MITE Filbert bud mite, *Phytocoptella avellanae*, feeds inside the hazel buds, causing them to become swollen and rounded. Such buds fail to open and blind shoots can result. The mites can also damage the male catkins and the female flowers but, overall, little loss of cropping appears to follow the damage.

Control: If necessary for very severe attacks, prune out all the infested buds in early spring or whenever they are seen.

FIREBLIGHT Fireblight, caused by the bacterium *Erwinia amylovora*, attacks apple and pear, as well as various ornamental trees and shrubs belonging to the rose family. 'Laxton's Superb' pear is particularly susceptible to attack by fireblight. Initial infection is often spread by pollinating insects to late blossoms, and the first indication is the sudden dying back of shoots and branches with the leaves looking as though they had been scorched by fire. Leaves on these branches tend to stay on rather than being shed (as with apple canker, for example). Fireblight cankers develop on the wood in autumn and from these 'holdover cankers' masses of bacteria ooze out in humid, spring conditions to spread the infection. A severe attack of fireblight can kill a mature tree within six months.

Control: There is no cure for this disease. Avoid excessive applications of nitrogen to reduce any sappy growth, and hand pick any summer flowers on apples and pears where possible. Should an attack occur, prune out the affected parts to around 60cm (2ft) below the lowest visible sign of death.

FROST Frost after bud break causes the leaves and flowers to blacken and die, while a severe winter frost can result in large fissures in the bark of fruit tree trunks. Peach, nectarine and almond, followed by pear, are the earliest trees to flower and they tend to suffer more than the later-flowering apples. Damage to the floral parts prevents pollination and subsequent fertilization so no fruit will develop. A frost after fruit set can cause the apples or pears to become distorted and they will often show vertical corky fissures on the sides or a circular mark close to the eye of the fruit. Avoid planting fruit in any known frost pocket and where late spring frosts are known to be common choose later-flowering varieties which may escape damage. 'Cox's Orange Pippin', 'Spartan', 'Worcester Pearmain' and 'Gala' are among the latest-flowering apple varieties, and 'Williams' Bon Chretien', 'Beurre Superfin' and 'Doyenne du Comice' among the latest-flowering pears.

Control: Should there be a late frost, try to put a lawn sprinkler on to the trees before the sun gets on them. This will slow down the rate of thaw and may be enough to prevent the worst of the damage. Overnight sprinkling when frost is forecast would be even more effective, although expensive where metered water is concerned.

FRUIT TREE RED SPIDER MITE Fruit tree red spider mite, *Panonychus ulmi*, will attack apple, plum and damson and has also been found on pear. (Peaches and relatives are attacked by the two-spotted mite, *see below*). The mite overwinters in the egg stage, the eggs being a dull red and clustered in large numbers around fruit spurs and on younger shoots. They hatch out over a six week or longer period during spring and early summer and feed on the plant sap. There are normally four or five overlapping generations per year. Infested leaves show a light stippling of the upper surface, gradually lose their bright green colour and, as damage increases, the leaves turn brown or bronzed. In severe attacks, all the leaves may fall before the end of summer. When day-length falls to about 14 hours in early autumn, normal breeding ceases and winter eggs are laid. Fruit tree red spider mites have several natural predators, the most effective of which is a predatory mite, *Typhlodromus pyri*. Anthocorid bugs and the black-kneed capsid also feed on red spider mites, but tend to be less helpful to the gardener as they are mainly attracted to trees with dense populations of the pests. They then leave the tree when the spider mites have been reduced to low levels, thus allowing the survivors to build up again.

Control: Bifenthrin is probably now the most effective pesticide for severe attacks of red spider. Fatty acids and pyrethrins will give control, but need more thorough and frequent applications to ensure good contact with the pests. Sprays for red spider mite are likely to affect the natural predators, so would best be reserved for severe attacks.

FRUIT TREE TORTRIX MOTHS Several different species of tortrix moth attack the leaves and fruits of apple, cherry, pear and plum. Typically, eggs are laid in late spring or early summer and the emerging caterpillars feed first on the leaves, which they web together, and then on the fruit. The caterpillars spend the winter hidden away safely and become active again in spring, feeding on leaves and fruitlets. The bud moth bores into the young buds, which it hollows out, causing serious losses in some years. After the spring feeding, the tortrix caterpillars pupate and emerge as adult moths in late spring to early summer and restart the life cycle. The typical tortrix caterpillar is found underneath a leaf, webbed either to another leaf or to a fruit, will wriggle rapidly backwards when disturbed, and will drop off the tree to hang on a silken thread. When danger has passed, it climbs back up the thread to the tree.

Control: For most tortrix species, a spray at green bud will catch the caterpillars emerging from hibernation, and two further sprays, in mid- and late summer, will control the next generation. For fruitlet-mining tortrix, spray at petal fall and fruitlet stages with insecticides like bifenthrin, fatty acids, permethrin, pirimiphos-methyl and pyrethrins. Several tortrix species can now be controlled by pheromone traps, each with their own, specific pheromone *(see pp. xv–xvi)*.

Main tortrix species:
- Bud moth, *Spilonota ocellana*, attacks apple, cherry, pear and plum.
- Fruit tree tortrix moth, *Archips podana*, occurs most widely on apple, cherry, pear, plum plus a range of soft fruit crops and ornamentals.
- Fruitlet-mining tortrix, *Pammene rhediella*, is mainly a pest of apple and pear but also occurs infrequently on cherry, pear and plum.
- Plum tortrix moth, *Hedya pruniana*, attacks apple, cherry and nut as well as its main host, the plum.

- Summer fruit tortrix moth, *Adoxophyes orana*, attacks apple, cherry, pear and plum.

GOAT MOTH Goat moth, *Cossus cossus*, is a widespread but relatively unusual pest of apple, cherry, plum and walnut trees among others. Eggs are laid in batches of 50 or so on tree trunks, and each female can lay several hundred eggs. The caterpillars bore down through the bark and feed on both hard wood and sap wood for up to four years before pupating just under the bark. It is not unusual for the trees to be killed by an attack from this type of pest.

Control: Rarely possible, but felling and burning of infested trees when detected is advised.

GREENFLY (*SEE ALSO APHIDS, ABOVE*)

HONEY FUNGUS Honey fungus, *Armillaria mellea*, is a widespread and damaging fungus, capable of killing mature fruit trees. The fungus can be quite common in gardens sited on old orchards or old woodland, and spreads through the soil by means of bootlace-like growths, known as rhizomorphs, which penetrate into the new host plant at, or just below, soil level. The bark at the tree base dies and under the dead area will be found a white web of fungal strands, the mycelium. After the tree has died, toadstools appear in large clumps. The toadstools are honey-coloured, giving rise to the name of honey fungus, and they can be identified also by the presence of a paler collar around the stem just below the cap. All kinds of fruit trees, bushes and plants can be attacked and killed by honey fungus (*see also Honey fungus, p.182*). Removal and burning of all dead wood is an essential part of treatment, as is removal of as much of the root system as possible by digging out, or by chipping the stump to as low a level as can be reached where root removal is not possible. Where an attack has been identified it may be possible to isolate the area by sinking sheets of corrugated iron or other strong material into the ground around the site. It may be necessary to have such a barrier down to 1m (3¼ft) into the soil.

Control: Try a phenol drench to protect trees from attack by honey fungus and also to control light attacks in the absence of any other available chemical treatment. If planting up a site where honey fungus has been active, it would be wise to change the soil to a depth of 1m (3¼ft).

IRON DEFICIENCY Iron is not very mobile within the plant, and when a deficiency occurs the iron stays in the older leaves, resulting in a yellowing of the youngest leaves, with the veins remaining green except in severe deficiency. Shoot growth is restricted and shoots may later die back. Pear fruit develop brightly coloured fruits, often with red shades present. Most iron shortage occurs in alkaline, chalky soils where any iron is rendered insoluble and so unavailable to plant roots. In acid soils, the iron in the soil can be used up by the fruit trees, resulting in a deficiency. (*See also Iron deficiency, p.182.*)

Control: Water leaves and soil with a chelated or sequestered iron solution. This supplies iron in a form that is available to the plant but that cannot be rendered insoluble by the alkalinity of the soil. Specialist fertilizers are now available which contain iron in sequestered form in addition to the main nutrients, plus sulphur which helps to make the soil more acid.

JUNE DROP June drop is the name given (in the northern hemisphere) to the fall of apples, that occurs a few weeks after petal fall. It is a perfectly normal occurrence and is generally a reflection of the volume of fruit that has been set. Too heavy a set will often result in some of the fruitlets running short of nutrients and falling from the tree. Where inadequate numbers of fruits remain after this drop, lack of complete pollination or pest damage may be involved, or there could be a root problem.

Control: If thought necessary, check on pest control and for any indications of soil waterlogging.

LACKEY MOTH Lackey moth, *Malacosoma neustria*, is a pest of many trees including apple, cherry, pear and plum. Eggs are laid in autumn in wide bands around young shoots. Each band may contain as many as 200 eggs and they remain dormant until the following spring. The caterpillars have bright red, white, blue and black stripes and feed gregariously in a silken web. Such tents may be over 30cm (1ft) long, and are extended as the caterpillars move along shoots and branches to seek new leaves to eat. Trees can be completely defoliated.

Control: Seek out and prune off the egg bands during winter, and the tents in summer.

LEAFHOPPERS Several different species of leafhopper attack fruit tree leaves. Feeding underneath the leaves results in a pale stippling on the upper surface. The adult leafhoppers are variously striped and patterned and they take short leaping flights when disturbed. The young are mainly found along the veins and dead, cast skins are usually present.

Control: Rarely necessary. If damage is severe, insecticides recommended for caterpillars (*see also Fruit tree tortrix moths, above*) would give good control.

LEOPARD MOTH Leopard moth, *Zeuzera pyrina*, attacks a number of trees, including apple, cherry, pear, plum and walnut. Normally attacks are limited to trees from around 10 to 15 years of age. Eggs are laid in summer and the caterpillars feed for a while on the foliage before boring into the wood, typically selecting branches no greater than 10cm (4in) in diameter. The caterpillars, which in later stages are yellow with black spots and brown head, feed for two or three years before moving towards the outside of the branch to pupate. The feeding results in a withering and die-back of the infested branches.

Control: If the damage is spotted sufficiently early, it is often possible to extract, or to kill, the caterpillars with a piece of strong, flexible wire. Otherwise, cut off wilting branches to below any sign of boring, and check other trees at the same time for similar symptoms.

MAGNESIUM DEFICIENCY Magnesium deficiency is common on alkaline soils and in wet years as it is readily leached from the soil. It results in a yellowing, followed by a browning, of the leaf areas between the veins of the oldest leaves. Magnesium is quite mobile in the plant, unlike iron, and so in cases of deficiency the available magnesium is moved to the new growth, leaving the older leaves deficient. Leaves may also roll and develop a purplish tint, and by mid- to late summer defoliation of the older leaves will have occurred, leaving little tufts of leaves at the tops of the shoots. Magnesium deficiency can be caused by excess applications of potassium fertilizers.

Control: Spray the leaves a few times with a solution of magnesium sulphate (Epsom Salts) using 100g per 5l (4oz/1gall) of water, plus a wetting agent. Apply at petal fall and, if necessary, repeat a few times at 14 day intervals. Avoid excess potassium applications.

MANGANESE DEFICIENCY Manganese deficiency is often difficult to distinguish from magnesium deficiency, but tends to appear on trees growing in soils with highish alkalinity plus plenty of organic matter.
Control: Spray at petal fall with a solution of manganese sulphate at 15g per 5l (½oz/1gall) of water plus a wetting agent.

MARCH MOTH March moth, *Alsophila aescularia*, belongs to the geometer moth group, along with mottled umber moth and winter moth (*see below*). One characteristic feature of these moths is that the caterpillars move by a looping action, having no prolegs between the normal three pairs of true legs at the front and just two pairs of prolegs at the rear. A further distinctive feature of March, winter and mottled umber moths is that the adult female moths only have vestigial wings and so cannot fly. The female moth has to climb up the tree to lay her eggs, which she does in a large band around suitable twigs. The larvae feed on blossom and leaf trusses on apple, cherry, nut, pear and plum.
Control: Females can be trapped on bands of sticky grease put round the trees in late autumn. To control the caterpillars, however, spray before flowering with bifenthrin, fatty acids, permethrin, pirimiphos-methyl or pyrethrins. Repeat this spraying regime if necessary after petal fall.

MILDEW (*SEE ALSO POWDERY MILDEW, BELOW*)

MOTTLED UMBER MOTH Mottled umber moth, *Erannis defoliaria*, is similar in life cycle and other details to March moth (*above*), but the eggs are laid in crevices in the bark and not in bands.
Control: As for March moth (*see above*).

NITROGEN DEFICIENCY Nitrogen deficiency results in small, pale leaves and shoots, bright yellow or red tints to the foliage in summer and premature defoliation. Pears often have bright red or orange skins, and flowering is reduced. Nitrogen deficiency is most frequent on trees growing in grass and where no fertilizer applications are given.
Control: Apply a nitrogen fertilizer to the soil or grass under the branch spread, using sulphate of ammonia or a proprietary lawn fertilizer (not including weedkiller). For a rapid response, spray the foliage with a urea solution using 25g per 5l (¾oz/1gall) of water plus a wetting agent. Spray at petal fall and repeat, if necessary two to three weeks later.

NUT WEEVIL Nut weevil, *Curculio nucum*, is widely distributed and can be quite a serious pest of hazel. The adult weevil bores a small hole in the nuts before the shell hardens and the larva feeds on the developing nut kernel. When fully fed, the larva squeezes out through the initial egg-laying hole and enters the soil where it spends winter in an earthen cell, pupating in spring.
Control: Cultivating the soil under the bushes during winter and early spring will expose or kill many of the overwintering weevil larvae or pupae. It may also be helpful to shake the nut branches over a plastic sheet in late spring to dislodge and catch the adult weevils.

PAPERY BARK Papery bark is a growth disorder in which the bark of apple trees peels off in a thin, pale brown, sheet. Apple canker and silver leaf disease have both been suggested as being involved, but it is generally considered now that papery bark is a response to waterlogged soil conditions and associated faulty root action. Normally the damage is superficial and of minor importance, but in severe cases the bark can be killed to some depth, and there may then be considerable die back.

Control: Remove dead bark and any dead or dying branches, painting any large areas with a wound paint, if necessary. Take any available measures to improve drainage.

PEACH LEAF CURL Peach leaf curl, *Taphrina deformans*, attacks almond and apricot as well as peach, resulting in a bloating and discolouration of the leaves. Infected leaves fall prematurely and the effect can be quite weakening on the trees. The fungus spends the winter between the bud scales and, in early spring as the buds start to open slightly, the spores germinate and infect the new foliage. A white 'bloom' of spores develops on the discoloured leaves and these infect further leaves. In autumn, the spores lodge in the winter bud scales to complete the cycle.

Control: It has been found that moisture is essential for the establishment of peach leaf curl in spring. Where the peach is growing against a wall, a temporary or permanent cover to keep off the rain in the spring will reduce, and may prevent, the disease. Otherwise, spray with a copper fungicide or mancozeb in late winter as the bud scales start to loosen and again at leaf-fall time in autumn. With small trees, pick off affected leaves, ideally before any white 'bloom' appears.

PEAR LEAF BLISTER MITE Pear leaf blister mite, *Phytoptus pyri*, is a common pest of pear and a minor, occasional pest of apple. In spring, the new leaves show a pale green pimpling, and as the season progresses the spots change colour through yellow and pink to brown to black. In severe attacks the fruit is also spotted by the tiny blisters. The underside of each blister has a tiny hole through which the next generation of mites disperses to new shoots and then to the winter buds.

Control: Hand picking the infested leaves on smaller trees may eliminate the attack if done thoroughly for a few years. Chemical control is unreliable, although pirimiphos-methyl, applied for control of aphids, may reduce the blister mite and protect against new attack.

PEAR MIDGE Pear midge, *Contarinia pyrivora*, is perhaps the most damaging of all the pests of pear fruit. The female midge lays up to 30 eggs in a single blossom bud at white bud stage, or sometimes in newly-opened flowers, and as many as 100 eggs may be found if other females lay eggs in the same blossom. Infested pear fruitlets swell up rapidly and generally in a rounded, rather than pear-shaped fashion, but then turn black and fall from the tree. The yellowish-white larvae, having fed on the tissue of the fruitlet, move out of the pear and into the soil. There is only one generation per year.

Control: Picking off the unusually rounded fruitlets, and gathering up the fallen ones from the ground, as soon as possible after they fall, will remove a lot of the local infestation. A spray of permethrin at early white bud should also be effective, and once an attack has been experienced, spray for the next two seasons to complete the control.

PEAR SCAB Pear scab, *Venturia pirina*, is virtually identical in biology and control to apple scab (*see above*). The only major difference as far as control requirements are concerned is that the pustules of wood scab persist on pears for four or five years, but on apples they die out in the second year.

Control: Treat as for apple scab, paying special attention to pruning out cankers on the young wood.

PEAR AND CHERRY SLUGWORM Pear and cherry slugworm is the name given to the larval stage of the pear slug sawfly, *Caliroa cerasi*. Apple and plum can also be attacked. The black, slug-like larvae feed on the upper surface of the leaf, leaving 'windows' of tissue from the lower surface. The window soon turns brown and in a severe attack, which most tend to be, the whole leaf will blacken and fall. Once fully fed, by midsummer, the larvae pupate in the soil and a second generation emerges later. In some years there is even a partial third generation which appears in autumn.

Control: Dimethoate, permethrin or pirimiphos-methyl would control; apply as soon as the pests are seen.

PEAR SUCKER Pear sucker, *Psylla pyricola*, is widely found on pear and can be a serious pest. Unlike apple sucker which overwinters in the egg stage (*see above*) it is the adult pear suckers that survive the winter. Eggs are laid on the spurs in early spring and the young nymphs feed on the developing buds and flowers. Small,

badly-shaped fruit and premature leaf fall can follow a severe attack, and copious honeydew is produced. This is colonized by sooty mould fungi to turn leaves and fruits black, and it also attracts ants, wasps and flies to the site. Summer eggs are laid to continue the cycle and there are normally three generations each year, building up very large populations which may greatly reduce flower bud production for the following season.

Control: For heavy infestations, spray at petal fall and again three weeks later with dimethoate or pirimiphos-methyl. For light attacks, omit the petal fall spray.

PHOSPHORUS DEFICIENCY The main distinguishing feature of phosphorus deficiency is a purpling of the veins, together with poor, pale or dull green growth. Trees on heavy, calcareous soils and in high rainfall areas are most at risk.

Control: Bonemeal or superphosphate applications to the soil are usually sufficient, but for rapid results also apply a foliar feed.

PLUM FRUIT MOTH Plum fruit moth, *Cydia funebrana*, is often found in the wild on blackthorn and is an important pest of plums is some areas. Eggs are laid in summer on the developing fruits and the caterpillar (known as red plum maggot) feeds inside the plums. In some years there is a partial second generation. Damage is done later in the season than plum sawfly, *see below*, and the damage can be more severe.

Control: Larvae overwinter under rough bark, so scraping to remove this in winter may also remove some of the pests. A winter tar oil spray for dormant egg control may also reduce plum fruit moth numbers. The plum fruit moth pheromone trap should be used where the plum fruit moth has been a problem in previous years. (*See pheromones pp. xv–xvi.*)

PLUM SAWFLY Plum sawfly, *Hoplocampa flava*, lays eggs during flowering time and the larvae tunnel into the young fruitlets, moving from one to another over a period of about a month. Attacked fruitlets, recognisable by the entry hole made by the pest and by the exuded gum, drop early and very heavy losses occur in some years. Mid-season flowering varieties, including 'Czar' and 'Victoria', are more subject to attack than early or late flowering varieties. When fully fed, the larvae enter the soil and emerge as adults one or two years later.

Control: Spray seven to ten days after petal fall with dimethoate, permethrin or pirimiphos-methyl. Winter cultivations under the trees may help by disturbing the overwintering larvae.

POCKET PLUM Pocket plum is the name given to the damage caused by the fungus *Taphrina pruni*. The fungus passes from infected spurs into the young plums which elongate and then become hollow on one side and rather boat-like. A white 'bloom' of spores then develops on the fruit and this infects the new growth. No stone is formed and the damaged plums shrivel and fall.

Control: Prune out infected spurs where pocket plums have developed. It may also be worth applying a copper fungicide between bud break and flowering where the disease had been serious the year before.

POTASSIUM DEFICIENCY Potassium deficiency often occurs on light soils and results in a browning and death of the leaf margins, thin, restricted growth and shoot die-back. Leaves are a dull bluish-green and leaf drop often occurs from the tips of shoots downwards. Fruits remain small.

Control: Apply sulphate of potash (potassium sulphate) each spring. For rapid effect, apply a foliar feed when symptoms first seen.

POWDERY MILDEW Powdery mildews attack most kinds of fruit trees, but apple mildew, *Podosphaera leucotrica*, is the only really serious one. It causes severe damage and crop losses on apple and slight damage on pear and quince. Peach mildew, *Sphaerotheca pannosa*, affects peach, particularly under glass, and can be quite damaging. Apple mildew is evident at pink bud stage when infected blossom and leaf trusses become coated with a white, powdery deposit of spores. This constitutes the primary infection and from there it spreads to new leaves and shoots and can also cause a russetting of the skin of the fruit. Infected winter buds appear thin and pointed and the shoots have a distinct silvery appearance.

Control: a) For apple, in winter, prune out all infected shoots, cutting back to three buds below the lowest sign of infection. At pink bud stage, remove all blossom and leaf trusses showing signs of powdery spores and then spray with a benomyl or carbendazim fungicide. Repeat a few times at 14 day intervals. Sulphur fungicide can be used where the variety is not sulphur-shy.

b) For other crops, cut out any severely mildewed growths and spray as for apple.

QUINCE LEAF BLIGHT Quince leaf blight, *Fabraea maculata*, has had at least four different Latin names in recent

years. It causes dark, irregular spots on quince leaves, twigs and fruit. Small black dots develop in the spotted areas, the leaves then turn yellow and fall prematurely. Re-infection occurs from fallen leaves in spring and infected twigs.
Control: Pick up and burn fallen leaves and prune out infected shoots during the winter.

R**ABBIT** Rabbits damage young and older fruit trees in winter by stripping off the bark. Damage can be very serious in hard winters. If damage is done, paint over with a wound paint to protect the exposed wood from infections. Where the bark is removed completely from the trunk, bridge graft in early spring to bypass the damaged area and save the tree.
Control: Protect young trees with spiral plastic rabbit guards or with netting, bearing in mind that with deep snow the rabbits will be able to reach quite high up the trunk. In severe winter snow conditions, pruning the trees and leaving the prunings lying around for the rabbits to eat may save the trees from damage. Pick up and burn once the snow has gone.

RUSSETTING Russetting is the term used to describe the roughness of the skins of fruit. Russetting is quite natural with some fruit, most typically 'Egremont Russet' apples, but with others it can be due to mildew, frost or to the use of an unsuitable chemical, particularly sulphur fungicide on a sulphur-shy variety of apple. Most pear varieties can be subject to damage by sulphur, as can the following apples: 'Beauty of Bath', 'Blenheim Orange', 'Charles Ross', 'Cox's Orange Pippin', 'Lane's Prince Albert', 'Newton Wonder' and 'Peasgood Nonsuch'.

Control: Avoid using sulphur on sulphur-shy varieties.

RUST Rust fungi can attack pear and peach but is only a problem on plum trees. Small bright yellow spots appear on the upper surfaces of the leaves, while underneath can be seen the orange-brown, powdery spots of the rust spores. The rust spore spots turn to black by autumn, leaves turn yellow, and premature leaf fall may occur.
Control: There is no recommended chemical treatment for plum rust. Plum rust alternates between plum and species of anemone, so elimination of any infected anemone plants from the garden will be of help.

S**CALE INSECTS** Scale insects can be found on the bark of most fruit trees, where they feed on the sap. The young disperse on to young growths and fruits. On apple and pear, the most usual species is the mussel scale, *Lepidosaphes ulmi*, while on peach and relatives, plum and on nuts the brown scale, *Parthenolecanium corni*, is the species concerned.
Control: A winter application of tar oil will kill the scale insects on dormant shoots. For control during the growing season, dimethoate or malathion would be effective.

SHOTHOLE Shothole on peaches, cherries, almonds and nectarines is mainly due to attack by the fungus, *Stigmina carpophila*. Rounded brown spots appear on the foliage and later fall away giving the appearance of the leaves having been peppered by shot. Poor growth and waterlogging may encourage this fungal condition.
Control: Feed well to encourage stronger growth. Summer applications

of a copper fungicide, as for bacterial canker, will also be helpful.

SILVER LEAF Silver leaf fungus, *Chondrostereum purpureum*, can attack all trees but plums are most severely affected, and in particular the variety 'Victoria'. In the summer, the foliage on one or more branches appears to have a silvery sheen, due to a separation of the upper epidermis and penetration by an air layer. The affected leaves may later develop a tattered and brown appearance. Branches die out after one or more years and, when cut across, a brown stain can be found in the tissue. After a year or more, purplish, flattened or bracket-type fruiting bodies appear on the dead wood (*see also Silver leaf, p.78*).

Control: The silvered leaves are not infective, but all dead wood should be cut out to 15cm (6in) or so beyond any sign of discoloured wood. All the removed wood should be burned to prevent spore production from the fruiting bodies. It is advisable to remove all dead wood by midsummer to avoid the main spore-production period. Carry out any necessary pruning of stone fruit at the same time, and protect large cuts with a wound paint. It is now possible to control silver leaf by means of the antagonistic fungus *Trichoderma viride*. Pruning wounds are protected from silver leaf attack by being painted with a suspension containing the *Trichoderma* fungus, while to cure an existing attack, wooden pellets, on which the Trichoderma has been cultured, are driven into the tree trunk. The fungus works its way through the tree and attacks the silver leaf infection. At one time, vertical slitting the bark of infected trees was used to encourage renewed vigour, and seemed to clear up silver leaf on some occasions.

SOOTY MOULD Sooty mould, *Cladosporium* spp., grows on sugary honeydew which is excreted by aphids, suckers, scale insects, and a number of other sap-feeding insects.

Control: Control of the pests producing the honeydew will prevent sooty mould growths. Existing moulds can be sponged off leaves and fruit with tepid water.

SPIDER MITE (*SEE FRUIT TREE RED SPIDER MITE, ABOVE, AND TWO-SPOTTED SPIDER MITE, BELOW*)

SPLIT STONE Split stone is a physiological disorder found in peaches just before harvest time. The stalk end of the fruit splits and the stone opens into two halves. Earwigs are commonly found feeding or hiding in the open fruit, and the kernel rots. Infection by brown rot fungus often follows. Lack of lime and inadequate or fluctuating water supplies, aided by poor nutrition, are responsible. Poor pollination may also be involved.

Control: Prevent split stone by hand pollination, feeding well and supplying adequate water when required.

STONY PIT Stony pit is a virus disease found in pears. It causes a distortion and dimpling of the fruit, while inside the fruit are numbers of hard, gritty cells. It will slowly spread through the tree.

Control: There is no cure and affected trees should be grubbed out and burned. Ensure that replacement pears are guaranteed virus-free.

TORTRIX (*SEE CHERRY BARK TORTRIX AND FRUIT TREE TORTRIX MOTHS, ABOVE*)

TWO-SPOTTED SPIDER MITE Two-spotted spider mite, *Tetranychus urticae*, is

a common greenhouse pest that also attacks peach, nectarine and walnut and, to a lesser extent, can be found on apple, cherry, pear and plum. Feeding results in a pale stippling of the foliage as the mites feed underneath the leaves. Severe attacks take all the colour out of the leaves and cropping will be reduced. There can be as many as seven overlapping generations of mites in a year before the female winter forms arise to hide away in cracks and crevices until spring.
Control: Two-spotted spider mite is resistant to many of the available chemicals, but bifenthrin should be effective, as should good, drenching applications of fatty acids or pyrethrins. Ideally spray the plants while the infestation is still at a low level.

VOLES Voles will eat the bark from around the base of fruit trees and can cause considerable losses in some years. They are, however, normally only troublesome where long grasses and weeds are allowed to grow around the base of the tree.
Control: Keep an area around the trunks free of all grass and weeds so there is no hiding place for the voles.

WALNUT BLISTER MITE Walnut blister mite, *Eriophyes erineus* (also known as walnut leaf gall mite), feeds on walnut leaves that react by developing large, raised galls. The underside of the galls is coated with pale hairs amongst which the mites live. Galls can be very numerous, but general growth appears to be unaffected.
Control: None is necessary.

WALNUT LEAF BLOTCH Walnut leaf blotch, *Gnomonia leptostyla*, attacks both the leaves and the young walnuts,

eventually causing a dark spotting and premature defoliation. The fungus continues to develop on the fallen leaves and spores from the leaves infect the new growth in spring.
Control: Gathering up and burning the fallen leaves is often sufficient to control the attack.

WASP Wasps are quite useful to the gardener in spring and early summer, when they feed their young on caterpillars and other pests. They are not as welcome when they attack ripening plums and apples. Wasps will cause the initial damage to soft-skinned plums but on apples are more usually found where birds have pecked and made the first hole.
Control: It is rarely possible to keep wasps away from ripening fruit, although individual fruits can be enclosed in ventilated plastic bags, muslin bags or nylon tights. Jars of water mixed with jam, hung in the trees will catch and kill large numbers of wasps, but have little overall effect on wasp numbers. Any wasp nests can be killed with a carbaryl or rotenone insecticide dust applied in and around the nest in the evening. Alternatively, grow small, trained fruit trees in a fruit cage to avoid bird damage.

WATER CORE Water core is the name given to a condition of apples when parts of the flesh become water-soaked in appearance. Also known as glassiness, this is a physiological disorder which is more severe in apples from young trees and in seasons of extreme variations of water supply and temperature.
Control: There is no real control possible. The condition may disappear during storage if the fruit is kept cool and well ventilated, although severely affected apples are more likely to rot in store.

WATER FLUCTUATIONS Water fluctuations are responsible for a number of problems, but the most common is the splitting of ripening fruits. The skins of the various fruits can become hardened by a spell of hot, dry weather and then cannot cope with a sudden upsurge of water into the fruits following heavy rains. Cherries also crack under conditions of high humidity close to harvest because the fruits cannot evaporate sufficient water.

Control: There is no easy or complete answer to this problem, but adequate watering during dry spells and mulching the soil surface to even out water supplies will help.

WINTER MOTH Winter moth, *Operophtera brumata*, is the most common of the geometer moths (*see also March moth and Mottled umber moth, above*). All fruit tree types can be attacked. The wingless female moth climbs up into the tree in early winter and lays up to 200 eggs among the buds and on the shoots. The eggs hatch in early spring and the looper caterpillars feed on developing leaves and blossoms. Where they feed on young apple fruitlets, the apple may not be destroyed but will carry a round scar, and sometimes quite a deep indentation, until harvest time.

Control: Trap the female moths in bands of sticky grease applied a metre (a yard) up from soil level to the bark, or use proprietary bands supplied for this purpose. The bands must be in place by late autumn. To control the caterpillars, spray with bifenthrin, fatty acids, permethrin, pirimiphos-methyl or pyrethrins before flowering and repeat, if necessary, after petal fall.

WOOLLY APHID Woolly aphid, *Eriosoma lanigerum*, feeds on apple trees, plus a small number of other host plants. The insect was introduced from North America in 1787, and is still referred to as 'American blight' by some. The purplish-coloured pests feed on the sap on young shoots, and around pruning cuts and callus formations on old wood, and can be identified by the copious woolly strands which they secrete. Where the insects feed, the tissue tends to swell up into small galls and these later crack open, allowing access to apple canker and other diseases. As with other aphids, ladybird adults and larvae and the larvae of hoverflies and lacewings feed on the pests and there is also a more specific predator, *Aphelinus mali*, introduced to help with control. This is now established in warmer areas.

Control: Spray with bifenthrin, dimethoate, fatty acids, heptenophos, pirimiphos-methyl, pirimicarb or pyrethrins as necessary. Apply as good, drenching sprays to penetrate the waxy woolly coating.

WITCHES' BROOMS Witches' brooms are found on cherry and plum trees and consist of tufts of small, closely-growing shoots. Various causes have been suggested over the years, including adverse weather damage, virus or pest attack, but on cherry the usual cause is attack by the fungus, *Taphrina cerasi*, and on plums by *Taphrina insititiae*. These are both relatives of the peach leaf curl fungus, but are much less common.

Control: The witches' brooms do no actual harm, but look rather odd and can be cut out. Remove them during early summer to avoid the cut being attacked by silver leaf disease.

FRUIT 2

ROOTS

DISCOLOURED	Strawberry: central tissue red	red core
	Strawberry: roots black	black root rot
NO SPECIAL DISCOLOURATION	Dying, no pests	drought, waterlogging
	Strawberry plants wilting	Verticillium wilt
	White, legless grubs feeding	strawberry root weevil, root weevil
	Large, off–white caterpillars feeding	swift moth, cutworms

PLANTS, CANES, STEMS

DYING BACK	Plants stunted	eelworm, mites
	White mould at plant base	honey fungus
	Purple lesions around cane buds	spur blight
	Canes become brittle, snap at soil level	cane blight
	Silvery areas with clumps of grey mould	grey mould
	Shoot-tips partially severed, larvae in wilted tips	strawberry rhynchites
SPOTTED	Pink pustules	coral spot
	Purple spots with grey centres	cane and leaf spot
TUNNELLED	Raspberry	raspberry moth
	Currant, gooseberry	currant clearwing moth
	Pink maggots under bark of raspberry	raspberry cane midge
GALLED	Distorted shoots	leafy gall
	Lumpy galls	crown gall
PESTS VISIBLE	Hard, shell-like objects	scale insects
	Pinkish, woolly-covered insects	mealy bug

LEAVES AND BUDS

PESTS VISIBLE	Stationary green insects under leaves and on shoot tips	aphids
	Pale stippling of leaves, active pests underneath, making short leaping flights when disturbed	leafhopper

PESTS VISIBLE cont.	Cuckoo spit at junctions of leaves and stems	*froghopper*
	Black-spotted, pale green caterpillars defoliating bushes	*gooseberry sawfly*
	White caterpillars with black and orange markings eating leaves	*magpie moth*
	White to pale green caterpillars webbing strawberry leaves or flower petals together and feeding on leaves, flowers and fruits	*tortrix moths*
NO PESTS VISIBLE LEAVES SPOTTED	Purple spots with grey centres on raspberry, loganberry	*cane and leaf spot*
	Small purple spots on strawberry	*strawberry leaf spot*
	Irregular brown spots on currants and gooseberries	*blackcurrant leaf spot*
	Irregular grey spots on grape	*anthracnose*
	Yellow blotches on cane fruits	*leaf and bud mite*
	Irregular yellow spotting and leaf distortion	*mosaic*
	Irregular brown blotching on strawberry	*leaf blotch*
	Small yellow spots on upper surface, rusty pustules below	*rust fungi*
NO PESTS VISIBLE LEAVES DISCOLOURED	Brown edging, leaves wilting	*frost*
	Yellowing between veins of youngest leaves	*iron deficiency*
	Yellowing between veins of oldest leaves	*magnesium deficiency*
	Leaves silvered	*silver leaf*
	Coated with white, powdery fungus	*American goose-berry mildew, powdery mildew*
	Pale green blotching of upper surface, greyish powdery fungus below	*downy mildew*
	Pale stippling of youngest growth followed by fine webbing	*two-spotted mite*
NO PESTS VISIBLE LEAVES DISTORTED	Deformed leaves and shoots, twisted growths	*lawn-weedkiller damage*
	Currant leaves with few veins and nettle-like appearance	*reversion virus*
	Leaves with small holes and tattered look	*capsid bug*
	Leaves in tips fail to open, twist and turn black	*blackcurrant leaf midge*
	New growths crumpled and puckered	*strawberry mite*

BUDS

	Grossly swollen buds fail to open in spring	*blackcurrant gall mite*
	Buds eaten away in winter and early spring	*birds*

	Flower stalks partially severed	*strawberry blossom weevil*

FLOWERS AND FRUIT

FLOWERS DISCOLOURED	Black centres on strawberry	*frost*
	Green petals on strawberry	*green petal mycoplasma*
FRUIT WITH FUNGAL GROWTHS	White, powdery coating	*powdery mildew*
	Grey, furry growths	*grey mould*
FRUITS DEFORMED	One-sided or uneven development	*poor pollination*
	Fruits split	*splitting*
	Grapes shrivel from stalk end	*shanking*
FRUITS EATEN	Strawberry: irregular holes, slime trails present	*slugs*
	Currant: fruit and leaves eaten, small snails on shoots	*snails*
	Raspberry, blackberry: brown grubs in fruits	*raspberry beetle*
	Grapes: berries hollowed	*wasps*
FRUITS DISCOLOURED	Uneven ripening on blackberry	*red–berry*

AMERICAN GOOSEBERRY MILDEW American gooseberry mildew, *Sphaerotheca mors-uvae*, attacks both gooseberry and currants and is a more serious disease than European gooseberry mildew, *Microsphaera grossulariae*. It first came to Europe around 1900 from North America. A white coating appears on leaves, shoots and young fruits in late spring and during the summer the mildew develops into a brownish felting. On gooseberry, the fruits are generally more severely attacked than the leaves but on currants, the shoot tips are attacked more than the fruits.
Control: Pick up and burn fallen leaves in winter and prune out felted shoots. Avoid excess applications of nitrogen. To prevent attacks, spray three times at 14 day intervals starting just before flowering, using benomyl, carbendazim or sulphur. 'Careless', 'Leveller', and several other traditional varieties of gooseberry, together with 'Wellington XXX' and several other blackcurrant varieties, are sulphur shy, so should not be sprayed with that fungicide. When planting new bushes, choose an open site and a new, mildew-resistant variety such as 'Greenfinch' or 'Invicta' gooseberry or 'Ben Lomond' or 'Ben More' blackcurrant.

ANTHRACNOSE Anthracnose, *Elsinoe ampelina*, is a fungal disease of the grape vine that causes an irregular spotting of the leaves. The grey spots have a darker margin and often fall out, leaving a series of holes. The fruit is also attacked and bears rusty spots.
Control: Cut out and burn affected shoots. A copper fungicide may also be of use.

APHIDS A number of different aphid species can be present on soft fruit bushes (*see also Aphid, p.154*).
Control: Spray as necessary with bifenthrin, dimethoate, fatty acids, pirimicarb,

pirimiphos-methyl or pyrethrins. In winter treat with a tar oil spray (not on strawberries) to kill overwintering eggs.

Main aphid species on soft fruit:

- Large raspberry aphid, *Amphorophora idaei*, and small raspberry aphid, *Aphis idaei*, are important as potential carriers of virus diseases of raspberry and loganberry. Small raspberry aphid causes leaf curling in the tips of new canes.
- Red currant blister aphid, *Cryptomyzus ribis*, is a widespread and damaging species. On red and white currants the aphids feeding under the leaves results in red to purple blisters appearing on the upper leaf surfaces. On blackcurrants the blisters are pale green to yellow.
- Shallot aphid, *Myzus ascalonicus*, attacks strawberry as well as shallots and causes a marked and severe stunting and distortion of the plants.
- Strawberry aphid, *Chaetosiphon fragaefolii*, is a widespread species and serious as a spreader of virus diseases.

BIRDS Bullfinches can eat and damage large numbers of dormant fruiting buds.
Control: Growing crops in a fruit cage is the only complete solution, but netting, or the use of humming or buzzing lines may be sufficient. Gooseberries are often severely attacked and it is wise to delay winter pruning of unprotected bushes until bud growth starts so that lengths of shoot without viable buds can be pruned out.

BLACKCURRANT GALL MITE Blackcurrant gall mite, *Cecidophyopsis ribis*, is a common and damaging pest of blackcurrants, resulting in fruit bud loss and the spread of reversion virus (*see below*). The

mites migrate from infested buds at the 'grape stage' (just before flowering, when the flower buds look like small bunches of grapes) and are carried on the wind and on legs of insects to new bushes. New buds start to swell in summer and are very obvious by leaf fall.
Control: Pick off infested, swollen buds during winter. If leaves show typical reversion symptoms, cropping will gradually decrease, and removal and burning of the bushes is the only action to take. Replace, on a fresh site, with certified, virus-free bushes. There are no chemical controls for blackcurrant gall mite, although the fungicides recommended for powdery mildew may have some controlling effect.

BLACKCURRANT LEAF MIDGE Blackcurrant leaf midge, *Dasineura tetense*, can be a serious pest of blackcurrants. Attacks result in the terminal leaves becoming distorted, folded to one side, and failing to develop fully. These leaves generally turn black by midsummer. There are three to four generations per year, so damage can be considerable unless controlled.
Control: Sprays for aphid control containing dimethoate, applied just before flowering occurs, should also control leaf midge.

BLACKCURRANT LEAF SPOT Blackcurrant leaf spot, *Drepanopeziza (Pseudopeziza) ribis*, attacks currants and gooseberries. The leaves develop scattered, dark brown spots and the leaves gradually turn yellow before falling prematurely. Wet spring and summer weather encourages the disease. Severe attacks have a marked weakening effect on the bushes.
Control: Gather up and burn fallen

leaves during winter to prevent the release of infective spores in spring. Pre- and post-blossom sprays of fungicide for powdery mildew should check attacks, and a spray after picking the crop will also help. Alternatively, spray with man- cozeb before and after flowering and after picking with mancozeb. The new 'Ben' varieties of blackcurrants are less susceptible than many older varieties, but are not truly resistant.

BLACKFLY (*SEE APHIDS, ABOVE*)

BLACK ROOT ROT Black root rot, *Thielaviopsis basicola*, attacks strawberry roots and has been reported on raspberry. Plants wilt and generally die, but there are few specific symptoms visible to the naked eye.
Control: Remove dead or dying plants. Change the soil or use a new site for fur- ther plantings of strawberries.

CANE AND LEAF SPOT Cane and leaf spot, *Elsinoe veneta*, is commonly found on raspberry and loganberry but rarely on blackberry, which has its own cane spot fungus, *Septoria rubi*. Raspberry cane spot appears first as small purple spots on canes and leaves. The spots elongate as the canes grow, and the cen- tres of the spots become grey as the wood dies. The fungus spends the winter on the canes and infects the new growths the following year. Blackberry cane spot is virtually identical.
Control: Cut out spotted canes down to soil level in autumn or winter. With blackberry, training one year's growths in one direction and the following year's in the other reduces the chances of dis- ease spread. To protect the new growth from attack, spray when the buds on the old raspberry canes have grown out

about 2cm (¾in) and repeat just before flowering, using a copper fungicide, benomyl or carbendazim.

CANE BLIGHT Cane blight, *Lep- tosphaeria coniothyrium*, attacks only raspberries, causing the canes to become discoloured and cracked at the base, very brittle, and easily snapped off at soil level. Leaves wither and droop and the infec- tion can spread rapidly. The same fungus can cause a root disease of strawberry and a canker on apples. Attacks on raspberry often follow damage by raspberry cane midge, giving a complex known as midge blight (*see also Raspberry cane midge, below*).
Control: Cut off and burn all diseased canes as soon as the damage is seen, and take action to control raspberry cane midge where this is involved. As infected stools can spread the disease, do not propagate or transplant from the infected area. Disinfect secateurs after cutting out canes affected by this disease. There is no effective chemical control.

CAPSID BUG The common green cap- sid, *Lygocoris pabulinus*, is the main species involved and it will attack all the soft fruits as well as top fruit. Where the pests feed on the sap the punctured tissue turns brown and dies out, resulting in a series of small brown holes. As the leaves expand the damaged areas become tat- tered and distorted. Weeds and garden flowers are attacked as well as fruit crops, and there are two generations of the pest each year. The winter is spent in the egg stage, eggs being inserted into one or two-year-old shoots of currant, goose- berry or other woody plants. Apple capsid also attacks currants and goose- berry in similar fashion (*see also Capsid bug, p. 161*).

Control: Spray before and after flowering using permethrin, pirimiphos-methyl or fatty acids.

CORAL SPOT Coral spot, *Nectria cinnabarina*, is mainly a disease of dead or dying shoots. Infection gains entry through wounds, including pruning cuts, and results in the death of the shoot. Coral-red pustules then arise on the dead wood and produce spores to spread the infection further.

Control: Cut out and burn infected and dead wood, try not to leave snags above buds when pruning, and check other dead wood in the garden, including pea sticks, for signs of coral spot pustules.

CROWN GALL Crown gall, *Agrobacterium tumefaciens*, can attack cane fruits and causes lumpy outgrowths on the stems. This bacterial disease is soil-spread and infects through wounds on the cane.

Control: Take care when cultivating around the canes to avoid damaging the stems. Only propagate from healthy plants and, if necessary, move the cane fruits to a different part of the garden, starting off with new, healthy plants.

CURRANT CLEARWING MOTH Currant clearwing moth, *Synanthedon tipuliformis*, is mainly found on blackcurrant, but redcurrant and gooseberry are also attacked from time to time. The adult moth, which looks more like a wasp than a moth since it has a black body, yellow stripes and partially uncoloured wings, lays eggs on the shoots in early to mid-summer. The larvae bore into the pith of the stems as soon as they hatch and feed inside the stems during summer and winter. Leaves wilt and fruit fails to develop fully on infested shoots. In late spring the following year, the larvae pupate and

emerge shortly afterwards to start the cycle off again.

Control: Cut out wilting shoots. If hollowing is found, cut further back until the pith is sound.

CUTWORMS Cutworms are the caterpillars of certain night-flying moths, including the turnip, the heart and dart and the yellow underwing moths. The caterpillars are plump and relatively large, around 4.5 to 5cm (1¾–2in) when fully fed, and range from brown to green to off-white. They can be serious pests of strawberries on occasions, eating the roots and crown. Typically, cutworms will work their way along rows of plants, eating them off around soil level. Vegetables and ornamentals are often subject to attack.

Control: Frequent cultivations will disturb or expose the larvae. A soil insecticide could be applied for severe attacks, or the crop could be netted to prevent adult moths laying eggs in summer.

DOWNY MILDEW Grape downy mildew, *Plasmopara viticola*, attacks the foliage and flowers, causing an off-white mould under the leaves and pale patches on the upper leaf surfaces. Infected fruits become hardened and fail to develop. This disease came from North America to Europe around 1880, but is unusual in Britain.

Control: Cut out and burn any infected shoots, and spray with copper or mancozeb a few times after flowering.

DROUGHT Drought can affect all plants, but strawberries suffer more than most fruit crops. Plants wilt, fruit development comes to a standstill and, in severe cases, permanent damage can be done.

Control: Incorporate plenty of organic

matter into the soil when preparing the beds for planting. Mulch well in late spring after some good rains or waterings.

EELWORM Eelworms, or nematodes, are microscopic creatures that move in natural films of moisture to invade plant tissue. Strawberry plants are attacked by at least six different eelworms. The most damaging ones are shown below.
Control: There is no chemical control. Burn suspect plants and propagate only from healthy plants, or buy in guaranteed healthy plants from a reputable source.

Main eelworm species on soft fruit:
- Leaf eelworm, *Aphelenchoides fragariae*, attacks strawberries, resulting in a puckering and distortion of the foliage, reduction of leaf edge serrations and a lengthening of leaf stalks. Developing flower trusses and whole plants may be killed.
- Stem eelworm, *Ditylenchus dipsaci*, causes the leaves to become dark green and puckered. Runners, flower and leaf stems become thickened and stunted. Plants can be killed by a severe attack.

FROGHOPPER Common froghopper, *Philaenus spumarius*, is an occasional pest of strawberry and soft-fruit bushes. The larval stage produces the 'cuckoo spit' seen at the junctions of leaves and stems and on young growth. There is a little leaf distortion at the feeding sites, but the froth, produced by the larvae as they feed, can be a nuisance at picking time.
Control: A forceful spray of water from a hose is normally sufficient to dislodge the pests. In severe cases a general insecticide could be used.

FROST Frost causes browning or bleaching of the young leaves of raspberries and the condition known as 'black eye' in strawberries, where the centre of the flower turns black. Such flowers are unable to set fruit. Frost can also damage currant flowers and reduce fruit set.
Control: Avoid planting in any known frost pockets. Covering the crops with a woven fleece will keep out all but a very severe spring frost. Using a water sprinkler on the leaves in the early morning after a frosty night will slow the thawing process and so reduce damage. Where a severe frost is forecast, leaving a lawn sprinkler on the crop overnight would be effective, although expensive in areas subject to water metering.

GOOSEBERRY SAWFLY Gooseberry sawfly, *Nematus ribesii*, is the most damaging of a small group of sawflies that feed on gooseberry. Attacks start in late spring to early summer, but always in the centres of the bushes, so the start of the damage may be missed. The pale green caterpillars, with dark heads and black spots on the body, feed voraciously and can strip a bush of all foliage in a day or two. There are three broods per year although the first is normally the most severe. The larvae pupate in the soil. Bushes of two or three years of age are more seriously attacked than older or younger bushes.
Control: Hand-picking of the caterpillars is possible, but this is a very prickly job. Spraying with fatty acids, permethrin, pirimiphos-methyl or rotenone would be a better option. Look out for signs of early feeding at the centres of the bushes and apply a thorough spray immediately.

GREENFLY (SEE APHIDS, ABOVE)

GREEN PETAL MYCOPLASMA Green petal mycoplasma affects strawberries. A mycoplasma is similar to a bacterium, but without a cell wall, and the symptoms they induce are more like those of a virus. With green petal mycoplasma, the petals take on a green colouration and fruit fails to form or remains small and hard. Leaves are stunted, yellow or red, and the plants are not worth keeping.

Control: The disease is spread by leafhoppers, and is usually carried from clover plants, so good pest control should reduce the chances of infection. Always purchase guaranteed disease-free plants when establishing new beds.

GREY MOULD Grey mould, *Botrytis cinerea*, attacks ripening fruits, and also invades the stems and canes of soft fruit. It is normally a wound parasite, so careful pruning, and good husbandry by way of feeding and site selection, will help to avoid attacks. Attacked tissue develops a characteristic grey, fluffy mould and in the later stages of damage on stems and canes, black masses of fungal threads may develop. On fruits, the grey fungal coating develops rapidly, together with a soft rot. Grey mould is worse in wet weather and often follows damage by hailstones or pests, particularly slugs and snails (*see below*).

Control: Prune out dead or diseased canes and shoots. Protect fruits from pest damage with appropriate pesticide treatments, and control the fungus with benomyl, carbendazim or sulphur. Apply the fungicide immediately before flowering and repeat as necessary after fruit set.

HONEY FUNGUS Honey fungus, *Armillaria mellea*, attacks fruit bushes and canes; it also invades and kills strawberry plants (*see also Honey fungus, p.165*).

IRON DEFICIENCY Iron deficiency is often a problem with gooseberries and raspberries, particularly when grown on chalky or alkaline soils. Any iron present is in the form of insoluble salts. The youngest leaves turn yellow between the veins, and then overall (*see also Iron deficiency, p.165*).

LAWN WEEDKILLER DAMAGE All plants are damaged by contamination by hormone-type lawn weedkillers, but vines are particularly sensitive. Leaves loose their characteristic shape to become more rounded or fan-like, stems may produce warty outgrowths and usually spiral as they grow. Contamination can result from spray drift during application, or from a watering can or sprayer used for weedkiller treatment and then for fertilizer, insecticide or fungicide.

Control: It is virtually impossible to wash out every last trace of some weedkillers from equipment and only minute traces are needed for some extreme effects. The only proper course is to have different cans or sprayers for weedkiller, and to mark them clearly. There is no treatment for weedkiller contamination; whether plants recover or not depends on the degree of contamination, but total recovery to normal growth is unusual.

LEAF AND BUD MITE Leaf and bud mite, *Phyllocoptes gracilis*, is a common pest of raspberry, and a less common problem on blackberry. Attacks cause the foliage to become distorted with a yellow discolouration on the upper surface and an unusual hair development under the leaf. Terminal buds are sometimes killed, resulting in the growth of more laterals than normal. Severe attacks on the fruits result in malformation and irregular ripening. The raspberry 'Malling Jewel' is particularly susceptible to attack.

Control: No effective chemicals exist, but fortunately the pest is often kept in check by the predatory mite *Typhlodromus pyri*.

LEAF BLOTCH Leaf blotch, *Gnomonia fruticola*, (although it can be found under a number of different names) affects strawberry and appears as large brown areas surrounded by purple and yellow borders. The fruit and leaf stalks may also blacken and rot, resulting in a withering of fruits and foliage. The old varieties 'Cambridge Favourite' and 'Redgauntlet' are particularly prone to attack.

Control: Remove and burn affected parts. Sprays of fungicide for grey mould control should also reduce or control.

LEAFHOPPER Several different species of leafhopper can attack soft fruit, and they are to be found feeding under the leaves. Where they feed on the sap, a pale stippled spotting appears on the upper leaf surface, and in severe attacks the whole leaf colour may be affected. Nymph stages of the pests are present alongside the adults together with cast skins. The adults make short, leaping flights when disturbed.

Control: Insecticides applied to control aphids will normally take care of leafhoppers at the same time.

LEAFY GALL Leafy gall, caused by the bacterium *Corynebacterium fascians*, is mainly a problem on ornamental plants, but it can also attack strawberries. When the bacterium and a nematode (eelworm) attack strawberries the resulting proliferation of shoots is known as 'cauliflower disease'.

Control: The bacterium persists in the soil, so crop rotation, or removal of the strawberry plot to a different part of the garden and starting again with new, healthy plants, is the best solution.

MAGNESIUM DEFICIENCY Magnesium deficiency shows up as a yellowing of the older leaves with the veins staying green. Being a soluble element, magnesium is quickly washed out of the surface soil layers in wet weather.

Control: Spray the foliage with a solution of magnesium sulphate (Epsom Salts) using 100g per 5l (4oz/1gall) of water plus a wetting agent. A few fortnightly treatments, starting at the first sign of the yellowing, will assist the leaves to green up. For longer-term correction of magnesium deficiency, apply a dressing of magnesium limestone to the soil.

MAGPIE MOTH Magpie moth, *Abraxus grossulariata*, is a frequent pest of currant and gooseberry, although damage is not as serious as that caused by gooseberry sawfly (*above*). The caterpillars are white with black markings and an orange stripe down each side. They hatch from eggs laid in late summer and feed till late autumn, hibernate and then feed again in early spring. Magpie moth caterpillars can be distinguished from gooseberry sawfly by the earlier start to feeding, by the orange stripes and by the fact that, when disturbed, the magpie moth caterpillars drop from the plant on a silken thread.

Control: Treat as for gooseberry sawfly (*see above*).

MEALY BUG Various mealy bugs, but mainly *Pseudococcus* spp., attack grape vines, although attacks are largely limited to greenhouse culture. Pinkish, mainly immobile insects cluster in leaf axils, and in severe attacks among the developing berries. Mealy bugs are coated with strands of white wax which they produce from their bodies, and they also produce masses of sugary honeydew. This makes leaves, stems and fruits sticky, and encourages the growth of sooty moulds.

Control: Spray with dimethoate, heptenophos or pirimiphos-methyl, ensuring good penetration of the mealy coating. Under glass, an alternative method is to introduce the mealy bug predator *Cryptolaemus* (*see Biological control, pp. xvi–xxi*).

MITES (*SEE BLACKCURRANT GALL MITE, LEAF AND BUD MITE, ABOVE, AND REDBERRY, STRAWBERRY MITE AND TWO-SPOTTED MITE, BELOW*)

MOSAIC Mosaic is probably the most common symptom of virus attack on raspberries. Attack results in a yellow discolouration and distortion of the leaves and a gradual falling-off in crop yields. The virus types that cause mosaic are carried by aphids as they feed, although other viruses can be spread by eelworms in the soil.

Control: The simplest solution is to grow only the newer varieties of raspberry that are resistant to aphid attack, and which, therefore, can be expected to remain free from aphid-transmitted diseases. 'Autumn Bliss', 'Joy', 'Leo' and 'Malling Delight', for example, are all listed as aphid-resistant, and reliable suppliers will be able to offer advice on new varieties as they become available.

POOR POLLINATION Poor pollination is generally due to adverse weather conditions during flowering time which keep bees and other pollinating insects away. It shows up in the form of lack of fruit on parts of the flowering stalks, or uneven fruits.

Control: Hand-pollination of soft fruit flowers is impracticable, so no treatment is possible.

POWDERY MILDEW (SEE ALSO AMERICAN GOOSEBERRY MILDEW, ABOVE). Leaves and fruit become coated in a white, powdery covering. Powdery mildew is less severe on plants receiving adequate water, so watering well in dry weather and mulching to conserve moisture will help to keep it in check.

Control: Spray at the first sign of attack with a benlate, carbendazim or sulphur fungicide. Repeat a few times at 14 day intervals.

Main mildew species:

- Strawberry mildew, *Sphaerotheca maculans,* shows first as an upward curling and purpling of the leaves. The typical mildew symptoms then appear on the undersides of the leaves and on any fruit present. The fruits stay firm, unlike those that have been attacked by grey mould. This fungus spends the winter on the old leaves, so cut or burn them off after picking the crop.

- Vine powdery mildew, *Uncinula necator,* attacks leaves, shoots and the developing grapes. When the grapes are attacked early they stop growing, crack, and are then subject to infection by various rotting fungi. Cut out and burn infected shoots as soon as seen.

RASPBERRY BEETLE Raspberry beetle, *Byturus tomentosus,* attacks raspberry, loganberry and blackberry. The adult beetles appear in spring and feed on apple, pear and hawthorn blossoms before moving to the soft fruit flowers. There, the beetles feed on open and unopened flowers. Each female beetle will lay about 100 eggs, one per flower, over a two to three week period. The larvae feed externally on the young fruits and at pink fruit stage of raspberry they bore into the basal plug. They then feed in the fruits for a number of weeks before dropping to the ground where they pupate.

Control: Regular winter cultivations will expose and may kill the beetles but very good control can be achieved with just one or two sprays in summer. Using bifenthrin, permethrin or rotenone, spray raspberry at the first pink fruit stage, loganberry when 80 per cent of the blossom is over and again two weeks later, and blackberry immediately before the first flower opens.

RASPBERRY CANE MIDGE Raspberry cane midge, *Resseliella theobaldi*, attacks raspberry and occasionally loganberry. The adult lays her eggs in natural splits on young, 20 to 30cm (8–12in) high raspberry shoots, and the pinkish larvae feed underneath the rind. As many as 100 larvae can be found on a single young cane and with three generations of the midge in most years, there can be several hundred larvae per cane by autumn. The actual midge damage is fairly superficial, but the attacked areas are frequently invaded by fungal diseases which combine to create a disorder known as midge blight, and this may kill the canes. Varieties with naturally splitting canes, including 'Glen Clova' and 'Malling Promise' are more subject to attack than the older 'Norfolk Giant'.

Control: Spray with a contact insecticide, such as permethrin when the canes are about 25cm (10in) high and repeat two weeks later. One cultural method used in commercial plantations is to cut out the first flush of canes from 'Glen Clova' and any other variety found to be very susceptible. The following canes will then develop when there are less cane midge adults around.

RASPBERRY MOTH Raspberry moth, *Lampronia rubiella*, is quite widespread and can be a serious pest of cane fruit in some years. The caterpillars feed on the developing fruits in summer, but cause little harm, and then move down into the soil where they stay over the winter. In spring, the caterpillars climb to the tops of the new canes and bore into the tips. Infested canes wither and may send out side shoots but these too are often be invaded. With a severe attack, few new canes will develop sufficiently to carry a crop the following year.

Control: Remove old canes and stakes from the bed in winter, and cultivate lightly, without damaging the canes or roots, and apply a tar oil spray as for aphid control, drenching it into the bases of the canes. Alternatively, spray in late spring as the caterpillars are moving from the soil to the new cane tips, using a contact insecticide like permethrin or fatty acids.

RED-BERRY Red-berry is a condition found on blackberry where only part of the fruit ripens to the normal black colour, with the remainder staying green or red and hard. The damage is caused by feeding by the blackberry mite, *Acalitus essigi*. The adult mites come out of hibernation in early spring and build up on the leaves and leaf stalks. At flowering time the mites enter the flowers and feed on the developing fruits, particularly those at the base of the berry. The mites migrate to the bud scales in late summer, where they spend the winter. Damage varies from light to very severe, possibly depending on autumn and winter weather conditions.

Control: No chemical is effective against red-berry. Pruning out severely affected shoots immediately after picking the crop should also remove a lot of the mite population.

RED CORE Red core, *Phytophthora fragariae*, is a fungal disease that attacks the roots of strawberry. Patches of stunted strawberry plants can be seen in early summer, the outer leaves being stiff and brown and the inner, newer ones being small and having a red colouration. The roots are rotted and brown, but when the outer layer is pulled off the inner tissue is seen to be red in colour.

Control: The infection is in the soil and there is no satisfactory control. Fortunately, there are some resistant varieties, including 'Bogota', 'Tantallon' and 'Tristar'. If there is any suspicion that your soil may be infected it is better to use another area of the garden, as well as seeking advice from a reliable supplier on the best resistant varieties available.

REVERSION VIRUS Reversion virus affects blackcurrants and is spread by the blackcurrant gall mite. The most easily recognised symptom is a reduction in the number of lobes of the leaf, giving a nettle-leaf appearance, accompanied by fewer side veins arising from the main central leaf vein. Healthy leaves will have five or more side veins, reversion-infected leaves less then five, and infected flowers are almost hairless and appear more brightly coloured. Bushes infected with the reversion virus are more susceptible to attack by blackcurrant gall mite, thus compounding the problem.

Control: Dig out and burn infested bushes. Always destroy the old bushes before planting new and certified healthy ones.

RUST FUNGI Rust fungi produce orange, brown or black powdery patches on the leaves and sometimes on the fruit. Some species of rust alternate between different host plants, others stay on one host while yet others have two different life-cycle stages that can persist on two different hosts.

Control: Cut out and burn badly-infected shoots. Try to protect from attack by spraying with mancozeb or with a copper fungicide a few times from spring onwards. Some varieties of gooseberry are copper shy, including 'Careless' and 'Leveller'.

Main rust species:

- Blackberry stem rust, *Kuehneola uredinis*, produces orange spotting of the leaves and yellow spots on canes.
- Blackberry common rust, *Phragmidium violaceum*, produces purple spots on the upper leaf surfaces with an orange or black spotting below, and can also produce orange pustules in splits in the canes.
- Gooseberry cluster-cup rust, *Puccinia caricina* var. *pringsheimiana*, alternates between sedges and gooseberry. On gooseberry the fungus starts as deep orange or red pustules on fruits and leaves in summer. The pustules then produce cup-like growths, the leaves curl, and stem swellings appear. The next stage in the life cycle has to take place on sedges before the fungus can return to gooseberry. Removal of any sedges present in the garden is an essential part of the control. Glyphosate would be a suitable weedkiller to use.
- White pine rust, *Cronartium ribicola*, alternates between white pine, *Pinus*

strobus, and currant, but the damage is normally far more severe on the pine than on the currant.

• Raspberry rust, *Phragmidium rubi-idaei*, develops as yellow pustules on the upper surfaces of the leaves followed by orange spores. Later, black pustules appear on the lower surfaces.

S**CALE INSECTS** Scale insects have hard, shell-like coverings of the body, composed of old cast-off skins and wax. They can be found on those types of fruit which have a permanent branch framework. The young hatch from eggs under the female scale and may migrate to newer wood or stay in the same spot, depending on the species involved. Scale insects feed on the sap but cause little real harm.

Control: Tar oil winter sprays for aphid control will also kill any scale insects present on the bark.

The main species on soft fruit bushes and grape vines are:

• Brown scale, *Parthenolecanium corni*, which attacks all fruit types.
• Mussel scale, *Lepidosaphes ulmi*, found on currant and gooseberry.
• Oyster scale, *Quadraspidiotus ostreaeformis*, which attacks currants.
• Woolly currant scale, *Pulvinaria ribesiae*, found on currant and gooseberry.

All the above can also be found on various top fruit trees (*see pp.151–174*) .

SHANKING Shanking is the name given to a growth disorder of greenhouse-grown grapes which results in the fruit stalks of individual berries turning black and shrivelling. The grapes then fail to develop fully and remain sour. White varieties of grape appear translucent and black varieties turn red. Shanking is associated with poor root activity and lack of nutrient uptake. Waterlogging or drought may be involved.

Control: Good soil preparation before planting is essential and will help to prevent later problems with shanking. Where it does appear, apply more, or less, water depending on conditions, cut out the affected berries and apply a few sprays of a complete foliar feed to put nutrients into the plant quickly.

SILVER LEAF Silver leaf, *Chondrostereum purpureum*, shows up as a silvery sheen on the leaves and a die-back of shoots. Brown staining of the wood is visible when dead shoots are cut across.

Control: The silvered leaves are not infective, but all dead wood should be cut out to 15cm (6in) or so beyond any sign of discoloured wood. All the removed wood should be burned to prevent spore production from the fruiting bodies. It is advisable to remove all dead wood by midsummer to avoid the main spore-production period. It is now possible to control silver leaf by means of the antagonistic fungus *Trichoderma viride*. Pruning wounds are protected from silver leaf attack by being painted with a suspension containing the *Trichoderma* fungus. The fungus works its way through the plant and attacks the silver leaf infection.

SLUG Slugs are mainly a problem on strawberry fruits where the damage caused by their feeding can also provide a point of entry for grey mould disease. There can be as many as 200 slugs per square metre (square yard) of soil and slug activity increases in wet weather. The field slug, *Deroceras reticulatum*, is probably the most damaging and also feeds on currants, gooseberries and raspberries. Other species found to be damaging are the black slug, *Arion ater*, and the garden slug, *Arion hortensis*.

Control: Scatter metaldehyde or methiocarb pellets thinly over the strawberry beds in advance of fruiting and repeat as necessary during picking. Alternatively, use the nematode *Phasmarhabditis hermaphrodita*, which seeks out slugs in the soil. The nematodes enter the slug via the breathing hole and carry with them a bacterium which kills the slug (*see Biological control*, pp. *xvi–xxi*).

SNAILS Snails can damage soft fruit crops, but are normally less of a problem than slugs. The strawberry snail, *Trichia striolata*, and the garden snail, *Helix aspera*, can both attack strawberry, gooseberry and currant, while the smaller banded snail, *Cepaea hortensis*, and the larger banded snail, *Cepaea nemoralis*, can be found in blackcurrant bushes and may get picked along with the crop.

Control: Use metaldehyde or methiocarb pellets as for slugs, *above*.

SPLITTING Splitting of ripening fruits is normally due to heavy rain or applied water after a drought. Skins hardened in the dry conditions are unable to cope with the sudden intake of water.

Control: Incorporation of plenty of organic matter into the soil before planting and regular mulching after will help to even out water supply. In prolonged drought, try not to let the soil dry out completely. A few good soakings are more effective than several light waterings.

SPUR BLIGHT Spur blight, *Dydimella applanata*, is a serious disease affecting raspberry and loganberry. Infection occurs in late spring to early summer, but is not really evident until late summer, when the purple lesions appear on the canes. The infections are centred on the buds and during winter the lesions turn silvery and the buds are killed. Fungal bodies on the silvery areas produce spores in spring and these infect the new canes. Both dense stands of new canes and wet weather encourage the spur blight fungus.

Control: 'Malling Admiral' and 'Leo' have some inbred resistance to spur blight. Remove any canes with silvery markings during winter and thin out the new canes in spring. A few sprays with benomyl or carbendazim, starting when the new canes are about 15cm (6in) high, would protect them from attack.

STRAWBERRY BLOSSOM WEEVIL Strawberry blossom weevil, *Anthonomus rubi*, can be a locally important pest in strawberry-growing areas. Raspberry and blackberry are also attacked. The female weevil lays her eggs singly in unopened flower buds and then makes a ring of punctures round each flower stalk. The buds fail to open and the weevil larvae complete their development inside.

Control: An application of permethrin at green bud stage should stop most of the damage.

STRAWBERRY LEAF SPOT Strawberry leaf spot, *Mycosphaerella fragariae*, causes small red spots on the leaves. Later, the spots turn grey then almost white with a red border. With a severe attack the spots may join up, and the leaves will then turn brown and die.

Control: Cutting or burning off the old foliage after cropping will take care of much of the infection. For severe attacks, applications of fungicide, as for grey mould control (*above*), should help.

STRAWBERRY MITE Strawberry mite, *Tarsonemus pallidus fragariae*, is a serious pest of strawberry plants. The mites inject a toxic substance into the plant as they feed and the leaves become crinkled, discoloured and brittle. Plants become severely stunted and may die. If they survive, fruits are small and poor.

Control: Do not take runners from infested plants. Infested plants are best removed and burned, and new, healthy plants set out in a new site. Bifenthrin may be of value as a spray against light attacks.

STRAWBERRY RHYNCHITES Strawberry rhynchites, *Rhynchites germanicus*, is a damaging pest of strawberry, raspberry, loganberry and blackberry. This weevil used to be known as 'elephant bug' by former generations of strawberry growers. The adults feed first on the foliage in late spring and then on flowers and shoots. The females lay their eggs in the runners of strawberry, in the terminal blossom trusses of blackberry, and in tips of shoots of raspberry and loganberry. In a similar fashion to strawberry blossom weevil (*above*), a ring of punctures below each egg causes the shoot tip to wilt or fall off. The larvae complete their development in the tip and they then leave to pupate in the soil.

Control: Spray with permethrin at green bud stage. For attacks after flowering, spray at the first sign of damage and repeat as necessary.

STRAWBERRY ROOT WEEVIL There are several different weevils that feed on the roots of strawberry, typified by *Otiorhynchus rugosostriatus*. Eggs are laid by the female weevils (no males are known) in late summer and autumn, either in the soil or on the lowest leaf stalks. The larvae feed on the roots through to spring and then pupate, and some slight damage is done to the leaves

by the adult weevils. The root feeding can be severe and plants will wilt and may die. The white, legless larvae have brown heads and can be found feeding on the roots of wilting plants.

Control: The most satisfactory control will be obtained by using one of the nematode biological control agents, *Heterorhabditis megadis* or *Steinernema carpocapsae*. These nematodes invade the tissue of the weevil larvae and infect them with a bacterium. The bacteria attack and kill the larvae and the nematodes feed and build up their numbers on the breakdown contents. Moisture and a reasonable soil temperature, between 10 and 25°C (50 and 77°F), are required for the nematodes to flourish.

SWIFT MOTH Swift moths, both the ghost swift moth, *Hepialus humuli*, and the garden swift moth, *Hepialus lupulinus*, fly at dusk in summer and scatter their eggs around suitable host plants which include strawberry. The whitish, semi-transparent larvae feed on plant roots through to spring. Garden swift moth larvae feed for one, and sometimes two years, while ghost swift moth larvae feed for two and sometimes three years. Root damage can be severe and plants may die. Garden swift moth larvae wriggle backwards vigorously when disturbed, while ghost swift moth larvae retreat into their silk-lined feeding tunnels.

Control: Thorough soil preparation before planting will expose the larvae, which can then be removed. After planting, the nematodes recommended for strawberry root weevil (*above*), will probably prove effective. Alternatively, apply a soil insecticide.

TORTRIX MOTHS Various species of tortrix moth can attack soft fruit, but the strawberry tortrix, *Acleris comariana*, is probably the most damaging. It is most severe in low-lying areas where its natural food plants, marsh cinquefoil, water avens and wild strawberries are to be found. There are two generations of this pest per year and the caterpillars feed on leaves and flowers, often webbing leaves or petals together and feeding below. Fruits can also be attacked.

Control: Spraying with bifenthrin or permethrin just before flowering should stop most of the damage.

TWO-SPOTTED MITE Two-spotted mite, *Tetranychus urticae*, feed on blackcurrant and strawberry leaves, resulting in a stippling on the upper leaf surfaces. In severe cases there will be a fine webbing over the plant, and the leaves will take on a bronzed appearance. Early leaf fall follows and cropping is reduced. Each female is capable of laying up to 100 eggs, and with seven generations produced per year, populations can increase to pest levels very rapidly.

Control: Two-spotted mite is resistant to a great many chemicals, but bifenthrin should be effective. Spray before flowering in most seasons. The predatory mite *Phytoseiulus persimilis* can be introduced into soft fruit crops and may keep two-spotted mite in check, particularly in warm summer weather.

VERTICILLIUM WILT Verticillium wilt, *Verticillium* spp., attacks through the soil via the root system and causes a wilting and death of strawberry plants. The infection spreads through the soil to affect a whole bed of plants.

Control: Remove and burn any suspect plants, and replant new, healthy strawberries on a new site.

VINE WEEVIL Vine weevil, *Otiorhynchus sulcatus*, attacks the roots of currants, gooseberries, raspberries, strawberries, vines and other plants. Each female weevil lays several hundred eggs without recourse to mating, as males are unknown. The larvae feed on the roots, and plants may be killed.

Control: Treat the soil with a nematode biological control agent as described for the control of strawberry root weevil (*above*).

VIRUS (*SEE MOSAIC AND REVERSION VIRUS, ABOVE*)

WASP Wasps, both *Vespa vulgaris* the common wasp and *Vespa germanica*, the German wasp, attack ripening fruit in autumn. In spring, however, wasps prey on caterpillars and other harmful insects, so are beneficial creatures at that time.

Control: If numbers are too great in autumn, seek out the nests and dust in and around the entrance holes with a carbaryl or rotenone preparation.

WATERLOGGING Waterlogging shows up in the form of poor growth, wilting shoots and nutrient-deficient leaves. When plants die after periods of heavy rain, and no obvious symptoms are present, suspect waterlogging of the root system.

Control: There is no easy answer for existing plantings, but thorough soil preparation and the provision of soakaways will help to avoid problems in future.

WEEVILS (*SEE STRAWBERRY BLOSSOM WEEVIL, STRAWBERRY ROOT WEEVIL AND VINE WEEVIL, ABOVE*)

APPENDIX

The lists that follow show representatives from all the different types of garden plants, grouped under ornamentals, lawns, vegetables and fruit. The more important pests, diseases and other disorders that may affect them follow each plant name.

ORNAMENTALS

AFRICAN MARIGOLD (*TAGETES ERECTA*)   Aphids, damping off, slugs

AFRICAN VIOLET   *See Saintpaulia*

ALDER (*ALNUS*)   Caterpillar, heart rot, leafhopper, scale insects

ANEMONE   Aphids, cutworm, downy mildew, grey mould, rust, slugs and snails, swift moths, virus

ANTIRRHINUM   Aphids, damping off, leaf spot, powdery mildew, rust

AQUILEGIA   Aphids, leaf spot, powdery mildew

ARABIS   Virus, white blister

ASTER (ANNUAL)   Aphids, damping off, grey mould, leaf spot, powdery mildew, virus, wilt

AUBRIETA   Downy mildew, white blister

AZALEA   *See Rhododendron*

BAY (*LAURUS NOBILIS*)   Scale insects, bay sucker

BEECH (*FAGUS*)   Aphids, coral spot, heart rot, leaf spot, powdery mildew, scale insects

BEGONIA   Aphids, cyclamen mite, grey mould, leaf spot, mealy bug, powdery mildew, slugs, two spotted (red) spider mite, vine weevil, wilt

BERBERIS   Leaf spot, rust

BIRCH (*BETULA*)   Bracket fungi, sawfly caterpillar, leaf spot, rust, witches' broom

BROOM (*CYTISUS*)   Broom gall mite, rust

BUDDLEIA   Capsid, virus, weevil

BUSY LIZZIE (*IMPATIENS*)   Aphid, damping off, grey mould, glasshouse leafhopper, leaf spot, springtails, two-spotted (red) spider mite

CACTI & SUCCULENTS   Mealy bug, oedema, root mealy bug, root rots, scale insects, snails

CAMELLIA   Bud drop, iron deficiency, leaf spot, oedema, scale insects, sooty mould, vine weevil

CARNATION & PINKS (*DIANTHUS*)   Aphid, tortrix caterpillar, grey mould, leaf spot, powdery mildew, rust, thrips, two-spotted (red) spider mite, virus, wilt

CARYOPTERIS   Capsid

CHAMAECYPARIS   Aphid, honey fungus, phytophthora

CHRISTMAS ROSE (*HELLEBORUS NIGER*)   Leaf spot

CHRISTMAS TREE (*PICEA*)   Spruce pineapple gall adelges

CHRYSANTHEMUM   Aphid, bloom damping, capsid, earwigs, eelworm, leaf miner, leafy gall, petal blight, powdery mildew, rust, virus, wilt

CINERARIA   Aphids, crown rot, leaf miner, powdery mildew, sciarid fly, waterlogging

CLEMATIS   Aphid, earwig, powdery mildew, slugs and snails, wilt

COLEUS   Mealy bug, waterlogging

COTINUS   Powdery mildew

COTONEASTER   Fireblight, woolly aphid

CROCUS   Aphids, birds, drought, mice

CUPRESSUS   Aphid, honey fungus, phytophthora

CYCLAMEN   Cyclamen mite, grey mould, vine weevil, waterlogging

DAFFODIL (*NARCISSUS*)   Bulb mite, eelworm, narcissus fly, smoulder, virus

DAHLIA   Aphid, capsid, crown gall, earwig, two-spotted (red) spider mite, wilt

DAPHNE   Leaf spot, virus

EUONYMUS   Aphid, caterpillar, scale insect, powdery mildew

FICUS   Dry air, thrips, waterlogging

FORGET-ME-NOT (*MYOSOTIS*)   Powdery mildew

FORSYTHIA   Birds, capsid, fasciation

FREESIA   Aphid, corm rots, grey mould, leaf spot, virus

FUCHSIA   Aphids, capsid, rust, two-spotted (red) spider mite, whitefly

GLADIOLUS   Aphids, corm rots, grey mould, thrips, virus

GOLDEN ROD (*SOLIDAGO*)   Powdery mildew

HEBE   Leaf spot

HOLLY (*ILEX*)   Leaf miner

HOLLYHOCK (*ALCEA*)   Capsid, caterpillar, rust, slugs and snails

HONEYSUCKLE (*LONICERA*)   Aphid, powdery mildew

HOSTA   Slugs and snails

HYDRANGEA   Capsid, iron deficiency, leaf spot

IRIS   Caterpillar, leaf spot

LAUREL (*PRUNUS LAUROCERASUS*)   Powdery mildew, vine weevil

LABURNUM   Leaf-cutter bee, leaf miner

LAVENDER (*LAVANDULA*)   Cuckoo spit, shab disease

LILAC (SYRINGA)   Leaf miner, lilac blight

LILY (*LILIUM*)   Grey mould, leaf blight, lily beetle, slugs and snails

LILY-OF-THE-VALLEY (*CONVALLARIA*)   Peony blight

LUPIN (*LUPINUS*)   Aphid, crown gall, leaf spot, powdery mildew

MAPLE & SYCAMORE (*ACER*)   Gall mites, leaf hopper, sooty bark disease, tar spot

MICHAELMAS DAISY (*ASTER*)   Cuckoo spit, eelworm, powdery mildew

MOUNTAIN ASH (*SORBUS*)   Fireblight, pear leaf blister mite

MULLEIN (*VERBASCUM*)   Mullein moth caterpillar

NASTURTIUM (*TROPAEOLUM*)   Aphid, caterpillar

ORCHID   Aphid, leaf spot, scale insects, two-spotted (red) spider mite, virus

PEONY (*PAEONIA*)   Peony blight

PANSY (*VIOLA*)   Aphid, leaf midge, wilt

PASSION FLOWER *(PASSIFLORA)*   Virus

PELARGONIUM   Aphid, black leg, oedema, rust, whitefly

PRIMULA   Aphid, leaf spot, vine weevil

PRIVET (*LIGUSTRUM*)   Honey fungus, thrips

PRUNUS   Aphid, bacterial canker, rust, shothole

RHODODENDRON & AZALEA   Azalea leaf gall, bud blast, leaf spot, vine weevil

ROSE *(ROSA)*   Aphid, black spot, sawfly caterpillars, powdery mildew, rust

SAINTPAULIA   Cyclamen mite, sun scorch

SALVIA Capsid	
SOLOMON'S SEAL (*POLYGONATUM*) Sawfly caterpillar	
STOCK (*MATTHIOLA*) Club root, flea beetle, white blister	
SWEET PEA (*LATHYRUS*) Aphids, pollen beetle, powdery mildew, root and foot rot, wilt	
SWEET WILLIAM (*DIANTHUS BARBATUS*) Leaf spot, rust	
TULIP (*TULIPA*) Aphid, fire, bulb rots, eelworm	
VIBURNUM Aphid	
VIOLET (*VIOLA*) Leaf midge	
WALLFLOWER (*CHEIRANTHUS*) Cabbage root fly, club root, downy mildew, white blister	
WATER-LILY (*NYMPHAEA*) Aphid, water-lily beetle	
WILLOW (*SALIX*) Anthracnose, aphid, heart rot, scale insects	

LAWNS

Ants, chafer grubs, dollar spot, earthworms, fairy rings, fusarium patch, leatherjackets, mining bees, moles, red thread

VEGETABLES

ASPARAGUS Asparagus beetle, slugs	
AUBERGINE Aphid, grey mould, two-spotted (red) spider mite	
BEANS Aphid, chocolate spot, halo blight, pea and bean weevil, pea midge, wilt	
BEETROOT Aphids, bolting, heart rot, mangold fly (leaf miner)	
BROCCOLI *See Cauliflower*	
CABBAGE, KALE & SPROUTS Aphid, cabbage caterpillars, cabbage root fly, club root, flea beetle, white blister, whitefly, wirestem	
CALABRESE *See Cauliflower*	
CARROT Aphid, carrot fly, motley dwarf disease	
CAULIFLOWER, BROCCOLI & CALABRESE Aphid, blindness, cabbage root fly, cabbage caterpillars, pigeons, whiptail, white blister, whitefly	
CELERY & CELERIAC Aphid, celery fly (leaf miner), leaf spot, slugs	
COURGETTE, MARROW & PUMPKIN Aphid, capsid, magnesium deficiency, powdery mildew, virus	
CUCUMBER Aphid, dry air, grey mould, powdery mildew, two-spotted (red) spider mite, whitefly, wilt	
JERUSALEM ARTICHOKE Slugs, swift moth caterpillar	
KALE *See Cabbage*	
LEEK Leek moth caterpillar, onion fly, rust, thrips, white rot	
LETTUCE Aphids, bolting, cutworm, grey mould, downy mildew, root aphid, virus	
MARROW *See Courgette*	
ONION & SHALLOT Bolting, eelworm, grey mould, leek moth, neck rot, onion fly, thrips, white rot	
PARSNIP Aphids, canker, carrot fly, celery fly (leaf miner), slugs	
PEA Aphids, leaf and pod spot, marsh spot, pea and bean weevil, pea moth, thrips, wilt	
PEPPERS Aphids, two-spotted (red) spider mite	
POTATO Aphids, blackleg, Colorado beetle, eelworms, frost, potato blight, scab, slug, storage rots, virus	

PUMPKIN   *See Courgette*

RADISH   *See Turnip*

RHUBARB   Crown rot, leaf spot, rosy rustic moth, virus

SHALLOT   *See Onion*

SPINACH, SPINACH BEET & SWISS CHARD   Aphid, manganese deficiency, mangold fly (leaf miner), slug

SPROUTS   *See Cabbage*

SWEDE   *See Turnip*

SWEET CORN   Frit fly, mice, seed rots, smut

SWISS CHARD   *See Spinach*

TOMATO   Aphids, blossom end rot, eelworm, grey mould, leaf mould, magnesium deficiency, potato blight, stem rot, tomato moth, two-spotted (red) spider mite, whitefly, wilt, virus

TURNIP, SWEDE & RADISH   Brown heart, cabbage root fly, club root, flea beetle, mealy cabbage aphid, powdery mildew

FRUIT

APPLE   Aphids, canker, capsid, caterpillars including codling moth, fruit tree red spider mite, powdery mildew, scab, storage rots, woolly aphid

APRICOT & ALMOND   Aphids, bacterial canker, iron deficiency, peach leaf curl, scale insects, shot hole, two-spotted (red) spider mite

BLACKBERRY & LOGANBERRY   Aphids, cane spot, capsid, raspberry beetle, rust

CHERRY   Aphids, bacterial canker, various caterpillars, silver leaf

CURRANTS   Aphids, capsid, gall mite, leaf spot, powdery mildew, scale insects

GOOSEBERRY   Aphids, sawfly caterpillars, leaf spot, powdery mildew, rust

GRAPE   Powdery mildew, scale insects, two-spotted (red) spider mite

PEACH & NECTARINE   Aphids, bacterial canker, peach leaf curl, scale insects, shot hole, silver leaf, two-spotted (red) spider mite

PEAR   Aphids, fireblight, leaf blister mite, midge, scab, sucker

PLUM & DAMSON   Aphids, caterpillars, rust, silver leaf

QUINCE   Leaf blight

RASPBERRY   Aphids, cane spot, raspberry beetle, spur blight, virus

STRAWBERRY   Aphids, tortrix caterpillar, grey mould, powdery mildew, slugs and snails, two-spotted (red) spider mite, virus

WALNUT   Leaf blotch, leaf gall mite

INDEX

NOTES

AMATEUR GARDENING

Hamlyn in association with **Amateur Gardening** also publish Stefan Buczacki's 'Best' series. A complete range of these titles, along with the handy Pocket Reference series, is available from all good bookshops or by Mail Order direct from the publisher. Payment can be made by credit card or cheque/postal order in the following ways:

By Phone Phone through your order on our special CREDIT CARD HOTLINE on **0933 410511**. Speak to our customer service team during office hours (9am to 5pm) or leave a message on the answer machine, quoting your full credit card number plus expiry date and your full name and address. Please also quote the reference number shown at the top of this form.

By Post Simply fill out the order form below (it can be photocopied) and send it with your payment to: Reed Book Services Ltd, PO Box 5, Rushden, Northants NN10 6YX.
Special Offer: Free Postage and Packaging for all orders over £10, add £2.00 for p+p if your order is for £10 or less.

ISBN	Title	Price	Quantity	Total
0 600 57698 1	Hellyer Pocket Guide	4.99		
0 600 57697 3	Gardener's Fact Finder	4.99		
0 600 58187 X	Dictionary of Plant Names	4.99		
0 600 58427 5	Pests, Diseases and Common Problems	4.99		
0 600 58428 3	Garden Terms	4.99		
0 600 57732 5	Best Climbers	4.99		
0 600 57735 X	Best Foliage Shrubs	4.99		
0 600 57734 1	Best Shade Plants	4.99		
0 600 57733 3	Best Soft Fruit	4.99		
0 600 58337 6	Best Water Plants	4.99		
0 600 58338 4	Best Herbs	4.99		
		Postage & Packaging (add £2 for p+p if your order is £10 or less)		
		GRAND TOTAL		

Name .... (BLOCK CAPITALS)

Address ....

....

.... Postcode ....

I enclose a cheque/postal order for £ .... made payable to Reed Book Services Ltd or

please debit my: Access ☐   Visa ☐   AmEx account ☐   Diners ☐

by £ .... Expiry date .... Signature ....

Account no ☐☐☐☐☐☐☐☐☐☐☐☐☐☐☐☐

Whilst every effort is made to keep our prices low, the publisher reserves the right to increase the prices at short notice. Your order will be dispatched within 28 days subject to availability.
Registered office: Michelin House, 81 Fulham Road, London SW3 6RB. Registered in England No 1974080
THIS FORM MAY BE PHOTOCOPIED